D0582094

THE CRAFT OF WRITING

The National Curriculum recommends that children, from the earliest age, learn to write texts for real purposes and real audiences. The real writing approach has been welcomed by teachers, but it raises some difficult questions to do with what we now call 'compositional skills'. How do we decide which are the most important of the forms of writing which we meet in real life? What are their characteristics and how do we teach them? How do we design a simple version for young children and then stretch the ability of the older and more able? What are the skills of the writer's craft?

This book answers those questions with a wealth of practical suggestions for teachers of writers from NC level 2 through to GCSE and into adult life, for teachers of English as a foreign language, and for language study courses in higher education. It sets out the major categories of writing, highlighting essential similarities and differences. It identifies the key features of the most significant forms by analysing examples of published material from a wide range of real-life sources. The author compares published writing with the work of children from across the key stages of schooling. Within a readable and informative commentary, essential information is summarised to allow for easy access, making this an essential reference book for the busy teacher – and the developing writer.

Stephen Parker is a lecturer at the School of Education, University of East Anglia. He has taught English to all age ranges and lectured widely in North America and Europe on children's language development.

THE CRAFT OF WRITING

STEPHEN PARKER

Paul Chapman
Publishing Ltd

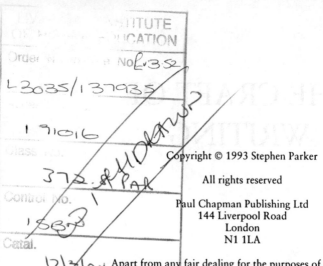

Paul Chapman Publishing Ltd
144 Liverpool Road
London
N1 1LA

British Library Cataloguing-in-Publication Data

Parker, Stephen
Craft of Writing
I. Title
372.6

ISBN 1-85396-200-7

Typeset by Inforum, Rowlands Castle, Hants
Printed and bound by
Athenaeum Press Ltd, Newcastle-upon-Tyne, England

A B C D E F G H   9 8 7 6 5 4 3 2

To Hannah
and the many young people
who helped me to write this book

CONTENTS

1 THE STORY SO FAR   1

2 THE WRITING GENERATOR   7
   Topic   8
   Audience   9
   Form   9
   National Curriculum   11

3 REAL WRITING AND THE WRITER'S PURPOSE   16
   A Range of Real Forms   16
   A Model of Primary Purpose   17
   Informative Purpose   21
   Persuasive Purpose   22
   Evocative Purpose   23
   Affective Influence   24
   Implications of the Model   24

4 LAYING THE FOUNDATIONS   26
   Introduction   26
   Kinds of Plan   28
   The Planning Sequence   38
   Review   39

5 THE BLANK PAGE: CHOOSING OPTIONS   40
   Introduction   40
   Voice   41
   Register   43
   Tone   43
   Length   44
   Detail   44
   Tense   45
   Structure   45
   Persuading the Reader: Rhetoric   48

6   INFORMATIVE WRITING   53
      Introduction   53
      Explanation   57
      Instruction   61
      Reporting   66
      Exposition   75
      Criticism   78
      Propaganda   85
         Developing Skills   87
         Promoting Critical Reading/Writing   88

7   PERSUASIVE WRITING   90
      Introduction   90
      Argument   92
      Assertion   98
      Appeal   104
      Advertisement   108
      Description   117
         Developing Skills   126
         Promoting Critical Reading/Writing 127

8   EVOCATIVE WRITING   128
      Introduction   128
      Poetry   130
      Story   142
      Drama   155
      Biography   164
         Developing Skills   171
         Promoting Critical Reading/Writing 172

9   INTO ACTION   174
      Pre-Writing Stage   175
      Drafting Stage   180
      Post-Writing Stage   186
      Towards Independence   191

Appendix 1:   THE WRITING GENERATOR   192
Appendix 2:   LINKING IDEAS   197
Appendix 3:   PARAGRAPH STRUCTURES   200
Appendix 4:   THE WRITING PROCESS   203

Bibliography   204
Acknowledgements   209
Index   211

1

THE STORY SO FAR

> Growing mastery of written language entails mastery of a variety of
> types of writing. (DES, 1989, para 12.1)

The last twenty-five years have been a fascinating time for teachers of
English. Dynamic change seems to be on us with a rush at present,
and the definition of English to be the subject of heated debate, but
looking back it is possible to see our present position as more the
result of evolution than of revolution. Within that debate, this book is
an attempt to map out the field of writing, placing the requirements of
the National Curriculum in the context of what we know about 'real
writing' and about the development of children's ability.

When I began teaching in 1967 in a grammar school in the north of
England, life was relatively simple. For us, English was defined by the
textbooks of Ronald Ridout, with their analytical approach to language, and by the classics of English Literature which I had studied
through 'A' level and university. My teacher-training year had en-
dorsed that classic model, in spite of notorious evidence that it did not
work on teaching practice at Stockton-on-Tees Secondary Modern
School for Boys. The first sign for me of changing times was my friend
George. We arrived to begin our probationary teaching year together
but George came inspired by the training of one of the key figures of
the new creative writing movement, Geoffrey Summerfield. Being en-
ergetic and imaginative, George spiked up the Ridout diet with pep
pills of creative writing, some of which were bizarre especially by the
conservative traditions of that time and place. I don't think he ever
used the apocryphal stabbing of a dagger into the desk so that

children could write as it quivered of what it suggested to them, but the head, walking past the windows of the classroom one day, saw George squatting on the teacher's desk imitating a chicken to fire up Ridout-jaded imaginations. The head was near to retirement so he walked on, but had a quiet word with the Head of Department later. George used to leave the results of his lessons around the staff-room coffee-tables for marking, and his classes certainly produced some inspired writing, the title of Alex Clegg's book *The Excitement of Writing* capturing the spirit of the age. In the present, more functional, age let us hope that we never lose sight of the fact that children are capable of a freshness of vision and power of expression when given a strong stimulus and freedom to say what they feel.

The 1960s were a time of great enthusiasm for 'creative writing', by which was meant writing a personal response to a strongly perceived stimulus. Stories, poems and free-form 'purple prose' became the major forms of writing for all ages of children, displacing the traditional essay. The movement placed its major emphasis on the quality of perception expressed through writing rather than on the form which the writing took. Although we have retained high motivation as a foundation for work in language, that narrow focus on poetic forms and the lack of concern for structure came to be seen as a weakness. The seeds of a counter-movement were also to be found in the 1960s when the increasing interest in socio-linguistics focused attention on the wider range of registers of language in the world outside school, a comparison which suggested that creative writing was too narrow a focus. Doughty, Pearce and Thornton (1971) produced a key text in *Language in Use* which proposed a great many real-life language topics for study and imitation. For those who accepted Chomsky's suggestion that all language use is creative, not solely the poetic, this was not a contradiction but a considerable expansion of the range of acceptable forms of writing. Research by James Britton and his team in the 1970s (Britton *et al.*, 1975) suggested that writing could be divided into three categories: Expressive, Poetic, Transactional. As such his model of writing functions made obvious the narrow focus of the creative writing approach, where writing was predominantly in the Poetic mode, the writer taking the viewpoint of a spectator of experience. In the Transactional mode, he proposed, the writer takes the viewpoint of a participant in life's transactions, such writing serving a wider range of purposes, and additionally a wider range of audiences than the 'teacher as examiner' which he found to be the norm in the classroom.

His model was eventually highly influential in widening the scope and in sharpening the definition of purpose and audience in writing in schools. By the time of the Bullock Report in 1975 there was increasing criticism of spontaneous-response writing as a major target for children's writing development. The Bullock Report (DES, 1975) with its title *A Language for Life* shifted the emphasis away from the Poetic onto the Transactional, though still stressing high motivation and active learning methods. It suggested that children learn about language by using it in contexts which have real meaning, not by analytical grammar exercises and out-of-context writing assignments. It gave official endorsement to the widening of the range of written forms seen as appropriate in the classroom, such forms to be more specific than 'the essay' and for audiences wider than 'teacher as examiner'.

Although 'creative writing' was not officially rejected, the creative process was now seen as serving other than poetic forms. Although the report was relatively tentative about the relationship between the classroom and the real world, the seeds of the present position are clear in such relatively muted statements as:

> There is often great excitement and high motivation in simulation, role-playing, and constructing imaginary situations, but activities based on actualities ought not to be neglected.
> (DES, 1975, para 10.14)

During the pragmatic 1980s the notion of 'a language for life' was given an increasingly functional interpretation. There was a steady increase in emphasis upon the triangle of forces seen as influencing the shape and extending the range of writing: function–form–audience. The HMI (DES, 1984) summarised developments in thinking on the general principles of English in all four modes since the Bullock Report: 'Essentially, then, the objectives can best be attained by setting tasks which require communication for real or realistic purposes and in which particular skills need to be used' (para. 2.1). Government initiatives and funding which targeted vocational education at the top end of secondary schooling gave 'real or realistic' a highly specific direction. Peter Medway (in Hayhoe and Parker, 1992) describes a TVEI development project in Leeds during which year 10 and 11 writers produced marketing and publicity material for local enterprises, community newspapers, stories for special needs children, recommendations for a school librarian, an evaluation of care facilities in the area, an investigation of school-leavers' experiences, and finally a bound report distributed to administrators and teachers across the city. Such genuinely real and purposeful contexts clearly give powerful motivation to the socio-linguistic function–form–audience theory, which is now the predominant influence in language development throughout schooling, as all schools have increasingly formed positive links with the community at large and as teachers have come to devise suitable activities and resources for younger children.

The National Curriculum (DES, 1989) has been built upon these principles and practices which have evolved over the last twenty-five years, namely that all forms of writing are valid material for the classroom, that they should arise in contexts which are meaningful for the children, be for real audiences and serve real purposes. Although these principles are widely accepted, there is a long-standing and heated debate over the role of knowledge about language in relation to the production of real writing. The difficulty is most apparent when considering how examples of authentic texts should be presented in the classroom; does it help children as writers to have the terms and techniques of linguistic analysis, and if they do, does such knowledge improve their writing? Favouring the teaching of specific linguistic knowledge, Gunther Kress (1982, p. 99) noted:

> The major genres which the school teaches are taught by the way, implicitly: descriptive, scientific, technical, historical writing. This is also true of creative writing: children are asked to write 'stories' – with whatever motivation or purpose – without being given any teaching about the appropriate type of genre, or its main structural features.

The teaching of traditional grammar and the use of formal exercises were attacked from the 1960s on (see Wilkinson, 1971 for a summary of the arguments) on the grounds that the approach had little positive effect on children's ability to write. Explicit teaching of grammatical knowledge subsequently went into a rapid decline. The Bullock Report (DES, 1975), while not advocating a return to the teaching of prescriptive grammar, did suggest a compromise in recommending a climate of 'language awareness' in which children's intuitive knowledge about language was 'raised to the level of consciousness'. It recommended that teachers should adopt a policy of 'planned intervention', i.e. that they should have exact knowledge of how language works but that their use of that knowledge would be indirect, guiding them in responding to children's needs as they arose. In such a spirit, in analysing the writing of children in relation to examples of authentic texts, I intend to offer to teachers explicit information about language to be used according to their professional judgement. Since the Bullock Report, however, there has been increasing official pressure to make the direct teaching of language knowledge as a body of fact a substantial component in the English programme. Whether children can achieve their highest potential using intuitive rather than conscious knowledge is still a matter for heated debate, though more ideological than scientific. In offering descriptions of features which experienced writers use to shape language for specific effects, I am not suggesting that children should rote learn and slavishly copy rigid protocols; the value of technical knowledge is not that children should know how to identify and name component parts so as to score highly in objective tests but that they should know that such patterns exist and what purposes they serve and have the opportunity to use them exploratively. Structured language work can allow children to play with the building blocks of language and explore their effects at a micro level released from the macro concerns of creativity and the communication of meaning.

Conformity and Resistance

Although we see ourselves as living in an increasingly televisual age, and talk of the future as a post-literate society, there is no sign yet that literacy is of diminishing importance. Quite the opposite. The adult world demands an increasingly skilled workforce, and that skill is communicated as much by print as by other means; our leisure time increases and with it specialist publications about our interests; the junk mail of consumerism lands daily on the door mat; as information technology increases so does the amount of print which flashes across the screens around the world. What we are seeing is not a contraction but an expansion of the importance of the written word. At the same time its use is becoming more and more sophisticated. Whereas in the past novelists, poets, dramatists were seen as the most sophisticated of writers, now there is increasing focus on the skill of writing in commercial and technical spheres for which special training is necessary. Writing is clearly an important life-skill. All children who leave school able to write will need to write at some time in their lives. Some of them will need to write across the full range of forms available; a very few will write a very great deal; some will earn a living in one way or another by writing. We have a responsibility to help them all to join what Frank Smith (1988) has called 'the literacy club' of reader-writers.

Although we have a responsibility to produce children who can 'do as they are told' in writing, we need to go further, without contradicting that first responsibility. In adult life we may write little and that within a narrow range of forms: letters, tax returns, shopping lists. But most adults read a much wider range of forms than they write: newspapers, magazines, novels, business letters, holiday brochures, junk mail and so on. If students learn how such writing is constructed by replicating the techniques of a wide range of writers, they are more likely to see through the page to the writer's intention and the artifice used to achieve it; they are less likely to be conned by the advertiser, seduced by the political sloganeer, misinformed by newspaper bias. They will become 'resistant readers', a notion recently developed by such literary response theorists such as Bill Corcoran (in Hayhoe and Parker, 1990). Such readers resist bias in what they read, the bias of sexism, racism, political ideology. It must be our fundamental aim to produce readers who are not only insightful but questioning, even sceptical. Nor should resistance be seen as appropriate only at a late stage of development. Brian Cox, chairman of the Cox Committee, commented (in Hayhoe and Parker, 1992, p. 9): 'The child in the classroom, just like a professional writer, needs to learn a craft, but very early on can begin to create his or her unique voice.'

We need to help children to find a personal voice in writing and we do it by giving them knowledge of available voices. Crafting does not threaten originality and creativity; it widens the writer's options, and this book explores that crafting process. In response to the National Curriculum challenge that 'Growing mastery of written language entails mastery of a variety of types of writing' (DES, 1989, para 12.1), it attempts to map as wide a range of real forms as possible, to describe the characteristics of major forms, to suggest what will make them easier to handle for young children, and what characteristics signify more advanced levels.

Chapters 6, 7 and 8 are based on the analysis of writing from two sources. Firstly examples of authentic texts by professional authors are analysed to reveal the techniques which make the text effective on the reader. Secondly examples of the writing of children across the years of schooling are analysed as they try to replicate those techniques in gaining 'mastery' of the craft. In both cases I have been limited to quoting the written text, without the typography or other presentational features of the original. In the case of the children's work I have corrected the spelling and punctuation, i.e. the so-called secretarial features, so as to better focus on the compositional features of their writing. This analysis has been arranged according to a theoretical model of writing for real purposes described in Chapter 3 and in the context of a model of the writing process in education described in Chapter 2.

2

THE WRITING GENERATOR

Since the 1960s our approach to writing development has been holistic; in the classroom we set up a motivating context within which children write and in response to their writing we teach them what they need to develop further. To this end we have played down the prescriptive approach of teaching by rules and set exercises in favour of generating a wide and meaningful variety of written forms. The forces which generate the variety and shape the form are generally acknowledged to be: topic, function, form and audience. Each of these forces has within it a range of options which multiplied together generate different forms of writing. We can illustrate this by adding some typical classroom possibilities to these categories:

Topic	Function	Form	Audience
TV chat show simulation	Persuade	Letter	Pop star
Nativity play	Inform	Poster	General public
Visit to younger class	Evoke	Story	Young reader

Each of these items can be substituted for any other within each column; a letter to an individual pop star about a TV chat show will not be the same in tone or structure as a letter to the general public announcing a nativity play. Through such substitutions we can generate a wide variety of written forms even in so short a list, and Appendix 1 gives many more alternatives for each category. If to this notion of breadth we add the notion of depth, we multiply the range of possibilities enormously, probably to infinity. Depth across a number of the major features of writing can be expressed like this:

	Simple	*Complex*
Audience	intimate	formal
Genre	open	closed
Length	short	long
Product	spontaneous	crafted
Purpose	sincere	assumed
Structure	linear	elaborate
Syntax	simple	complex
Tone	personal	impersonal
Topic	familiar/concrete	new/abstract
Vocabulary	vernacular	technical

From the writer's point of view, each line represents a set of questions to be asked: 'Who is the writing for – an expert or a novice? Someone I am familiar with or someone of high status?' and so on. From the teacher's point of view, determining the level of challenge for the young writer and the level of success in meeting that challenge is a matter of judgement. There are no precise measures, because a sophisticated writer may use the simplest of all forms to achieve the greatest effect; use of the qualities listed on the right-hand side exclusively does not ensure effective writing. Let us consider some of the features which might describe complexity, or depth, across three of the forces: topic, audience and form. The fourth, function, will be considered in detail in the next chapter.

Topic

In the holistic tradition the topic of the writing is determined by local circumstances, which takes it out of the reach of analysis, but the nature of the topic has a distinct bearing on the level of linguistic challenge. A significant factor is the extent to which the subject is known to the writer. Although there is no precise scale, it is generally felt to be easier for the writer where the topic is: concrete, personal experience, present at the time of writing. It is harder where the topic is: abstract, new information, a past event, of a technical/specialist nature. So for young children we expect that a great deal of their writing will concern concrete personal experience, but at the higher levels of schooling the child will be called on to write more and more exactly about subjects outside direct experience – in the historical past, or about a distant place, or a complex scientific process – which increases the level of difficulty. James Britton's (1975) taxonomy suggests that the distance of the writer from the subject represents stages of increasing difficulty:

(1) record what is happening
(2) report what has happened
(3) generalised narrative or description
(4) generalisation at a low level
(5) classification – generalisation at a high level
(6) speculation on what might happen
(7) theorising on what has or might happen

It is essential to make a distinction here between facile and informed speculation. We can all speculate with ease at the level of fantasy: 'If I ruled the world . . .' and so on. What Britton means by speculation is where factual knowledge is used to guide detailed consideration of possibilities. This is seen as high-level thinking, and so a high-level target for writers of all stages.

Audience

Martin Joos (1962) suggested that there is a spectrum of formality in writing determined by the relationship between the writer and the reader, and he suggested five stages to which I have added examples:

(1) Intimate: 'Gone to Jo's for p.m. Drop in if poss.'
(2) Casual: 'It seems ages since I saw you. Why don't we meet at Jo's like we used to?'
(3) Consultative: 'We are forming a discussion group and would be very pleased if you would join us.'
(4) Formal: 'Your application has been considered by the committee, but I regret to inform you that at the present time the membership list is complete.'
(5) Frozen: 'The Cringleford Philosophical Society requests the pleasure of the company of S. Parker, esquire at its annual charity luncheon. RSVP.

Possible audiences which might help to generate such a range of tones and registers might include: one/many; known/unknown; layman/expert; sympathetic/hostile; younger/older; friend/examiner. Appendix 1 lists many more.

Form

There continues to be a heated debate about the nature and significance of form or 'genre' in writing. Supporters of the genre cause claim that all texts can be classified according to predictable characteristics which can be taught to children. Certainly genre labels such as novel, poem, news report, horoscope are in general use and if, like a wine-tasting, we held a blind test in which a group of readers tried to identify samples of such forms, we could expect a high degree of agreement. In certain ritualistic social contexts, the writer is under a great deal of pressure to conform to highly specific structures, such as the conventional wedding invitation:

> Mr and Mrs S. J. Parker request the pleasure of the company of Mr and Mrs D. Reader on the occasion of the marriage of their daughter Hannah Louise to Mr Peter Jackson at Intwood Church on Saturday August 3rd at 11.00 a.m. and afterwards at a reception to be held at the Red Lion, Cringleford. RSVP.

The recipient of such an invitation, the reader, has specific expectations in such a context, which puts heavy pressure on the writer aspiring to a position in society to follow the well-trodden path, the ways that writers in the past have worked out as securing desired effects on the reader. Where genre characteristics have been thus determined over time by reader-writer agreement, such forms can be classed as 'closed'; poetry has many of them, for instance the sonnet or limerick.

At the other end of the scale, though, there are forms with so few predetermined characteristics that they can be classed as 'open': diary, personal letter, and free verse for instance. In between closed and open are forms where certain conventions are expected, as small though perhaps significant features within the text; for example, the greeting 'Dear' to open a letter, no matter how inappropriately. In a business letter additional conventions might also be respected, such as the arcane 'your esteemed order of the 15th inst.' However, such conventions are of minor significance as carriers of the writer's meaning in the letter. Indeed, many conventions can be regarded as options for writers as they shape their meaning in language. It would, for instance, be perfectly possible to break with convention, to invite wedding guests with:

> Hi there, you lovely people! Want to come to a wedding? We've got just the thing for you. Little Han is marrying Jacko . . .

Such a departure from convention would signify either a very particular relationship with the intended reader, or a writer with a very particular personality, but nonetheless such a departure is possible. Genre alone cannot adequately explain the written product; it can describe at least some of the reader's expectations and some of the options available to the writer in the process of composition but not the writer's potential for creating uniqueness, an infinite variety of written products. This will be discussed further in the next chapter.

National Curriculum

The National Curriculum recognises the holistic tradition, with the major forces of function, form and audience as reference points, for instance sub-titling the writing section 'a growing ability to construct and convey meaning in written language matching style to audience and purpose.' However, the NC document takes a major step towards placing the holistic model within a structure, for instance attempting to identify specific kinds of writing as appropriate for specific developmental stages, so defining the breadth of the curriculum and the depth of children's ability. In general terms, it links the ability to generate language to increasingly explicit knowledge about the process of writing and the written product. The movement towards structure can be seen for instance in the section on 'Requirements of the programmes of study' of the non-statutory guidance:

> Key stage 2: Children's writing shows increased control. This is likely to be demonstrated by an understanding of the importance of planning to achieve shape and structure.
> Key stage 3: Pupils will be more aware of the purposes for which writing can be used and more capable of using written language to suit the circumstances.
> Key stage 4: Pupils should see writing as a craft. They will understand stylistic effects and will start to write in greater detail, where appropriate, demonstrating the ability to use different types of paragraph and more subtle sentence construction. They should be able to evaluate the success of what they have produced.   (p. B6)

And in the 'Implications for teaching and learning' section:

> KS4: Pupils will be able to identify the criteria which need to be applied to different types of writing and be able to use examples as models for their own work without being merely imitative. (p. B7)

Writing development in the National Curriculum is contained for the most part within Attainment Target 3 (En3) which specifies ten levels of attainment as an age-related line of development. In addition to En3 two further Attainment Targets concern writing: Spelling (En4) and Handwriting (En5), each with four levels. After their level 4 these two Attainment Targets are amalgamated to become Presentation (En4–5) which has a further three levels, namely 5, 6 and 7. In these three Attainment Targets there are 21 statements of attainment, but each statement has subdivisions, so that in fact the real total is 70 (42 in En3, 12 in En4, 5 in En5 and 11 in En4/5). That is still not the end of the count, though, because most of the subdivisions also contain embedded elements, for instance En3 8a: children are able to 'write in a wide variety of forms, with a clear sense of purpose and audience, demonstrating an ability to judge the appropriate length and form for a given task and to sustain the interest of the reader.' Such embedding makes for an uncountable multiplicity of objectives, though that is not surprising given the known complexity of the writing generator.

Maps of this complex terrain are now becoming available, though. The scope of writing within the National Curriculum for English has been usefully summarised in a booklet produced by the School Examinations and Assessment Council (1992) to illustrate the statements of attainment in relation to the written work of year 9 pupils in Key Stage 3. The booklet clusters the attainment targets for AT3 into 5 groups:

'Group A: Write in a variety of forms for a range of audiences and purposes (statements 4a, 4c, 5a, 6a, 7a, 8a).' The line of development is towards an increasing range, matching style to audience.

'Group B: Produce pieces of writing which are structured and organised so that the meaning is clear (statements 4b, 5b, 6b, 7b, 8b).' The line of development is towards use of more complex structures for more sophisticated purposes.

'Group C: Use standard English correctly and purposefully (statements 4d, 5c, 6c, 7c, 8c).' The line of development is towards a widening of vocabulary and the range of registers, with a decreasing number of errors in spelling, syntax and punctuation.

'Group D: Show an understanding of the need to redraft and revise work as appropriate to context and purpose (statements 4e, 5d, 6d, 7d).' The line of development is towards more exact process skills.

'Group E: Show some knowledge about language and the way it works in different contexts (statements 5e, 6e, 7e, 8d).' The line of development is towards increasingly explicit knowledge about language.

Additionally there are four groups of attainment target statements for Spelling (En4), Handwriting (En5) and Presentation (En4–5):

'Group F: Show knowledge of patterns in spelling and of the relationship between sound, spelling and meaning (En4 statement 4a; En4–5 statements 5a, 6a, 7a).'

'Group G: Check final drafts of writing for misspelling and other errors of presentation (En4–5 statements 5b, 6b, 7b).'

'Group H: Write fluently and legibly (En5 statement 4a; En4–5 statements 5c, 6c, 7c).'

'Group I: Present finished work clearly and attractively (En4–5 statements 6d, 7d).'

Much of this is self-explanatory, as it was intended to be, but the concepts which require further exploration are developmental stages, form and function.

Developmental Stages

The NC attempts to describe the developmental stages (called 'statements of attainment') which children need to master as they progress towards complete competence in writing ability. Such a description is problematic for at least two reasons: firstly it is not clear that all children do develop in the sequence that the statements of attainment suggest, and secondly it is difficult to give descriptive statements so exact a value that they are completely unambiguous. For instance, terms like 'developing ability', 'increased effectiveness' and 'appropriate length' are comparative; since they are not linked to an exact unit of measurement they are open to widely different interpretations by teachers and appraisers. If that is a weakness from the point of view of scientific measurement, it is a strength in allowing scope for the holistic approach. At the present time we do not have the necessary information to make either criterion or norm-referenced judgements across schooling, and in this book I will make only general comments on levels of attainment in terms of younger-older and simple-sophisticated.

Form

The detailed specification of writing across a range of forms begins at level 2 when children are able to 'produce simple, coherent non-chronological writing.' By level 5 the 'real writing' philosophy is approaching a description of full adult competence, since it suggests that children at that level are able to 'write in a variety of forms for a range of purposes and audiences, in ways which attempt to engage the interest of the reader.' Although the NC document is clearly not intended as an encyclopaedic description, it is not difficult to extrapolate specific forms which are mentioned at various places in the statutory or non-statutory sections. Some are listed more than once, but in the list below I have placed the form at the level for which it is first mentioned. As you can see, it is quite a comprehensive list:

L2: lists, captions, invitations, greetings cards, notices, posters, account of event, adventure story.

L3: plans, diagrams, description of person or place, notes for an activity in science or design.

L4: instructions, accounts, explanations (perhaps of a scientific investigation), expression of feelings (in forms such as letters, poems, invitations, posters).

L5: dialogue, script, report.

L7: personal letters, formal letters, essays, newspaper articles, reviews, biographies, playscripts, radio and TV scripts, news broadcast.

L8: editorial (broadsheet and tabloid).

Although it is not spelt out in the document, these forms reflect the notion of a taxonomy; those mentioned at the lower levels are seen as in some way intrinsically more easy than those at higher levels, and ability to handle them is seen as cumulative. There is no explicit clustering but four categories are mentioned: chronological, non-chronological, 'real life' and poetry. The most significant distinction is between chronological and non-chronological forms, reflecting the model suggested by Perera (1984). The non-statutory guidance for KS1 gives as examples of chronological writing: diaries, stories, letters, accounts of tasks or of personal experience. Non-chronological forms include: lists, captions, labels, invitations, greetings cards, notices, posters. We perhaps have more experience of teaching chronological structures, not least because story has played such a significant part in literacy development, so it is not surprising that story is the only form for which a clear line of development is described through the levels:

L2: write stories showing an understanding of the rudiments of story structure by establishing an opening, characters, and one or more events.

L3: more complex stories, with detail beyond simple events, with a defined ending.

L4: stories which have an opening, a setting, characters, a series of events and a resolution and which engage the interest of the reader.

L6: use literary stylistic features; write an illustrated story suitable for a younger reader.

L10: handle elements of a story which involve characters in very different contexts.

Such detail, though, indicates a weakness in the document, for, by contrast with story, non-chronological writing is a categorisation containing many forms, generally recognised as more difficult to teach, yet the document provides no guidance. There is the first mention of a wide range in level 2's 'produce simple coherent non-chronological writing' which develops in level 3 to 'produce a range of types of non-chronological writing', this being glossed as 'plans and diagrams, descriptions of a person or place, or notes for an activity in science or design.' However, the distinction of chronological/non-chronological, while on the helpful end of the scale, is frankly rudimentary as a model, and we will go on to describe non-chronological structures in Chapter 3 and analyse examples in Chapters 6, 7 and 8.

Function

That writing should have a purpose is a recurrent theme throughout the NC document, though without specific detail. At level 4, for instance, children are to write stories which 'engage the interest of the reader.' Elsewhere a variety of purposes is mentioned: plan, inform, explain, entertain, express attitude/emotion, compare and contrast, persuade, describe experience imaginatively, formulate hypotheses. These, however, seem to be samples of the possible rather than significant instances drawn from a logical model, hence in terms of their effect on written forms they are a wave in the direction of uncharted territory. It is the purpose of this book to explore in detail those two problematic areas of the National Curriculum: the writer's purpose and its effect on the crafting of the written product.

3

REAL WRITING AND THE WRITER'S PURPOSE

A Range of Real Forms

The central principle of the National Curriculum, that children should write across the range of real forms, is a daunting prospect if we take it literally, for Appendix 1 lists over a hundred kinds of writing. The total number is diminished if we regard some as sub-sets of others; for instance, ballad, lyric and sonnet are all forms of poetry while instructions are the substance of the instruction manual. Then not all of the remainder are significant, and I think we would all dare to make our personal exclusions. I do not feel compelled to teach the affidavit or the sermon, which belong to specific professional registers, and I doubt if many would disagree with me. But of those forms which remain, which do we choose? Those specified in the NC are not ranked as most to least important, so we have no clear picture of the relative importance of the many forms of writing specified. At the moment the approach is a shotgun – blast away at all of them in the hope that we hit some targets. Ideally we need a map of the territory, a model of writing to guide our choice. To be an operational model, though, it has to be simple, otherwise our task is like driving across the world with ordnance survey maps – too much detail is distracting.

In the last chapter we examined the major forces which shape written text: topic, audience, form or function. On which should we base a map? It would, of course, be possible to base a model on any one or more, in any combination, but topic and audience are static forces in that they are fixed beforehand and are unlikely to change during the writing; we would generally agree that it was a poor piece of writing which made an unstructured change of topic midway through, or which began informally as if to a known reader but then switched to formal address. As for form, it was suggested in the last chapter that this is not as clear a category as might at first appear. Take for instance a formal report; its basic content of material facts may be coloured by personal judgement, doubts, speculation, hypothesis, opinion. Short assertive sentences may be intermingled with extended imagery, metaphor, word pictures; it may contain within it a direct address to the reader. Our teaching model of writing has to feature an essential fact of writing: that the seemingly fixed boundaries of genre disguise fluidity and infinite potential. As Swales commented (1990, p. 37): 'At the end of the day genre analysis is valuable because it is clarificatory, not because it is classificatory.'

Knowledge about specific forms revealed by genre analysts is essential for understanding the crafting process, but it is not the fixed characteristics of written forms which is most striking, it is their uniqueness. No two pieces of writing are exactly alike. The old adage that if a thousand monkeys typed for a thousand years one of them would type *Hamlet* does at least suggest the totally divergent nature of written text.

A more reliable principle is that writing is a dynamic process with an infinitely variable product. The finite characteristics of a given form are not tramlines which lead a writer inexorably in a fixed direction; they are options which a writer may choose or disregard at will in order to serve the purpose of the writing. I will therefore not use the term 'genre' hereafter, preferring the rather vaguer term 'form'. In crafting a text it is the writer who is in the driving seat and the writer's purpose which sets the direction. In proposing a model based on purpose, I am making a distinction between purpose and function. Function seems to me to describe the effect which the finished product has on the reader, whereas my focus is to be on the writer's intentions which are the driving force during the crafting process. Function is at the output end of the writing process whereas purpose is at the composing end, where the crafting takes place.

A Model of Primary Purpose

Appendix 1 lists 35 possible purposes which might be in a writer's mind as the driving force, and the creative reader will no doubt be able to add to the list. However, to design an operational model we must reduce that number to manageable proportions, making the majority subservient to as few as possible. In analysing that list of real forms, I propose that they can be divided into three groups according to three *primary purposes* which writers might have: purposes which can be classed as seeking to inform the reader, or to persuade the reader or to evoke an aesthetic response. Others have reached similar conclusions (see, for instance, James Kinneavy, 1971). To emphasise the dynamic nature of the writing process, I have selected three active verbs as descriptors: *to inform (the informative), to persuade (the persuasive), to evoke (the evocative).* I must apologise for the somewhat abstruse term 'evocative' which is used because it describes an active process unlike the conventional terms 'literature' or 'the poetic'.

It is important to note that in this model the three primary purposes are not categories or boxes to put texts into, but forces which exert highly significant influence on a text as it is being composed. If we take travel as an example of a topic, we can see how it can be differently shaped by each of the three primary purposes. The purpose of the gazetteer writer is to give reliable information and so the form is a factual, objective account of the features of a place. The town guide writer intends to persuade the visitor that the place is interesting and so the writer selects the most positive features and describes them favourably. The travel brochure writer intends the description to go further, to persuade the reader to buy, hence the selection and description are noticeably more glowing. The writer of a journey novel tries to create the impression that the reader is actually taking part on the journey. For teaching purposes at least, all texts can be placed within the aegis of one of the three primary purposes, although most will reveal minor or secondary influences of the others, as I will describe later. Artists rarely paint only with primary colours, and likewise in real writing we find only rare examples which have one clear single purpose.

In the model each of the primary purposes is represented as a spectrum, subdivided into *fields*, representing specific aspects of a primary purpose. For instance, in the primary purpose of the Persuasive I have identified the fields of argument, assertion, appeal, advertisement, description. Within each field there are forms which share common characteristics because their writers wish to work a similar effect upon the intended reader. To choose an obvious example, the term 'advertisement' does not describe a single distinct form of writing, for advertisements come in all shapes and sizes. Advertisement is a field and the writer of a specific advertisement can choose from a range of known techniques which are available to writers in that field. I need to add the caveat here though that because written forms are so diffuse, with the potential for infinite variety, the degree of selectivity, even partiality, increases as the model becomes more specific. Others may consider that there are other or different fields than those I have selected; as with the spectrum of colour, where blue ends and indigo begins is a matter of judgement not of objective fact.

I have tried to use terms for the fields which suggest the active process of crafting. With regret, though, within the Evocative I have been obliged to use the conventional genre terms poetry, story, drama, biography, which do not have an active verb form. While 'to dramatise' is perfectly acceptable and 'to story' is possible, the others in the sequence, 'to poem' and 'to biograph' do not work.

In Chapter 6 on informative writing I have included a section on propaganda, which is a perverse kind of information with a concealed persuasive purpose. I have not assigned it to a field in the model below because it seems to me to be a special case, a kind of pseudo-field, pretending to be Explanation or Exposition. The same case could be extended to parody, which is not a field in its own right but takes the shape of whichever field is its satirical target.

To map all forms of real writing the fields chosen have to have wide tolerance, and the fourteen fields chosen for the diagram below are

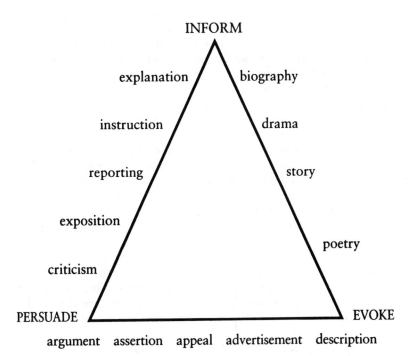

A model of primary purpose

intended to subsume the majority of the 100 plus forms listed in Appendix 1.

In the diagram, the three primary purposes have been arranged as a triangle of forces, with the fields arranged along each axis. A two-dimensional model such as this cannot truly represent a fluid relationship, and the positioning here is only indicative of one possible set – although it is one which I believe has wide validity. The fields are positioned along each axis so as to suggest that each is within the sphere of influence of one purpose while being also pulled towards another. For instance, within the field of Criticism a book review as a form is essentially informative, its primary purpose being to give information about the book concerned; but the writer will predictably have a personal opinion about it and wish to persuade the reader to that opinion, with a view to reading or not reading the book, so that Persuasion is a secondary purpose. Criticism has therefore been placed towards the Persuasive end of the Informative axis. However, it would be possible for the writer to Evoke the flavour of the book, and then the text would need to be represented in another position, perhaps within the triangle rather than on its perimeter.

On the model at the level more specific than field there are *forms*, i.e. real texts which are in some way representative of their field, as a book review is a form representative of the field Criticism. I have preferred the term 'form' because like field it is not precise; it is capable of admitting differing interpretations, blurring at the edges, overlapping like the Olympic rings with other forms. As the model thus takes on more detail, so the process of simplification involves greater selectivity and I have been able to select as illustrative only a very few real forms, though they are ones which I hope are the most appropriate for the classroom.

At the level of greatest specificity are the *options* available to the writer in the process of composing a specific form within a general field. For instance, among the options available to the writer in shaping an informative text are choices as to whether the information is given in concise or elaborated form, in active or passive voice, in personal or impersonal address. In the context of a formal (closed) genre a writer may be highly constrained to use specific characteristics, set phrases, structures, rhetorical figures, but despite greater or lesser constraint it is still more true to the process of composing to consider such language patterns as options from which the writer chooses. Composition is an immensely complex process since each word is an option as the text is built up. It is impossible to add such detail to the diagram above, but significant options are explored in Chapter 5 in terms of major choices the writer has to make in facing the blank page, and in Chapters 6, 7, and 8 in relation to specific fields and the real forms I have chosen to illustrate them.

It is only for the sake of producing an operational model that such options have been assigned to specific primary purposes as if they were their distinctive property. At any point in a text a writer may use techniques which I have here assigned as primarily associated with another field and purpose. For instance, I have designated Story a field in its own right in the Evocative, but the anecdote, a cameo story, is frequently used as an illustration within texts which are primarily informative or primarily persuasive. As another instance I have associated the option of 'rhetorical question' as most appropriate as a technique serving a Persuasive purpose, but a writer of an informative text would be free to choose such an option in order to provoke thought in the reader. Anecdote and rhetorical question are clearly free-floating options available to the writer of any kind of text, but in order to create a simplified map on which teaching strategies can be based, I have classified such techniques as if they were more fixed than they are in reality. The model of primary purpose is intended to give a simplified schema of what is in fact endlessly variable. Let us now look more closely at each of the three primary purposes and their implications for the writer:

Informative Purpose

Examples of forms primarily influenced by the Informative purpose include encyclopaedia entries, information books, instruction manuals, and (ideally) news reporting. In this field the writer's primary purpose is to transmit information to the reader, who is envisaged as actively seeking it. So the main concern of the writer in transmitting that knowledge is for accuracy, comprehensiveness, coherence, clarity, impartiality, objectivity. Such are the criteria by which the quality of informative writing should be judged above all. Beyond that the effect which the information has on the reader is not the primary concern of the writer, though where there are secondary purposes these will quite markedly affect the text. The weather reporter is primarily concerned with transmitting an accurate forecast, for instance that it is going to rain; whether or not the reader is persuaded to take an umbrella as a result of the forecast is a secondary consideration, and if the forecaster wishes to move the reader to act on the information then the tone, style and presentation might well be different.

Towards the Persuasive end of the axis the writer either selects the information or presents it in such a way as to encourage one particular interpretation of the results. This may be subconscious because of

an unwitting bias coming from sexism, ageism, racism, political in-
clination and so on. It may be conscious as in propaganda which
purports to be objective fact but which actually distorts by omission
or exaggeration or misrepresentation. Hence although reporting of
the news ought ideally to be placed unambiguously in the centre of
this axis, possible objections to its lack of impartiality are well
known. For instance, by selecting only the negative side of world
events (crime, disasters, war) newspapers give a pessimistic and hence
biased picture of the world. More specifically, certain newspapers give
a consistently favourable coverage to one or other of the political
parties. In such cases the writing may be primarily intended to inform,
but pulled further along the axis towards the Persuasive.

Crafting techniques can also reveal the Evocative as a secondary
purpose. Journalists speak of 'stories' and 'human interest'; direct
speech, background on personalities, purple-prose descriptions all
move outside the field of unalloyed fact. Journalism in fact has to
appeal to a readership, for each paper targets a defined readership
with an assumed set of interests, attitudes – and even reading age.
Appealing to a readership means that some stories are more appealing
than others, some literary styles more compelling.

Persuasive Purpose

Examples of forms primarily influenced by the Persuasive purpose
include advertising copy, feature articles, charitable appeals, campaign brochures. In this field the writer's primary purpose is to
change the opinion of the reader, who is envisaged as ignorant,
reluctant or sceptical in relation to the writer's message. Therefore
the main concern of the writer is to make an impact on the consciousness of the readership, to win it round to the writer's point of
view by appeal to reason and logic or to emotion and prejudice.
Writing in this field is, in the broadest sense, attempting to 'sell'
something, whether the object be a tangible product such as perfume
or a tourist attraction or intangibles such as a political ideology. The
persona of the reader is paramount: Who is the reader, what are his/
her views, preferences, beliefs, attitudes? These are the concerns of
costly market research by enterprises which seek to characterise a
target audience at whom the product, and hence the text, should be
most effectively aimed.

Advertising intends to persuade its readers into a certain course of
action; that is its primary purpose, and much advertising will contain
neither information nor evocation. But many reveal an informative
influence, containing genuine information about the product, and per-

suading through factual evidence and reason while others persuade through evocations of, for instance, golden childhood and images which appeal to the reader's emotions.

Evocative Purpose

Examples of fields primarily influenced by the Evocative purpose are poetry, story, drama and biography. The writer's primary purpose is to create in the mind of the reader a secondary world which is a representation through language of life in the world, in whole or in part. It may be the world of the here and now, of the past or future or a completely imaginary world as in science fiction and fantasy. Although there are exceptions to every rule, the content usually concerns living forms, particularly human, in relation to each other, moving through time and space, with some implication for the meaning of life. The main concern of the writer is to make the representation become real in the mind of the reader, who is envisaged as a traveller through this created world. However, as many interviews with novelists and poets have revealed, the persona of the reader is often not foremost in the mind of the evocative writer who writes primarily to create a secondary world with an integrity satisfying to personal rather than to public criteria. But as publishers readily point out, only writing which coincides with what they interpret to be reader interest will actually be published, no matter what the author intended.

An important option in this field is the aesthetic power of the language itself; the enjoyment or impact of musical effects such as alliteration and rhyme, and visual effects such as imagery. In poetry this shaping of language for aesthetic effect is usually more marked than in the crafting of prose, in which case it may become the main criterion for judging the success of the writing.

At the Informative end of the axis, biography uses the techniques of the Evocative but factual validity is an important principle of the form; it is a blend of story and history. The children's author Rosemary Sutcliff who wrote many novels about Roman Britain carried out detailed research into their factual background; their evocation of that past time relies heavily on the authenticity of its informational detail. Poetry is placed at the Persuasive end of the axis because of claims by poets through the ages that they seek to change ways of thinking and feeling. At a less elevated level there is clearly a link between poetry and advertising which share many of the same techniques, though incidentally the model of James Britton (1975) did not recognise that link.

Affective Influence

Linguistic models, being necessarily analytical and objective, can appear to heighten the importance of the intellect, suggesting that the writer constructs a text by constant reference to logic, rules, and stylistic conventions. By inference this plays down the role of the emotions in communication, which is misleading; the interaction between the cognitive and the affective for both writer and reader is inevitable. It is almost a rule of thumb for journalists that 'to be effective it must be affective', and much other writing deliberately seeks to touch the heart as well as the head. Aristotle in describing the purposes of poetry, joined the two domains together in his famous duality, translated as 'To delight and instruct'. However, in order to simplify the variables involved, the affective dimension has been assumed to be a secondary purpose. For instance, humour can be found in all three purposes. In the Informative and Persuasive its function will be to make the topic more attractive to the reader, but this is a supportive role, the primary purpose remaining to inform or to persuade.

Implications of the Model

If we attempt to teach written forms without reference to an overview we risk losing sight of the wood for the trees. By clustering forms firstly according to their primary purpose then placing them within a field of association, we are able to identify patterns of options which are available to the writer in the process of composition, such patterns being significant across a wider range of forms than we could include directly in the teaching programme. It is clear that we should focus children's attention on each of the three purposes, though in what ratio is a value judgement outside the scope of this book, but the allocation should be deliberate policy not random. Children should have a primary purpose in mind before they begin to write. They should know what field they are operating in, have experience of its typical forms and the kinds of options available to them in the process of composition. To that end it is crucial for them to study examples of real forms which fulfil the same purpose as the one they intend, to inform their choice as to available options which they might accept or reject as solutions to their own purpose.

The model of Primary Purpose does not comment directly on the relationship between language and thought, central to Britton's (1975) Expressive category, but that relationship is implicit in the model's essential concern with writing as a conscious crafting process. The model is, however, intended to fit into a teaching process, summarised in Appendix 4, in which thinking-writing is a distinct stage, and the following chapter considers how planning shapes the thoughts of the writer before detailed composition of the text begins.

4

LAYING THE FOUNDATIONS

Introduction

I once had an extension built onto my house, and to save money I first bricked in a doorway. The last course of my bricks did not fit in the remaining space so I had to cut each brick in half along its length, which looked odd. When the builder arrived I told him, 'I couldn't get the last course to fit in for some reason.' He explained in a very kind voice, 'It's not the last course you got wrong. Look down here,' and he pointed to the floor. 'You were wrong from the start. The first brick of the old wall isn't level with the floor, and you should have matched it. If you don't start off right you have the devil of a job to finish right.'

Just as I did with bricks and trowel, children prefer to pick up a pen and begin to write spontaneously, working out their ideas as they proceed. Usually that spontaneity shows in the results – the story which has a lame ending, the instructions with 'Oh, by the way . . .' inserts, the argument with one line in one paragraph and a jumble of unrelated ideas in the others.

Partly to allow for this spontaneity and harness it, current theory on writing emphasises the drafting process. It suggests that children should write not just one but several rough drafts, each an improvement upon the previous one until the final perfected stage is reached. The drawback with the theory is that children do not accept multiple drafting willingly, no matter what kind of writing is involved. This reaction is not limited to a particular age and stage; adults do not like drafting either. More significantly, when children do write successive drafts, they tend not to make changes after the first draft to major features such as sequence of ideas, structure and style without very specific advice; often new errors creep in to take the place of errors corrected in the earlier draft.

Successive drafting is not enough; it is the equivalent of my building my wall by trial and error, which would be vastly wasteful of time and effort. The solution comes before the drafting process, in spending more time and thought on the preparation: thinking about the subject, trying out ideas, talking with others and above all in making plans whereby thought and writing interact. Once the ideational structure of the writing has been worked out, drafting can focus more on the crafting of thought into language, and less on the crafting of thought itself. Planning ability, though, does not come naturally with maturation; it is a taught skill, best taught early on so that it becomes a habitual part of the writing process, which is unlikely if it is left until secondary school. There it is essential for more complex and lengthier writing tasks where the writer can easily lose direction during drafting, but if picking up the pen to begin spontaneous drafting has become the habit, planning will not be learned easily.

Young children also lose their way in writing, because it is difficult to hold a succession of points in the head whilst the demanding physical-mental effort of drafting takes place. Plans, on the other hand, are powerful devices which can contain dense information yet be seen at a glance by the writer, whose mind is then free to engage in the detail of composition, referring to the overall direction when necessary. With chronological writing a plan can help the child go beyond the tyranny of straight-line narrative, to explore more complex devices such as 'meanwhile', flashback and flash-forward constructions. Abstract ideas become more concrete and malleable and the writer more readily grasps the relationship between them. With a plan you don't lose sight of the wood for the trees.

Low-ability children frequently fail to finish their written work and over the years this succession of failure has a predictably depressing effect on their self-image. But many of them have excellent ideas which come out in oral sessions where pens are not used. Plans can be a creative and enjoyable exercise in themselves, balancing high-level thinking skills with a reduced literacy demand. Those which use fewer linguistic symbols and more symbols of other kinds, particularly the iconic, give the less linguistically able a chance to achieve success at the pre-writing stage and in the writing which follows.

Kinds of Plan

What constitutes 'a plan' is not usually finely focused in adult practice, for we allow personal preference and composition style to come into the formula. It might be a list of ideas in paragraph order or randomised key phrases arranged in any order on the page with esoteric arrows, signs and symbols. The essential features though are: inclusion of all major ideas; an indication of content order and relative emphasis; brevity; 'roughness' to accommodate alterations, speed and spontaneity.

Although it is possible to conceptualise planning structures in different ways, they are classified here into four types:

(1) The experiential – which clarify the meaning of the subject matter.
(2) The iconic – which express meaning through visual/graphic/ pictorial images.
(3) The conceptual – which highlight concepts and their relationships.
(4) The synoptic – which use language in abbreviated form.

Experiential Plans

Talk

Teachers probably spend more time thinking beforehand about topics they assign for writing than they realise. In addition they have vastly greater experience of life and writing to draw on, and hence they probably underestimate the amount of time children need to simply get into the way of thinking about a given topic. Talking about a new topic gives children the chance to make it their own. The talk may be with a partner, a group or the whole class. It might be about concrete experience immediately present, or the sharing of past experiences recalled in anecdotes, or talk of future hopes and fears. As Gordon Wells and his colleagues (1986, p. 130) explained:

> The advantage of oral monologue that we particularly wish to emphasise is that it provides an opportunity to develop some of the skills of composing – planning, selecting, marshalling and organising ideas that are so necessary for writing, and that it does so in a medium in which pupils feel more at ease and in which they are more likely to be successful.

Expressive talk brings the outside world into the classroom and gives children the opportunity to adjust their perceptions of it. Talk can also be structured. For instance, preparatory work might include asking an agreed series of questions of such people as grandparents or local shopkeepers. Small-group discussion might be firmed up into specific proposals through a formal report-back to the class. Episodes of formal talk such as report-back can be a useful way of revising and revisiting initial plans as a writing project proceeds.

Reading

Books of all kinds give children the material on which to work in their own writing, not just the information to include but also the knowledge of what writing is and what it does, how it is organised and crafted. Preparatory reading can be highly focused, to research exact information in specific books, to analyse a particular form; it can be browsing to get an overview of the subject, or an informal revisiting of books read in the past which find a new meaning through the writing project in hand. Reading might involve making written notes, which are then used in the plan.

Drama

Taking part in drama can extend a child's experience without leaving the school premises, through imaginative projection into other worlds, other times, inside the experiences of other people. The range of drama activity runs from interpreting scripts at the most formal end through simulation where significant parts of the experience are predetermined through to improvisation which allows participants freedom to design the nature and shape of the experience. Practical drama is clearly useful as a planning strategy in creating play-scripts, but more generally it will strengthen children's appreciation of experience which would otherwise remain outside their lives.

Imaging

It is very common for people to be able to recall past experience 'in the mind's eye' as if seeing people, places, events on a cinema screen. The most well known description of the phenomenon comes in William Wordsworth's poem 'I wandered lonely as a cloud' in which he describes the sight of the daffodils flashing on his 'inward eye'. Many people can also recall other sensory experiences – sounds, smells, tastes, touch. Young children will be prepared to close their eyes to help the process of imaging. Older children will be more embarrassed but most will know what is meant if they are asked to see in their mind's eye the people, places which are to be their subject. Without necessarily closing their eyes they will discover that description is so much easier when you can transfer directly what you see into word pictures on the page.

Iconic Plans

Children have a strong appreciation of the visual as a medium for conveying information, called by Jerome Bruner 'the iconic'. We praise certain kinds of writing in just those terms: 'graphic detail', 'vivid description', 'you can actually see it as you read'. Encouraging visualisation at the planning stage aims to help children to produce such writing.

Picture

In the early stages of learning to write it is common practice for children to draw a picture when they have finished their writing. Often the teacher has no higher objective than to fill in time or empty space on the page or to make the work look more attractive. But what if the child were to draw the picture first? Think what processes are going on. The picture in the mind's eye of what is to be written about becomes not only clearer, it becomes concrete, in Piaget's sense; it is here and apparent. Reversing the usual order of events, the picture becomes a plan of what is to be written about, whether it is about 'My House' for the beginning writer or 'Long John Silver' as the precursor to a character study by a high-schooler. One high school student began a study of Long John Silver by drawing an evil face on one side of the paper, then realising that Silver also had a vivacious character, turned over the page and drew him as handsome and smiling: two sides of the paper revealing the character as two-sided, two-faced.

Labelled Diagram

Any simple sketch can have labels attached to describe what its component parts are: a person's clothing, parts of a car, ground plans of a building. The labels act as a link between the physical actuality in the drawing and its representation in written symbols. This kind of plan is useful for technical writing such as the description of how a zip works quoted on page 59. The limitation of a diagram as a plan is that the picture usually contains no sequence in itself. However, if the diagram is of, say, a sledge that is being packed with equipment for an expedition, then the packed items might show the sequence of loading, and the extended writing might be a description of 'Packing for the North Pole'. Other possibilities are the ground plan of the scene of a crime, used as preparation for a key scene in a detective/crime story, or the stage set as a plan for a scene in a play.

Cartoon Sequence

A more elaborate use of the pictorial is in the cartoon sequence. One of the classic difficulties children find in writing stories is in maintaining the plot until the very end, and so the final section wilts badly. This is a sure sign that forward planning was missed. Young writers set off on extended story writing projects full of enthusiasm and good intentions, but the total task is too exhausting and they not only lose motivation, they lose sight of possible endings. Use of a cartoon sequence encourages planning of the overall shape of a narrative, as one 'scene' follows another.

Children have a great deal of experience of comics, not solely the *Beano* type. Raymond Briggs is the author of several picture books with a serious message, including *Gentleman Jim* and *Where the Wind Blows* which are aimed at readers in their teens and older. There are also cartoon versions of Shakespeare plays, which can be a source of comparative, contrastive analysis with the original.

The advantage of a cartoon strip is that it graphically shows the scenes of a story in a chronological sequence. It can cover an extensive range of events, more than a weaker writer might be capable of describing in words, and in a graphic detail which might be missing from a prose version. Written language can be integrated within pictures by using bubbles out of the mouths of characters to show speech or dotted bubbles to show thought. It can also include text within or below each picture, like the *Rupert the Bear* convention, to cover shifts of time and place or to add narrator commentary.

Disadvantages are that for all but a few children drawing is a slower medium than writing, and as they get older it is very common for people to feel insecure about their drawing ability. For them pinmen are usually an acceptable alternative. On the other hand, a few children are fanatical about cartoons and can become very involved, more so than in the writing to follow. A limit has to be set on the amount of time and detail given to such planning, though time spent in making the drawings is also time spent in thinking about the possibilities for the narrative.

The form can be used not only to create stories but also very effectively to summarise a book which has been read. If the task is syndicated, i.e. one child or group summarising one chapter each, the whole class can produce a cartoon summary of a complete novel in a very short time. The quality of the work lies in selecting the most significant detail in what is said and represented in the written text.

Storyboard

Storyboard deserves special mention as a planning strategy because of its importance in the real world of film and television making, where it is used after the script has been written, to guide the filming. Conventions for layout vary but typically the page is divided up into such columns as:

Visual	Camera angle	Sound effect	Script

In the visual column is a series of sketches of significant moments of what the camera sees, shot by shot, and in this it is similar to the cartoon sequence. In the next box across the page is the description of the shot, whether close-up or long shot and so on. If there is any additional sound effect this is described (e.g. 'door creaks'), and in the right-hand column the script which is spoken by the actor or voice-over at that moment of the film. It is the visual which leads, and in film-making the sketches might be of every camera shot, though in the classroom there is rarely either the need for such detail or the time. The technique is also used to promote active response to literature, to project the pupil into imagining how a film would interpret the text. As with cartoon sequence response, the quality lies in the selection of detail. The completed storyboard might be a finished product in its own right or the plan for a film review, a play-script or scene for a story.

Map

For some texts a map can be a useful planning medium because unlike other iconic plans it can suggest a sequential structure such as the description of a journey from home to school; place names and map symbols act as an aid to memory of features passed on the way. A map is also a good basis for the kind of tourist guide which takes the reader on a tour of major attractions, such as the guide quoted on pages 118–9. Many children's novels use maps to illustrate the movement of the plot, particularly those with a journey theme such as *The Silver Sword* by Ian Serraillier, *The Book of Three* by Lloyd Alexander or *The Hobbit* by J. R. R. Tolkien. They can excite the imagination like the chart in *Treasure Island*. When children are setting out to write an extended story, a map is one kind of plan which can prompt ideas about setting and plot; notes on events can be jotted in along the route, together with drawings of monsters and villains. This might then be developed into a board game, to stimulate oral or written story-telling.

Like the picture, this kind of work is often saved until after the writing is completed, as a filler, but that misses its potential for guiding the structure, prompting visualisation of detail before the writing begins, not to mention exciting interest if a map is stained in cold tea, rolled up and charred at the ends so that it imitates parchment, stuck down with sealing wax and tied with ribbon. When they are reading journey stories which do not have a map created by the author, creating an appropriate map from the text is an active comprehension assignment as they translate the detail given in the text into the visual medium.

Conceptual Plans

Conceptual plans are based on language in its briefest form, and as such some people will find them too abstract. However, they are among the most powerful in terms of density of information and speed of use.

Brainstorming

The technique of brainstorming is usually used as an oral planning technique with a group or whole class, though it can be a solo written form as well. The aim is to produce as many ideas as possible, as quickly as possible, noting them as they occur, to be later sorted out into some sort of shape, order of priority or sequence. It is the speed of response which is critical, as if the response were coming from the subconscious under the heat of inspiration, perhaps with the pressure of competition or collaboration with others. The 'association of ideas' effect will encourage both convergent and divergent thinking. Distinctions, selections, refinement can be made once the flow of ideas has dried up. It is best used as a pre-plan, for anything which slows down or distracts from this spontaneous flow reduces the impact, so in oral brainstorming the standard teacherly questions such as 'What do you mean?', 'Can you say more?', 'Does that really fit in here?' should be saved for a later stage when the ideas are opened up for all to discuss; it would be psychologically threatening to conduct an autopsy of the 'Who said that? What did you mean?' kind, and would perhaps limit future participation by those who had felt threatened.

Outlining

Outlining is the closest to the 'rough notes' which most adults claim to be their favoured form of planning. The process is to write down ideas in brief form as they occur, as key words or phrases. The disadvantage of this in the 'rough notes' approach is that such a spontaneously generated list is unlikely to create an overall shape for the intended writing, since ideas will occur in random order. The writer has to review the notes and sequence them either by numbering, underlining, highlighting (with a marker pen), or by arrows forward and backward to show sequence. The sequence becomes the outline of the writing, hence the term 'outlining', though it may be known also as 'key-notes'.

Most people consider this to be the 'natural' approach to planning and the only kind of plan that even older children need, but the feeling of naturalness may come from never having been taught alternative approaches. It is in fact a clumsy way of planning complex material because possibilities for large-scale revision are limited.

Web Chart

Alternatively called a spidergram or concept map, this is an immensely powerful and flexible planning device. The main concept is written in the centre of a blank page. Supporting concepts are then written around it, in any order as they are thought of, linked to the central idea by lines like the spokes of a wheel or strands of a spider's web. To each of these concepts is added sub-concepts as supporting detail, then sub-sub-concepts, written in as they occur and linked with lines to the concept they support, so that gradually a map of the ideas involved in the subject is built up. To the words can be added visual symbols or sketches, and some people find it helps to use different colours for different areas of the chart. Finally the distinct areas can be numbered to show the order in which they are to be written.

It is a very powerful planning technique because it encourages a broad vision, even divergent thinking because of the movement outwards from the centre. It allows ideas to be inserted or deleted in any order and then a writing order established at the final stage without any rewriting. The writer can see at a glance as with a picture the complete ideational framework of even very long and complex documents, the main and subordinate concepts and the relationship between them. Writing the same ideas in more traditional fashion as a series of notes, either across or down the page, is a linear process which discourages forward-backward rethinking and tends to impose a sequence on the text at an early, perhaps too early, stage.

The web chart can also be used as a memory aid for revision at higher levels of learning. If a different colour is used for each concept cluster, different print styles for main and subordinate ideas and additionally symbols in the form of simple sketches, the memory has even more visual clues of a distinctive nature, to aid recall.

Flow Chart

Widely used by computer programmers, the flow chart best suits a 'How to . . .' sequence of actions which may have 'either/or' consequences – if not this then that. At the simplest level, begin with a 'How to' sequence which is chronological. This allows you to list the main actions as boxes one below the other down the page. For more complex sequences where there are actions or instructions which are alternatives or which occur in parallel time the reader is guided by arrows to alternative boxes, then on along a different track. Giving directions to a robot is a fun target for this kind of plan. The most complex application I have encountered is in planning the design of a 'Fighting Fantasy Adventure Game Book', where the reader having read an introductory paragraph must choose what the central character should do next, being directed to another section of the book depending on what course of action is chosen, e.g. 'Stand and fight – turn to page 48'/'Take shelter in the enchanted forest – turn to page 12'.

Pros and Cons

Argument is often structured around two opposing points of view. Within a single sentence this can be expressed as 'on the one hand . . . on the other'. To plan an extended text the opposing ideas can be listed as two columns, one for the pros, the other for the cons. For each entry in one side it may be possible for the writer to think of one which counter-balances it, which illustrates the notion of a 'balanced' argument. The list can be in single words, though phrases and even complete sentences might help a younger writer beginning to learn the difficult field of Argument. For more experienced writers, the box structure described below is a more complex version of this kind of plan.

Boxes (windows or chocolate bars)

One of the simplest ways of teaching the concept of the paragraph is to describe it as a box to put things in, things which are in some way alike. This concept can be made concrete if a page is divided into four boxes by drawing one line across and one line down the page, so that the page looks like a child's drawing of a window. The number of boxes represents the number of paragraphs in the intended text. Each box is then given a heading or name, and into the box are put words, phrases, notes on that topic. For instance, for writing a letter about oneself to a new pen-friend, the four boxes might be called: (1) home life; (2) school life; (3) interests and hobbies; (4) hopes for the future. To these topics could be added sub-headings to prompt the thoughts of the writer – pets, jobs about the house, for instance, in box no. 1. Although such boxes do guide the response, they need not take away from the individuality or creativity of the writer who illustrates and expands the main idea with completely personal material.

For older children the 'window' of four boxes can be extended into a 'chocolate bar' as more paragraphs are added. If related ideas are clustered in this way at the outset by the plan then the writing which follows will be more likely to have a balanced paragraph structure.

Matrix

A matrix contains information classified according to two or more dimensions. For instance, if the class is to write adventure stories, planning might begin by discussing the qualities of characters they are going to create. This would raise possible headings for a matrix: appearance, age, friends, talents, personality and so on. The blank page is divided into vertical columns and each heading is written at the top of a column. Down the side of the page are written the names of the characters in the story, and for each character an entry is made in the appropriate characteristic column across the page. More detailed plans would need a separate matrix sheet for each character, and could then be alternatively called a character profile.

Synoptic

By synoptic is meant an abbreviated version of the intended text; this kind of planning involves more extensive language than the single concepts of conceptual plans.

Synopsis

The term synopsis is usually applied to the process of reducing a long text to a short one by selecting the key statements and ignoring all the rest. Book jackets can be good models of the form, offering at least a partial synopsis of the plot up to a dramatic moment, ending with a cliff-hanger. Selecting appropriate detail involves considerable judgement as to what is most and what least important, and skill in drafting so as to make a reasonably elegant text.

Used as a plan a synopsis sets out the main statements of the intended text, to be expanded later. The advantage is that the writer can play about with the rhetoric of the most important propositions, without being bogged down with the construction of the supporting detail, which is added later.

When they begin to write stories, young children tend to write unembellished story-lines, effectively a synopsis, being just the bare details of the plot even when one was hoping for a full evocation of life's rich pattern. This tendency can, however, be useful when applied to another context such as writing a play because if they write a plot synopsis first it acts as a plan which frees them to think about other matters such as characterisation and the difficulties of revealing that through speech alone. If they begin by writing speech first, they can become bogged down in trivial, quick-fire dialogue which does not take the plot forward.

Prompts

Prompts might in the first instance be given by the teacher to guide the shape of the writing. At the very briefest this can be words such as 'Where', 'Who', 'What happens', 'How does it end' set down the side of the page to draw out the substance and shape of a story. Prompts can be much more substantial than that. A classic prompt is for the teacher to provide the opening lines of, for instance, a horror story: 'It was in the crypt at midnight. An owl hooted and slowly a coffin lid began to open . . .' Further prompts can be given at significant points later in the story, the intention being to reduce the demands of creativity on the writer, demonstrating style and structure yet leaving freedom for individual imaginative projection.

Cameo Forms

Where children are reluctant to use the more abstract forms of plan, and resist successive drafting, they may find it more engaging to write a briefer form which, though complete in itself, prepares them for writing a more extensive and complex text. Such brief forms of writing, acting as miniature versions of a more extensive text, I have termed 'cameos'. For instance, a diary entry could be expanded into a story; a holiday resort poster might be the basis for a holiday brochure description; an epitaph could be reformulated as a poem or a brief biography. The diary, the poster and the epitaph here act as 'cameos' for the more extended forms which follow. A diary is a cameo form in another way in that its basic pattern is a chronological record of the events of a single day, a pattern which can be repeated to cover as many days as the writer chooses. In the classroom it can be held to a single day for the slow writers or continue for as long as it holds interest for the dedicated.

The advantage of cameos as a plan is that they are interesting and complete forms in themselves, so can be more satisfying to children than the more abstract forms. Importantly, slower or less able children may be able to do a good job on a cameo and so achieve success while the most able complete both the cameo and the main writing task for which the cameo was intended as the plan.

I have found the following forms useful as cameos: (1) book jacket; (2) concrete poetry; (3) diary; (4) epitaph; (5) greetings card; (6) letter; (7) memorandum; (8) minutes (of a meeting); (9) passport; (10) postcard; (11) poster; (12) telex.

The Planning Sequence

A planning sequence can involve a combination of more than one plan, for instance:

Model 1

Class discussion
Brainstorm ideas
Transfer ideas into a web chart
Cluster – sequence – prioritise ideas
Indicate paragraph order
Drafting

Model 2

Library-based research
Write list of key words
Review and edit the list
Number the items to show order
Add extension ideas
Drafting

Review

It is very important that plans are not seen as the first stage of the rocket, to be discarded once the mission is off the ground. They should guide the writing from start to finish, so should be there in evidence alongside the draft, to be consulted frequently. Once the drafting is finished and the text published class discussion can usefully focus on how helpful the plans were, how close the finished writing was to the plan and what difficulties were and were not solved by it. For children to see themselves as writers they need to be aware of every stage of the crafting process.

5
THE BLANK PAGE: CHOOSING OPTIONS

Introduction

On occasion we all feel a strong urge to 'write it down'. It may be in the form of a letter to the press or impressions of a holiday scene or a page in a diary. No matter how strongly we feel that first impulse, when we begin to write it often becomes clear that the brain does not unerringly direct the hand to write continuous lucid prose suitable to be read by someone else. Only for some people some of the time do words pour out fluently, so that on re-reading they hold up as a construct decodable by others. The poet William Wordsworth was said to have been able to compose poetry in his head whilst on his walks in the Lake District, later dictating it to his sister to transcribe. Enid Blyton is said to have composed her children's books at dictation speed to a secretary almost without revision; a cynic might say that it shows. Nonetheless such a facility must be very rare; most of us have a much more limited capacity to hold complete extended texts in the head in their formed state. Whenever we think we have a lot to write about we more often find that fluency holds for only a few lines; beyond that the structure of ideas may be complete but not the deathless prose that is needed to express them.

It is far more common to be aware from the outset of the blank page or screen impassively waiting for orders from a mind in which a jumble of ideas, images, feelings, intentions floats waiting to be realised through the medium of language. That blank page is a daunting reference point. In the guise of 'writer's block' it can recur at any moment in the writing process, and professional writers speak of it with dread. Many is the page, the letter, the great novel left unfinished because ideas or language or the interaction of the two would not flow. Some will know the trauma of the examination answer which just would not come. 'I know what I want to say but I just can't say it.' More will remember as a child having to write thank-you letters to little-known relatives at Christmas time.

Let us set out more optimistically here to see the composing process as a challenge, the blank page as a mind-game like chess which allows an endless variety of patterns of play discovered by those who have gone before. Available to us as options in the composing process are techniques and conventions to improve our chances of working the blank page into a communication which will achieve our purpose.

The first important point, for adult writers as well as for children, is that the macro-decisions should already have been taken at the planning stage: decisions to do with topic (what is the writing to be about, from start to finish), audience (who is it for, what is the reader's expectation), purpose (what effect do I want to achieve). It is from weaknesses at this macro-level that much of the writer's block problem can be traced rather than at the micro-level of composition. What now follows is premised on that; in facing the blank page to begin drafting, the writer already knows the answers to 'Who for?', 'What about?', 'What effect?' questions.

As described further in Chapter 9, it is extremely helpful for children to experiment with 'samples', that is short pieces of the intended text, before they attempt a complete draft. The brevity of a sample encourages them to experiment with such options as those listed below, to see which is most effective, and in the long term it is through such creative play that they develop skill in crafting.

Voice

The writer has the option of using the viewpoint (or 'voice') of first, second or third person, in the singular or plural. These are also described as the 'active voice' because the person who carries out the action is specified. Alternatively the writer might choose the passive or impersonal voice which takes the focus away from the person performing the action.

The most obvious to the young writer is the first person; the experience of the self is after all, without any accusation of egocentricity, the most direct to us all. In the example 'I got up and had my breakfast. . . ' the writer is recounting a personal experience in chronological order, but first-person viewpoint can be used effectively in fields such as Argument and Assertion as in 'I believe that it is wrong to kill baby seals . . . ' which suggests directness without formality and the 'sincerity' which the National Curriculum recommends. In some forms the 'I' persona licenses the informal vocabulary and syntax of everyday speech; the personal letter and diary forms are clear examples but beyond that such forms as travel writing and magazine feature articles often express the personality of the writer.

Related to first person singular but with a significantly different effect is the first person plural, the royal 'we'. This can have the effect of giving the writer more status since assertions and opinions are not so obviously those of a possible eccentric; two or more eccentrics are more authoritative than one. 'We' is used in advertising copy to suggest authorship by a group of concerned individuals not a faceless money-machine: 'We at Rattletrap Autos guarantee satisfaction.'

Use of the second person as in 'You like a lie-in on Saturday mornings . . .' can be effective because the writer assumes the views of the reader and suggests that the writing is a conversation between the two. It too can be used in serious writing as in 'You probably think it is wrong to kill baby seals . . .' but since it is more contrived than the first-person viewpoint it is more difficult to sustain in a longer piece of writing and tends to be used as an occasional insert such as the rhetorical question, used by advertisers to draw in potential customers.

The third-person viewpoint is very familiar to us not only through story structure but also through journalism and reportage of all kinds. It is a means of recounting the actions, thoughts and feelings of others, rather than the writer, e.g. 'He likes to lie in on Saturday morning . . .' or 'The students were protesting about the killing of baby seals.' Third-person viewpoint may seem less direct but since the device can take the reader into the innermost self of the third person it need not in fact be more remote.

Impersonal viewpoint takes the focus of the reader away from the viewpoint of a specific person; the actor (subject) of the action (verb) is concealed (passive). The last example above, which is in the active voice, would be transformed in the passive voice to: 'There were protests by students about the killing of baby seals.' It is considered more objective, impartial, scientific and hence more remote since less directly involving the persona of the writer.

A sustained impersonal viewpoint would be inappropriate for such genres as the story where the voice of an author or narrator is generally significant, but it is felt to be appropriate in such scientific writing as: 'The test-tube was placed in a clamp and heated to a temperature of $100°C$' where objectivity in reporting evidence is considered more important than the persona of the writer. In schooling the impersonal is considered to be an advanced option, difficult for young children to grasp and hence reached at a late stage by way of personal viewpoint: 'We placed the test-tube in a clamp.'

Register

The text has to be appropriate for the subject, for the intended form and the intended reader; together these three forces determine the register of the text. For instance, take the example of a description of an incident in an athletic event composed for: (1) a letter to an intimate friend; (2) a school magazine; (3) a scientific journal. The writer has won the race but has collapsed after the finish. In the first case to an intimate friend the writer might describe his/her physical state as 'totally knackered'. In the second it might be more appropriate for the school magazine to describe this as 'collapsing over the finishing line and needing help from a doctor'. For a scientific journal it might be more appropriate to describe it as a case of 'complete physical exhaustion requiring immediate medical treatment.' Because young writers have a limited word bank of alternative expressions and of experience of what is appropriate, they need to be guided in selection of vocabulary to fit the appropriate register. The National Curriculum suggests that by level 8 children should be aware of the appropriate vocabulary in five registers: colloquial, formal, technical, poetic and figurative. A thesaurus is essential in this respect; a dictionary will list alternatives for a given word, but a thesaurus explores the shades of meaning of a word and related concepts, across a range of registers.

Tone

Tone is a far-reaching term and notoriously difficult to describe briefly. To some extent the attitude of the writer will determine the tone, but it is created by the accumulated effect of the choices made above. Because of the multiple possibilities in the nuances of language the teacher will need to help pupils to match tone to intended reader by interacting with children as they write. Tone can be described through reference to a range of polar opposites:

formal – informal
hostile – encouraging
authoritarian – persuasive
neutral – biased
enthusiastic – dispassionate

Markers of a particular tone might come from the style of address:

Dear Sir/Madam   Dear Bill   Hiya Bill

Or from the vocabulary choice, as in this range of options from formal to informal:

youth	young man	yobbo
domicile	home	ours
exterminate	murder	bump off
extensive	large	ginormous
juvenile	adolescent	teenager

Or from balanced to biased:

Impartial	*Our side*	*Their side*
guerrilla	freedom fighter	terrorist
hostage	guest	innocent victim
press conference	press briefing	propaganda
loyal	patriotic	blindly obedient

Clearly it is important in the development of resistant readers that they should be able to detect such coloration in language which reveals or conceals the value-base of the writer.

Length

Although total length does not matter in such forms as the personal letter, which could be just a few lines or many pages, in most other forms it is important and sometimes highly significant as in for instance a classified advertisement where the writer is charged by the letter or word which gives a considerable incentive to be concise. News items are written so that they can be cut back from the bottom to fit available space, and journalists writing all forms within newspapers and magazines are given targets for word-length. Many forms of poetry are based on patterns of syllables or rhyme which determine the overall length. Length then should be one of the parameters of writing assignments given to children and be considered at the planning stage.

Detail

Writers probably do not begin by making a clear decision beforehand as to how much detail their writing is to include of, say, a description or the illustration of an argument. It soon becomes an issue though and children do need to be given guidance on the overall principle of detail; what is or is not 'key' in informing or entertaining the reader. Partly it is a question of how long the piece is to be, whether it is to gain an effect by being atmospheric or creating a word picture or detailing all the evidence. The range of options runs from full detail of every feature, through highlighting of the telling detail to use of symbol which leaves 'gaps' for the imagination. The normal characteristic of young children's writing is its lack of descriptive detail. 'A man walked down a street and he saw a bank raid. . . . ' 'We went on a school trip to the zoo and saw monkeys. . . . ' In both story and informative writing the tendency of young writers is to give an outline account using minimal detail. Development comes not only from increased word choice, but also from insight into the needs of the reader. The solution is to draw attention in their reading to the occasions when and the purposes for which detail is used; to give them chance to read other children's work and to learn how to look for such features; to make them critical readers of their own draft writing.

Tense

Young children often choose to begin a story with the continuous present, e.g. 'I am walking down the street when suddenly out jumps a robber. . . .' Although this seems the most direct and immediate to them, it is very difficult to sustain. A story after all is in some sense a history – an account of a past event, and the writer takes us into it by other means than the stream of consciousness. Only particular kinds of assignment will break that norm. For instance, the script of a Party Political Broadcast might have more frequent use of the future, e.g. 'When we come to power we will. . . .' A comment by a candidate who has lost the election might use more of the conditional, e.g. 'If we had been clearer we would have had more impact.' Children's ability to handle more complex tenses can be stretched by such specifically focused contexts.

Structure

At Sentence Level

We expect all continuous writing to proceed in terms of units of meaning which build up from words to phrases, sentences, paragraphs, chapters, volumes. These units are linked one to another in a relationship which creates a continuity of meaning. A complex sentence can be built up by adding onto the main clause one or more additional units (subordinate clauses) which support or amend the meaning of the main clause. The linking word (conjunction) indicates the relationship of ideas between the main and subordinate clauses. For instance, the conjunction 'when' indicates a time relationship, 'where' a place relationship and 'because' a causal relationship. The order of main and subordinate clauses can usually be changed, which allows the writer to vary the effect; for instance, one unit of meaning may be delayed until the end to create suspense or placed at the beginning for impact.

Modern linguists have greatly expanded and refined syntax descriptions but the distinctions made in traditional grammar are as follows. In all but one of the following examples the main clause is placed first, before the linking word:

(1) Clauses which are equal partners (co-ordinating) linked by: *and, but*, e.g.
  (a) I will clear the table *and* wash up the dishes.
  (b) I will clear the table *but* I will not wash up the dishes.
(2) Clauses which act like nouns (noun clauses) linked by: *that, what*, e.g.
  (a) (Noun clause object) I know *that* he is guilty.
  (b) (Noun clause subject) *What* they are asking is out of the question.
(3) Clauses which act like adjectives (adjectival clauses) linked by: *who, whom, which*, e.g.
  (a) We saw again the same man *who* had sold us the book last week.
  (b) I bought the book *which* she recommended.
(4) Clauses which act like adverbs (adverbial clauses).
  (a) Cause: *because, as, since*, e.g. The boss paid us a bonus *because* we had finished the work before time.
  (b) Comparison: *as . . . as*, e.g. She looked *as* white *as* a sheet (is).
  (c) Concession: *although, even though*, e.g. I will stay up late *although* I am tired.
  (d) Condition: *if, unless, provided that*, e.g. She would go to the cinema *if* a good film was on.
  (e) Manner: *as, as if, like*, e.g. He walked away from the court *as* a broken man.
  (f) Place: *where, wherever*, e.g. Give me a home *where* the buffaloes roam.
  (g) Purpose: *so that, in order that*, e.g. They went to the square *so that* they would see the procession.
  (h) Result: *so . . . that*, e.g. The rope had been *so* securely tied *that* no one could undo it.

(i) Time: *when, after, while, since, as, whenever*, e.g. They ended the meeting *when* they had completed the agenda.

Further detail of ways in which ideas are linked is given in Appendix 2.

At Paragraph Level

At the paragraph level Bissex (quoted in Gilliland, 1972) suggested twelve structural patterns used frequently by writers to shape their argument. What he called 'the classic' model is a three-part structure: a generalised statement, an expansion of that proposition and a summary. Other structures include: an anecdote followed by a moral; a two-part 'on the one hand . . . on the other'; a series of logical 'because A is true then B follows' steps. A fuller description is given in Appendix 3.

At Text Level

Wilkinson (1986a, p. 128) suggested three basic approaches to organising text: temporal, topical and logical. In constructing texts we find that it is easiest to write about things which can be put into a time sequence such as a narrative (temporal) or are immediately present (topical). Logical structure is generally felt to be more difficult, being less immediate or less obvious to our ways of thinking.

Concerning logical structure the National Curriculum document makes the distinction only between chronological and non-chronological writing. Although there are many kinds of logic other than the chronologic, at present we have no single agreed model to describe them. Some of those used by professional writers include:

(1) *Accumulation* – as in a newspaper article, the gist of the story is given first and further detail added thereafter.
(2) *Chain* – a sequential relationship between the ideas from one to the next, e.g. because one thing is true then another follows, e.g. 'First we . . . then we . . . .'
(3) *Cluster* – information is organised into sections according to a specific concept, e.g. the subject of clothing might be organised into sections or paragraphs on hats, jackets, trousers, shoes, underwear.
(4) *Comparison/contrast* – e.g. where all good points are described followed by all the bad points.
(5) *Highlighting* – each new item is marked as distinct by some graphic symbol:
    (a) Stars – alternatively a blob or any other non-sequential sign. It can only be used in relatively straightforward lists where the order is not significant.

(b) Typeface – a different print face such as bold or block cap-
    itals or a font such as Gothic.

(c) Colour – distinctive colours not only denote distinct ideas,
    they may also link related ideas across different parts of a
    text.

(6) *Headline* – each new item is introduced by a verbal sign such as a
    key-word or headline which signposts and summarises its
    distinctiveness.

(7) *Iconic* – where the written text uses systematic reference to a
    chart, diagram, illustration or map to which the reader refers in
    order to follow the logical argument of the text.

(8) *Impressionistic* – selected detail determined by the writer's
    personal choice; most likely to be where the personality of the
    writer is strongly expressed, as in travel writing.

(9) *Leading question* – a text sets up questions and then answers
    them. This is a device often used in promotional material given
    to potential customers who are anticipated as having predictable
    queries about the product. A series of questions that clients are
    likely to ask about a product acts as headlines for sections of
    information about the product, e.g. 'If I have sensitive skin will it
    cause a rash?'

(10) *Sequence* – where the main ideas are listed in a specific sequence:
     (a) Alphabetical order (e.g. an encyclopaedia);
     (b) Numbered steps (e.g. a car workshop manual);
     (c) Priority (e.g. an advisory leaflet on home insulation).

(11) *Signpost* – where the writing begins with a statement of what is
     to follow. The contents page at the beginning of a book is a
     larger-scale alternative showing the chapter headings and per-
     haps the sub-headings. The index at the end of a book is a
     detailed alphabetical listing of contents.

(12) *Visual* – where the writer controls the viewpoint like a camera
     lens, panning over a panorama, zooming in or out on detail,
     hardening and softening the focus.

Persuading the Reader: Rhetoric

The Greeks recognised the power of language to persuade, and identified by conscious analysis the crafting techniques used by orators who
were successful persuaders in public life. This study, rhetoric, was
defined by Isocrates as 'the science of persuasion', and in its origin it
was considered to be the essential study for the would-be successful
communicator. Over the ages rhetoric came to be identified with the
study of embellishments of flowery language rather than the cut and

thrust of persuasion in debate and as a discipline it fell into disfavour in modern times. Many of the Greek or Latin names for the so-called rhetorical 'figures' seem very remote from our own language, and hence the concern only of pedants. However, some have been adopted by our language and we can use in everyday speech without any raising of eyebrows such terms as:

(1) *paradox* – a seeming contradiction which intrigues the listener/reader and hence holds the attention.
(2) *metaphor* – an association of ideas through visual comparison, which helps the listener/reader to see a new idea in the mind's eye.
(3) *hyperbole* – a description of attributes which emphasises and simplifies by exaggeration.

Many teachers want their children to know those particular terms, and be able to use them in their own writing and identify them in the work of others. Other classical terms such as hendiadys, oxymoron, preterition are not terms in common parlance, even though they too identify distinctive features of crafted language which modern writers use. Should we add them to metaphor, hyperbole and paradox? There is no general agreement on which terms it is or is not appropriate to know and how far we should go in directly teaching such terms through the naming of parts or focused exercises. If precision in naming of parts helps children to resist the insidious use of rhetoric then the list which follows for their teacher's benefit will be useful; by it I do not intend to suggest that children should learn by heart lists of abstruse classical terms, or practise identifying them in ornate artificial examples. To lessen the resistance of those who oppose the very idea of rhetoric I have clustered this selection of rhetorical devices according to the desired effect on the reader, making a minor feature of classical terminology:

To Arouse Curiosity

(1) *Double meaning*: e.g. 'Everything we do is driven by you' (advert for Ford cars).
(2) *Oxymoron* (a sub-category of paradox): one concept is qualified by another which seems to contradict it, e.g. 'sweet sorrow.' A cynic once suggested 'military intelligence'.
(3) *Paradox*: a juxtaposed contrast with an apparent contradiction, e.g. 'Heathrow: the world's local airport.'
(4) *Pun*: a play on the meaning of words, e.g. 'As you see from the prose there aren't any cons.'

(5) *Rhetorical question:* a direct question of the reader, who cannot answer it but is provoked into thought, e.g. 'Have you ever thought what life would be like without the electric light?'
(6) *Suspension:* withholding vital information until as late in the sentence as possible, e.g. 'There on the doorstep, large as life with a bouquet of flowers in his hand, stood George.'

To Create Impact

(1) *Declamation:* an extreme assertion, e.g. 'Enough is enough!'
(2) *Hyperbole:* an exaggeration of the reality, e.g. 'This will be the meal of your life.'
(3) *Inversion* (fronting): transferring to the beginning of the sentence an element one would normally expect at the end so as to give it stronger emphasis, e.g. 'Chocolate, everyone's favourite treat.'
(4) *Preterition:* false modesty, e.g. 'Probably the best lager in the world.'

To Reduce Impact

(1) *Litotes:* to say one thing by negating the opposite, e.g. 'He is no longer alive' meaning 'He is dead.'
(2) *Circumlocution:* avoidance of a particular word or phrase, e.g. 'When a loved one passes away. . . . '
(3) *Euphemism:* using a more attractive term for a harsher reality, e.g. 'We are going to have to lose you' meaning 'You are fired.'

To Appeal to the Ear

(1) *Alliteration:* two or more words beginning with the same sound, e.g. 'To sit in solemn silence in a dull dark dock' (W. S. Gilbert, *The Mikado*).
(2) *Assonance:* two or more words with the same vowel sound within the words, e.g. the 'i' in 'Twinkle twinkle little star . . . Like a diamond in the sky' (Lewis Carroll, *Alice*).
(3) *Onomatopoeia:* the sound imitates the meaning, e.g. 'crash, bang, wallop'.
(4) *Rhyme:* two or more words whose endings sound similar, e.g. moon, June, soon, tune, croon.
(5) *Rhythm:* regular stress pattern in a series of words, e.g. 'Dirty British coaster with a salt-caked smoke stack' (John Masefield, 'Cargoes').

To Appeal to the Eye

(1) *Imagery:* a picture conjured up in words, e.g. 'Yet who would have thought the old man to have had so much blood in him' (*Macbeth*).
(2) *Metaphor:* an embedded comparison, e.g. 'He took it on the chin', 'The evening passed in a golden glow.'
(3) *Simile:* an explicit comparison, e.g. 'Oh my love's like a red, red rose.'

To Create Desirable Associations

(1) *Association chain:* e.g. 'Smooth, soft, mild, gentle for a baby's skin'.
(2) *Coloration of language:* e.g. 'Make your house into a home.'

To Make Connection with the Familiar

(1) *Familiar saying based on a concrete image:* e.g. 'Putting the cart before the horse.'
(2) *Synechdoche:* a part referring to the whole, e.g. 'Many hands make light work.'
(3) *Regional, grass roots sayings*, e.g. 'Many a mickle macks a muckle' (Yorkshire for 'Mighty oaks out of little acorns grow').

To Extend the Message

(1) *Accumulation:* a list of complementary attributes, e.g. 'We have suffered pain, sorrow, deprivation.'
(2) *Opposition:* e.g. 'He is not dead, he is still alive.'
(3) *Reiteration*, e.g. 'Your services are no longer required – your service is terminated, you are dismissed, fired, sacked.'
(4) *Repetition:* one idea represented by two nouns (hendiadys), e.g. 'The pain and suffering were soon over.'
(5) *Tautology:* repetition of a word, in a different sense, e.g. 'In these parts when it rains, it rains.'

To Contract the Message

(1) *Asyndeton:* omission of a conjunction, e.g. 'I came, I saw, I conquered.'
(2) *Ellipsis:* the omission of one or more words, e.g. 'Enjoy!' (i.e. enjoy your meal).

It is sometimes suggested that technical knowledge of language limits children's creativity. Whilst creativity is certainly possible without such knowledge, most rhetorical figures are slots into which creativity is fitted; the pun, for instance, is by its very nature creative play with words which turns cliché into original expression. Knowing that such kinds of play with words are possible can prompt children's creativity. Introduced with sensitivity as part of a climate of shared writing over the years of schooling, such knowledge will not stultify creativity. The terms are signposts not fences; they indicate directions not limits.

6
INFORMATIVE WRITING

Introduction

Informative reading and writing has somehow got itself a bad name. It has a reputation for being less 'user-friendly' than story which by contrast is considered to have universal natural appeal. I have no problem in resisting this stereotype because of overwhelming personal experience. My father-in-law's favourite reading is car workshop manuals and motoring maps; he will spend hours decoding their details, muttering juicy facts to himself. My wife loves dress-making instructions and consults them, scissors in hand, for long hours every evening. My daughter pores over 'how to make . . .' activities books, with glue and paper in dangerous liaison on the carpet. My son reads cycling magazines and catalogues until he knows them almost by heart. They all probably think that I have a similar obsessive relationship with newspapers. Each of us in our private life has an affinity with one or another form which has an Informative purpose; in spite of the acknowledged difficulties of such forms, we are driven by our interests to reach high levels of proficiency. If we were to swap reading matter with each other, though, the problems of the informative would be all too apparent. This chapter deals with the structural features of informative writing, but we have to keep in mind that it is interest in the subject matter which motivates the learner. Without that interest those features are a strait-jacket to the writer; with it they are a strength.

Objectivity

Factual knowledge has a high priority in education and for that reason informative writing has traditionally dominated the school curriculum. Where the primary purpose of the writer is to inform the reader, the writing is objective, functional, implicitly accurate; the reader expects the information presented to be complete, and impartial, the personality and opinions of the writer to be of no significance. This kind of 'pure' informative writing we expect to find in an encyclopaedia entry or a school textbook; or outside schooling in such forms as the car workshop manual, the 'how to' guides for hobbies, and the reports and technical instructions of working life.

Across the range of different forms of writing on the Informative axis, the primary purpose of informing the reader may be modified by a secondary purpose of persuading. As the scale shades towards this persuasive purpose, so the impartial representation of fact becomes coloured by the personality of the writer and rhetorical techniques used to shape the reader's response in a particular direction. Complete objectivity is rarely possible for informative writing, but it remains a potential usually unrealised, a touchstone by which writing in this range may be judged. It is an essential principle for the development of young writers that they should be made aware of the boundaries of scientific objectivity in informative writing.

Text Support

Over recent years there has been an amazing development in the range of approaches to informative texts, with the aim of making them more user-friendly. There has been a realisation that unambiguous communication involves attracting and holding the full attention of the reader. The dense prose of the Victorians has been replaced by such supportive techniques as colour photographs, charts and explanatory diagrams; the use of shorter, less complex sentences, shorter paragraphs, reduced number of technical terms; the use of narrative forms and personal viewpoint. This is an extension of the range, not a reduction. The notion of development still needs to include focus on reading and writing the dense prose of traditional forms of the Informative at the higher levels.

Terms of Reference

The degree of specificity required in the writing can be a major issue in informative writing, particularly when the subject is scientific or technical, where precise terms are necessary to convey the meaning. The more remote the subject, the more demanding it will be for the writer to be specific. Children can pick up the notion that everything can be expressed in plain English, and that technical terms must be 'jargon', to be scorned and avoided. That is an inappropriate notion here and their development must involve the learning of precise terminologies outside the registers of ordinary life. In teaching forms within the Informative range the necessary terms of reference will need to be made available to the writer, through direct teaching, reference books, glossaries of terms. For younger children the tolerance of inspecificity will be higher, perhaps very high, but the developmental scale should increasingly demand precision.

Writer Viewpoint

In informative writing, the writer's personality is not made one of the focuses of attention as a general rule. For instance, the reader is not made aware through the writing of who wrote the individual entries in an encyclopaedia, and it would take a skilled reader to detect the personal interpretations of the author of, say, a history textbook. Such writing hides the persona of the writer either because the focus of every sentence is a matter of fact distinct from the writer's experience, judgement, likes and dislikes; or because the persona is concealed behind an impersonal style by such phrases as 'It can be seen that . . .', 'Some people prefer . . .' rather than the personal 'I think . . .' and 'I prefer . . .' or such passive forms as 'The test-tube was heated to 100° C.'

On the other hand Perera's (1984) model suggests that children find writing easier if they can write from a subjective viewpoint. So it is helpful if they record findings in a science experiment as a personal account in what is called 'the active voice' as this year 5 group has done:

> We are testing how quick our reaction is. We have to hold the ruler and let go and somebody else had to catch it. We held the ruler at 30 cm and these are our results . . .

The writer here is an actor in the event, a concrete personal experience, described in a time sequence which offers a structure. The 'we' is not spurious because both the experience and the writing were the result of collaboration, which is again very helpful to the young learner. The writer has had difficulty with the tense, which slips from the present ('we are') to the past ('we held'), but nonetheless the form has enabled the writer to make a clear record of a scientific process. It is important to acknowledge that such an approach is possible and might be considered preferable at the most sophisticated adult level. However, traditionally the advanced level of scientific writing expects impersonal, passive constructions which conceal the persona of the writer behind demonstrable fact. One possible version of the above account transposed into an advanced form might be:

> In order to test the speed of human reaction a ruler was held at a height of 30 cm and dropped, to be caught by the subject. The results are as follows . . .

The distinction between simple and sophisticated forms is becoming more blurred, not least because school textbooks are using more narrative structures and personal style in order to reach children more directly. In journalism the traditional style is for reported speech to conceal the writer's persona ('A palace spokesman said that the Queen . . .'), but it is becoming increasingly popular for the reporter to write from first-hand experience, because it is more dramatic and moreover it reflects the practice of television news reporting, where presenters in the studio and on-the-spot reporters are not unseen 'voice-overs' without personality or presence, and can more naturally speak of 'I'. Another reason may be that the active voice and first-hand experience are understood by every reader, whereas it takes more advanced literacy skills to decode the impersonal.

Schooling trains us to expect that in reading, say, a story or a poem, the emotions will be an important focus of the content, but that in science, geography or history the writer should concentrate on objective fact. That is a limiting perspective. Children become very emotionally involved in any subject; good teaching will aim to do just that. So the emotions and reactions of the writer are usually a matter of the most obvious fact at the time of writing, no matter what the subject. The question we need to ask as teachers is 'Does the emotional response of the writer help get the message across?' A 'no' answer is likely to be because the writer's self becomes more important than the real subject. A 'yes' answer suggests that the writer is personally involved in the subject, which is usually essential with younger children and will remain acceptable to a diminishing extent throughout schooling, though at the top end of high school young writers will be learning through successive drafts to couch their enthusiasm in more technical language. Older children need to know how to hold back both negative and positive emotional involvement; that must be part of our teaching programme and one of the criteria by which success in informative writing is judged.

Bias

In its pure form informative writing seeks to be impartial, and the writer will attempt to avoid ambiguity, obscurity and misleading inference. In reality it is impossible for the writer to communicate exactly the objective, impartial message intended, because of the purely personal, esoteric meaning that particular words, phrases, associations have for each of us as readers and writers. In addition to this general tendency for language to shift away from impartiality, bias can be represented on a continuum which runs from notional objectivity at one end to propaganda at the other: impartiality – subconscious bias – conscious bias – disguised bias.

In subconscious bias the writer is not aware that his/her value system is affecting the construction of the text, but nevertheless signals of that value system are being sent to the reader for whom the information is not as impartial as intended. Recently we have become far more aware of implicit sexism, racism, ageism – terms such as 'chairman', references to the reader as 'he', to secretaries as 'she' and so on. Once aware of the possibility of such bias intruding, the writer can be on guard, though it may be extremely difficult to obliterate all traces since they may pervade the values, even the realities of our society. Bias is all-pervasive. For instance, how often do we notice that by definition the press concentrates more attention on the negative aspects of life – doom and disaster – than on happy events. That selection-deselection process is a kind of bias which we have been conditioned to accept as normal.

EXPLANATION

Introduction

Because of the complexity of modern life we frequently encounter writing which aims to explain a process or product; as a model for reading/writing development information brochures have the advantage not only that they are clear and distinctive forms but also that they are in plentiful supply from service industries (Electricity and Gas), tourism, public information and advice agencies and many more.

The reader is usually considered to be non-specialist, hence needing things to be explained simply, unambiguously and in a logical order. This makes them ideal for use even with the youngest children. When the text is actually too difficult for children, the teacher can still point out the basic principles of construction: how visual displays such as maps, photographs, diagrams can help us to understand the more difficult written text; how use of colour printing and different type faces make the text more attractive and readable by breaking it into shorter, more digestible parts; how headings divide the text into its main ideas and help us to skim for information we need.

Take, for example, this extract from a pamphlet in a dentist's waiting-room *Fluoride protection and the family; your questions answered*:

Q   What is fluoride?
A   There is nothing artificial about fluoride. It is a natural sub-stance, like iron and calcium, and is often found in fresh water streams.
Q   Is fluoride safe?
A   Yes. Doctors and dentists agree that the amounts recommended for family fluoride protection are completely harmless and cause no ill effects at all. (continued)

Although not reproduced here the Q symbol is in a red box and the A in a yellow box. The questions are in print double the size of the answers, so that the structure of the text is visually explicit, the questions acting like headlines for the specific pieces of information which make up the content. The fact that this informative text was in fact devised by a firm marketing fluoride products raises, of course, the issue of impartiality, though in this case it would need specialist medical knowledge to determine whether or not the information is reliable.

How to cope with doorstep salesmen by the Office of Fair Trading uses quotation as an alternative to the question and answer structure:

'Good evening . . . I'm doing some market research on how people spend their spare time . . . .'

A well-known opening to gain your confidence, get inside the door and see what sort of a home you've got. (continued)

Process

In education explanation writing most usually takes the form of a report, such as the report of a science experiment. For young writers a report is a series of statements in chronological order, describing in the first person what the writer did, ending with the result of the experiment. The structure is not usually a problem if it can be chrono-logical, first person and based on first-hand experience. More difficult is the report which is based on a process which cannot be represented as a time sequence. For instance, a boy in year 9 middle band was given a labelled diagram of a zip fastener and asked to describe how it worked. He wrote:

HOW A ZIP FASTENER WORKS

The slide in a zip fastener is usually made of metal. It works by pulling the piece of hanging metal upwards and the duct at the side of the slide pushes the teeth inwards so they grip onto each other. To undo the zip you pull the piece of metal downwards so the divider in the zip unfastens the gripped teeth and pushes them outwards. The slide in the zip fastener is made from metal. At the side there is a duct which pulls together the teeth. In the middle there is a divider to split the teeth apart.

The words 'slide', 'duct', 'divider' and 'teeth' were all on the labelled diagram, and all have a special technical meaning in the context. Without the cue of the diagram it is unlikely that the writer would have been able to write so clearly. Even so the overall piece is not as well organised as it could have been. The last three sentences are afterthoughts which could have been added in earlier to make a tighter structure. For instance, the third sentence from the end adds further detail on 'the slide' and so would have been better added into the opening sentence.

The moral is that although the visual helps a reader to decode a text, in general it is inadequate as a plan for the writer. The reader's eye can take in an illustration at a glance and can sweep back and forth over detail as need be. A written text is linear; the eye can only sweep back and forward with difficulty and so in addition to the illustration, this writer needed a plan such as a series of boxes to collect together the sub-categories of ideas about the zip.

Technical Terms

The examples quoted above raise the issue of technical language in informative writing. The Plain English Society was set up to campaign against the use by officialdom of language which is unnecessarily obscure because technical terms and complex syntax work against the comprehension of non-specialist readers. Certainly technical writers operating in specialised occupations develop highly esoteric ways of saying things. Education is no exception; an outsider would probably be mystified by such terms as SATs, profile components, coherent non-chronological writing (even Standard English), the language of the National Curriculum document for English. Such terminology is under-standable only to a specialist audience, and then not without debate, but in one sense that is its purpose; it is intended to focus the attention of the specialist reader onto very precise concepts which have an exact meaning. To an outsider the same terms might be considered 'officialese' and 'jargon', but that is because they are inappropriate for such a non-specialist audience, not because the terms in themselves are obscure or inappropriate. When teaching children we need to make a clear distinction between jargon and technical language. Certainly it should be a first principle for their writing that the reader should be able to follow the meaning, but to assert that in all circumstances there is a common word, or simple way of saying something which will replace a technical one is to seriously mislead them about both the power of language and the complexity of human activity.

Take, for example, an information brochure explaining the virtues of Champion double copper spark plugs, which includes the following:

> As a result of research and development, engines now utilize combustion chamber designs with higher compression ratios, increased gas turbulence, electronic engine management systems to prevent abnormal combustion conditions, and have the ability to ignite and burn leaner fuel/air mixtures. (continued)

If we underlined the technical terms in the passage we would have to underline most of it, because in the register of mechanical engineering it is bona fide. But if this information brochure was intended for amateur mechanics capable of changing their own car's spark plugs rather than for professional mechanical engineers, the level of technical terminology is certainly surprising, and whether you label it jargon depends on whether or not you understand it. It would be difficult to re-word the passage briefly in non-technical English and still say the same thing, though 'modern engines burn less petrol' conveys much of the meaning. In the complex adult world there are genuinely complex technical registers for which there is no adequate translation for the lay-person. The perennial problem in teaching is to decide how far to simplify such technical registers for all pupils. Certainly we should not pretend that technical terms have no real worth or that everything which is not instantly comprehensible must be jargon, to be dismissed as a confidence trick.

Small Print

Modern taste favours uncomplex syntax in all forms of writing, so that Victorian prose now seems highly convoluted by contrast. However, one form in which very complex style still notoriously remains is in so-called 'small print', ironically named in that the significance of what is being said is usually large. At the top end of the school we need to tackle the problem of decoding small print, because in adult life that is where so many adults find the outer limits of their literacy skills. We find the text so difficult in structure and so boring in subject matter that we ignore it and trust that the writer has our interests at heart. Usually, though, the small print is founded on legal language which is there to protect the writer's interests, and perhaps the reader's, though not necessarily. If by the time they are adults children cannot understand the legal language of small print, they will be at the mercy of those who can.

The term itself describes one important level of difficulty that readers have; the print itself is small hence difficult to read, and it is usually tucked away insignificantly at the end of a document, the main parts of which the reader may not have found a delight to read in any case, such as a contract, booking form, insurance document. This issue can only be briefly tackled here since it is so complex and the complete answer is legal training, but the points we need to get across to children are:

(1) Small print matters – you might be letting yourself in for something you would not want if you understood it.
(2) Skim read it, to get an idea of what it contains.
(3) Reading more slowly, put a cross in pencil beside what you do not understand and a tick beside what you do.
(4) Where the difficulty is with long sentences, identify the main statement and underline it in pencil. Read and re-read that part until you understand it; look words up in as large a dictionary as you can find.
(5) Once you understand the main statements, work on the supporting clauses and phrases; they qualify the main statement, and may change its meaning in significant ways.
(6) Parts you still cannot understand should now be underlined and a question mark put in the margin. Take the document to someone else who can help: a friend who is likely to know, the Citizen's Advice Bureau, the bank manager – or take it back to the writer and ask for a version in simple English.
(7) Don't sign the document until all your queries have been answered.

INSTRUCTION

Introduction

In the adult world we meet instructions in the form of cookery recipes, 'how to do it' articles in magazines and brochures, instruction manuals for machinery, knitting patterns, manufacturers' instructions for household goods, modelling and hobbies kit instructions, guidance on form-filling. How difficult we find them to read depends on our experience and our motivation. Most people would say that generally instructions are at the difficult end of what they read, because of the technical terms, the complexity of the processes involved, and the exactness of the actions required. We must all have tales to tell; anyone who has attempted to take a car engine apart using a manual, or tried to crochet from a knitting pattern will have stretched their literacy level to breaking point and perhaps beyond it.

In terms of children's development it is possible to find real writing examples across a range of increasing difficulty in the genre of instructions; from the Green Cross Code or a manufacturer's instructions for handling fireworks at the simplest level, to the manuals on Desk-top Publishing at the highest end. In between there are the many kinds of instruction, more or less complex: cookery recipes, construction kit instructions, rules of sports. In terms of children's learning, on the debit side there is the sheer baffling complexity of rules and instructions; on the credit side is the motivating force of a personal hobby which will inspire children of low ability to struggle until they can successfully decode technical texts on anything from fashion to fishing. We can only take them to higher levels of competence in such technical writing by building on their interest; by individualising their learning so that they bring in to class texts with which they need help and encouraging them to share their experiences as readers with the class.

Tone

Writers of instructions must of course know what they are talking about which makes the tone authoritative: directly telling someone less experienced how to do something – 'Make sure that you put the top back on the glue!' – the reader being directly addressed as 'you'. Technical terms are kept to a minimum or explained or illustrated in a diagram. For these reasons the field is ideally suited to pair work, with the writer trying out draft instructions on a partner who does not know how to carry out the routine described. Such direct experiment will give a real reason for redrafting to make the writing clearer.

Contexts which are associated with danger call for an assertive tone, as in this extract from an eight-page pamphlet designed to give instruction on the safe use of electricity in the garden, a potentially lethal context:

BEFORE YOU START

- Never use electrical gardening equipment when it is raining.
- When you go out and the garden is wet, wear rubber boots to increase your protection should an electrical fault occur.
- Dress properly! Never use any garden appliances barefoot or with open sandals. Wear trousers and strong flat-heeled shoes. Beware of flapping clothing and belts that might catch or trip you up. If you are using a rotary or hover mower it is important to wear very stout shoes or boots. (continued)

The main points are divided one from another by the use of dots. The first item is very short, which gives it a better chance of getting its message across and it might have been best to stick to that principle throughout; the third item here contains several separate points, which risks reader confusion. However, the attention-catching command 'Dress properly' does sum up the significance of what follows. That technique of making the first statement summarise what follows could have been applied to the second item so that it read: 'If the garden is wet, wear rubber boots. They will help to protect you if an electrical fault occurs.' The pamphlet is intended for an adult readership and the language used is not the simplest; with a class of children it would be helpful to check what they do not understand; 'should an electrical fault occur' is probably one trip-up point.

Older children will appreciate the range of tone possible in rules and instructions for different contexts, and can learn a lot by discussing which would be preferable in which circumstance in a list such as:

Prohibition: Smoking forbidden. Penalty £5.00.
Order: No smoking.
Request: Smokers please use rear seats.
Suggestion: We would prefer you not to smoke.
Subtle hint: Thank you for not smoking.

Structure: Sequence

Processes are usually carried out systematically in chronological order and so numbering will be the clearest indication of order. Otherwise the order might be:

Time sequence: First take a large saucepan.
Priority: Do A first, then B.
Clustering: 'Hutch', 'feeding', 'grooming'.
Contrasts: Six dos and six don'ts.
List: Three golden rules.

The Green Cross Code is an example of a time-related sequence of instructions, made deliberately simple so as to be understood by the youngest and least able reader:

(1) Find a safe place to cross, then stop.
(2) Stand on the pavement near the kerb.
(3) Look all round for traffic and listen.
(4) If traffic is coming let it pass. Look all round again.
(5) When there is no traffic near, walk straight across the road.
(6) Keep looking and listening for traffic while you cross.

On the basis of this example we can say that to simplify instructions the process should be divided into a numbered sequence of actions, written in the order that they are to be carried out. As far as possible each number concerns only a single action. Repeat instructions which are critical ('look/looking' occurs three times, 'listen/listening' twice). The instructions are addressed directly to a single reader, as if they are to be spoken to one person. Statements are positive, with the verb at the beginning of the sentence to emphasise the action concerned (e.g. 'Find . . .', 'Stand . . .', 'Look . . .'). Qualifications, alternatives and vagueness are avoided. Vocabulary and syntax are kept as simple as possible. This example contains two complex sentences ('If . . .' , 'When . . .') but this is unlikely to cloud the meaning. Item 4 contains two sentences, but the second is a repetition of 'look' so again the item is not overloaded with meaning.

A mixed ability year 5 class in a middle school were following a theme of Polar Exploration, which included simulating the planning of their own expedition. A discussion of what they needed to take with them led to a web chart (see Chapter 4) to encourage divergent ideas. These ideas were shared so that everyone could make the best possible listing. Then each person made a drawing of a sledge, with a labelled diagram of where the items in the web chart would be packed. One boy produced the following:

HOW TO PACK A SLEDGE FOR A POLAR EXPEDITION

(1) On the bottom you would put spare clothes and underwear, fuel and your diary. But I would be careful not to spill the fuel.
(2) In the middle you would put matches, drinks, soup, cheese, chocolate and meat but I wouldn't put the fuel with the matches because it might catch alight.
(3) On the top I would put my tent with the poles, an ice pick, first aid, sleeping bag and groundsheet.

In this example the writer has verbally duplicated the numbering system by adding 'on the bottom/middle/top'. This is not necessary but he has probably been influenced by the thought that he is giving the instructions verbally, person to person; we do not use '1/2/3' etc. when speaking to people. He has also used the direct address of 'you would/I would' throughout, softening the tone of command ('put', 'do not spill') into one of recommendation. Children are not used to giving orders, and they usually begin each instruction with 'You . . .' so as to stress the tone of direct address rather than the action word of the instruction, e.g. 'Put . . .'. This does suggest that in the planning and drafting stages children will readily take to working with a partner, the writer reading out the instructions and the partner carrying them out to see if they work unambiguously. The reader-writer interaction is this way made more direct than is usually the case in writing, and hence more helpful to the young writer in orienting and crafting the communication.

Structure: Clustering

The following information leaflet was enclosed in the packaging of a new personal stereo. Since the instructions are not describing a chronological process they have to be organised differently. In this case related points are clustered under headings:

READ THIS IMPORTANT INFORMATION BEFORE USING YOUR HEADSET

The portable headset is one of the most exciting and innovative consumer electronics products ever developed.
With it you can now enjoy listening to your favourite music wherever you go.
But, for your comfort and safety, be sure to observe the following guidelines.

Hearing comfort and well-being

● Do not play your headset at a high volume. Hearing experts advise against continuous extended play.
● If you experience a ringing in your ears, reduce volume or discontinue use. (continued)

Although this is an instruction leaflet, the first paragraph in fact demonstrates a Persuasive purpose. This is understandable in the circumstances because the leaflet is warning of the dangers of the product which has been purchased, yet the producer also wants to reassure purchasers that the product is the dream machine they expected. The remaining text is set out point by point for emphasis. The first main point begins 'Do not . . .', which is assertive and unambiguous. The supporting sentence, however, risks misunderstanding by using more complex diction: 'If you experience . . . discontinue use'.

The reader is addressed informally, as if known personally to the writer, a tone which is the most familiar for children. In other kinds of text this tone might appear as a direct address ('You might enjoy a visit to . . .') or rhetorical question ('Does that ever happen to you?'). If the reader is thought to be a stranger, either to a locality or to a subject, the sentence structures are likely to be simple, short and the vocabulary non-technical.

The Visual

If you have ever tried to include in a letter to a friend instructions on how to get to your new home, or worse still tried to give that information over the telephone, you will have realised how abstract language is as a system. The easiest solution by far is to send a map, for then you support the abstract of language with a concrete visual symbol. From a language point of view that is avoiding the problem, so a compromise is to have a map in front of you as you write or speak, which means that the brain has less to struggle with, translating the symbols of the map into words, rather than needing to first image the scene, then select salient detail to be finally translated into abstract language.

For the young writer the issues are exactly the same; a labelled diagram, chart, map or picture will help the writer to see the process, and so suggest both content and structure. Yet the classroom tradition is for the illustration to be added after the writing – 'When you've finished if you've space on the page and any time left you can draw a picture.' It would almost always be more helpful to the writer for the picture to come first, because any visual representation will contain a great deal of information, perhaps all of it, comprehended at a glance. Focusing on the visual will load the writer's mind with essential elements of the information-transmitting task. The visual aid need not be included in the final text, though modern taste favours the inclusion of illustrations in all kinds of text. See Chapter 4 for further examples of the role the visual can play in planning writing.

REPORTING

Introduction

The point has been made elsewhere that the term 'journalism' covers a very wide range of forms of writing. Newspapers are not a single model but contain such different forms of writing as advertisements, horoscope, features, weather report, etc. Appendix 1 contains a fuller list. Focusing here solely upon news reporting, it must be acknowledged that there is no single style even within one newspaper since there are different writing conventions for each of the following six major topics around which the news is generally organised: (1) politics; (2) the economy; (3) foreign affairs; (4) domestic news: (a) hard stories – conflict (e.g. crime, violence, industrial relations, education); (b) soft stories – human interest (e.g. animals, lost and found, pools win, humour); (5) occasional stories – disasters, celebrities; (6) sport.

These topics will be differently handled by national and local papers, tabloid and broadsheet, both in what they choose to report and how they report it. The different topics have their different approaches to objective fact; sports reporting, for instance, is usually a 'commentary' which indicates a personal judgement by the writer on the sports competition as well as the objective facts of the game. Each newspaper is likely to have a particular stance in interpreting economic affairs and a general political preference. In a local newspaper a degree of local knowledge is expected, so that many assumptions may have to be made. In a national paper there may be a degree of political and social bias in the choice of epithets. In both types of paper there may be a use of exaggerated language and attitude, often most marked in sports reporting.

Teachers may prefer the 'quality press' as the model for the classroom but its choice of the newsworthy, the complexity and density of its language and thought, will put it beyond the comprehension of all but the oldest or highest ability schoolchildren. In addition since the circulation of the tabloids runs to millions daily, the majority of children will absorb their style in the home context. Local papers are often a better choice as a model because they tend to centre on 'safe' content of local issues rather than on scandal in a sensational style, and their language is not usually complex.

Use of real models at earlier ages means selecting specific items from one or more papers, either local or tabloid. News items are not usually considered copyright, but it would be wise to contact the newspaper office concerned before photocopying items for class use. Rather than bringing in complete copies of newspapers, cutting out one individual news item and mounting it separately for close study is highly recommended since this focuses attention on the specific model and its characteristics in terms of tone, structure, and language. It also avoids the other kinds of writing which all newspapers contain, and which distract children's attention.

There are general principles and patterns which we can pass on as guidelines for young writers who are to become more discerning readers. Firstly since the newspaper is a commercial concern, the readership and its likes and dislikes are of prime concern. No matter how highbrow the newspaper, its readership is considered first and foremost to be in a hurry, hence to need attracting to all items. Consequently items which recur throughout the paper such as headlines, photographs and advertising all use eye-catching techniques, and the longer sections of text are broken up into short units easily followable by a reader who may literally be on the Clapham omnibus.

Secondly, contrary to the usual impression of informative writing, the tone of the big circulation newspapers is informal – to some people objectionably so. The objective, impersonal style of reported speech as traditionally taught in schools is a long way from the highly charged, personalised reporting of the popular press.

Thirdly the art of the journalist is to collect as much information as possible and by selection to précis it to what is essential. Therefore summary skills followed by organisation of the material through a web chart (see Chapter 4) will be helpful stages for children learning to construct a news story.

Structure

The essential principle of constructing newspaper copy is that it should be written in brief paragraphs, in diminishing order of importance. There are two reasons for this. Firstly news copy as written by the reporters is unlikely to fit exactly the available space on the page and so must be cut by the sub-editors at the news desk, taking into account how significant each news item is on that particular day, compared with other items. Since newspapers have to be produced to very tight deadlines, the sub-editors need to have a quick rule of thumb for cutting, and this is to cut from the bottom, from least to most significant information. Secondly the readership of a newspaper is envisaged as being in a hurry and skimming for essential information. Since we read from top to bottom of any text, the most important information will be easiest to find if it is consistently placed first in every news item. Readers who are still interested in the item after that and want to know more will be prepared to continue to add to this basic foundation of information by reading on. The basic structure of a news item is:

Headline
Strapline (i.e. subordinate headline)

Bodycopy:
(1) introduction (single paragraph of essential detail on who/what/when/where)
(2) amplification (paragraphs in order of importance)
Closure (single paragraph tying up loose ends)

Headline

In this hierarchic structure the first element, the headline, is considered to be of paramount importance in attracting the reader's attention, and sign-posting the theme of the story. Writing the headline is therefore the responsibility of the sub-editor, a higher authority than the reporter. In some cases a headline will be followed by a 'strapline' in similar style, which adds more detail. A brief statement to catch the eye and summarise a storyline is used in a wider range of forms: the billboard, the publicity flier, advertising copy, information leaflet.

Brevity and directness are the essential features of the headline and normal grammatical rules can be broken if the impact and density of meaning are thereby increased. As a general rule the headline should be in the active voice and present tense to give a sense of immediacy. Words should be the briefest available to compress meaning and suggest physical action where possible. Many headlines use sound effects, as reading them aloud will demonstrate, but if you draw up a list you can see many alternative patterns of appeal:

Personal	– I still love him
Third person	– She's left him
Colloquial	– He's a rum 'un!
Descriptive	– South swelters in heat haze
Direct speech	– No election this year, says PM
Dramatic	– Hanging by fingertips
Emotive	– Family pet a frenzied killer
Exaggerated	– Raining cats and dogs
Formal	– God Bless You, Ma'am
Informative	– Summit set for June
Narrative	– Happy ending for newly weds
Pun/wordplay	– Major upset
Sensational	– Government corruption revealed
Violent	– Bomb blast shatters home

To analyse this sub-form in class, examples may need to be chosen carefully to avoid the prevalent shock-horror sensationalism. Local newspapers may offer examples based on more 'normal' events. Try giving a class a local news item without its headline and asking them to compose alternatives which they compare with the original; or several articles to match with a range of headlines.

As for writing headlines, the subject can be created from almost any event in the school day and need not be part of a large-scale class newspaper project. Such writing can be a brief filler at the end of a lesson – a chance to play with language with a sharp focus for a specific purpose; writing out alternatives; crossing words out and replacing them; reading out the drafts to a partner; hearing the sound patterns in the head. Through this process children find out about such techniques as onomatopoeia, alliteration and assonance, not just through contact with poetry. The brevity of the headline as a sub-form should not make writing one a limited or low-level task; the intensity of word choice makes it a good cameo of the crafting process.

Introductions

The essential ingredients of the intro are that it should give only the essential details of the story in about thirty words, for the benefit of the reader in a hurry who might read nothing more. It should answer as many as possible of the five basic questions: who, what, when, where, how. It should tell the story in miniature and so be able to stand alone if necessary. It should give the most dramatic angle possible and so attract the reader's attention.

Bodycopy – amplification

The remaining paragraphs should amplify the who, what, when, where, how, information given in the intro. They are therefore increasingly optional for the reader. The following are common types of additional information and from these alternatives it is possible to construct a guideline paragraph structure for young writers:

(1) Further detail about the event.
(2) Alternative viewpoints on what happened, confirming or contrasting with the main viewpoint.
(3) Quotes of what was actually said by witnesses or those involved in the news event.
(4) Background information on the place or people involved (from newspaper's reference library).
(5) Reference to earlier events in a chain or in parallel occurrences (from newspaper's reference library).

Quotations of what people actually said are an important feature since they are direct evidence. Even though what is actually said may be subjective opinion, the reader is given the impression of hard fact. They also evoke an impression of immediacy and drama – as speech does in a play – which is an essential ingredient of the form.

Closure

The final paragraph will tie up the loose ends of the story and so particularly useful are comments from official sources (e.g. police, judge, MP) about what might happen next. 'Police are pursuing their enquiries', 'The judge will sum up tomorrow', 'The Summit will probably meet in the autumn.' No final twist or punchline is expected, though non-contentious human interest stories on the inside pages may be more adventurous, using a witty aside to round off the story, or saving the main item of interest to the end – a 'delayed drop'. They are unusual constructions, though, because they break the central principle of prioritising from the top.

Example

A year 4 class were given the details of a robbery in the form of a series of cartoons, eye-witnesses giving information in speech bubbles about what they saw. One boy wrote:

ROBBERY AT ARCADE JEWELLERY SHOP

A jewel robbery took place this morning at 10.30 a.m. in the Arcade Jewellery Shop.

Three men came running into the Jewellery Shop. They had stockings over their heads.

One of them had a flick knife which he flicked at the girl. 'Just keep still love,' he said.

The others had a big blue sports bag which they put the jewellery in.

The girl tried to press the alarm but she was too late.

The people were quite frightened and started to run out. They did not want to get stabbed.

Some detail supplied in the cartoons has not been used – the name of the girl and the name of the town where it took place, though the latter omission might be acceptable in local journalism if the address was well enough known. 'Quite frightened' misses the dramatic potential which the press would usually heighten in such a situation; 'terrified shoppers fled' would be more typical, and jewellery would more likely be 'crammed' into a bag to emphasise violent action, rather than the bland 'put'. Overall, though, the young writer has understood the principle of a series of short paragraphs, and the blend of reported and direct speech, which both dramatises and summarises the event reported.

Reported Speech

Traditionally classroom teaching of journalism concentrated on the principles of 'reported speech' – the changes to time, place and person which indicate that the information has been taken from its immediate context to a more remote context at a later date. For example, the direct speech:

> 'We have been having some production problems so I am going to call a meeting of all concerned here this afternoon.'

is transformed to:

> The manager said that because of recent production problems he was going to call a meeting between management and the workforce that afternoon at the firm's headquarters.

which could generate the headline and strapline:

FACTORY FEUD

'Try harder!' Boss tells workers

Although the process of direct translation from direct to reported speech is technically accurate, the overall effect is to make the information sound remote, formal and impersonal. Such a style would not be seen as a strong selling point by most newspapers, for whom the dramatic impact of immediacy is paramount. So although it might be helpful for children to know the technicalities of reported speech, it is far more realistic for them to appreciate how to give impact to reported events. School textbooks are often unhelpful about this, relying on exhortations to young writers to give their writing 'punch' or 'catch the reader's attention' which is vague advice. These are some of the 'slants' used by journalists:

(1) *Active verbs:* particularly in headlines verbs are usually in the present tense and active voice, suggesting immediacy and action. 'Sack', 'strike'.

(2) *Common touch:* remote figures are brought closer to the reader through use of nicknames – Prime Minister Margaret Thatcher becomes 'Maggie', Prince Charles 'Charlie'.

(3) *Conflict:* news items that have potential for drama, conflict, tension are those which are selected as 'newsworthy'. In the writing the sides of any conflict are heightened, even exaggerated to create effect.

(4) *Drama:* a vigorous debate in Parliament in which participants express strong views is likely to be reported as 'a heated exchange' or more concretely 'angry words' or even more vividly with the metaphor 'came to blows'.

(5) *Human interest:* an inference is made as to the emotional state of a participant; for example 'Looking tense and drawn the Foreign Minister said . . .', or 'Close to tears she described what had happened.'

(6) *Idiom:* 'hit out at' rather than 'rebutted'. The tabloid press in particular uses idiomatic or slang phrases to catch attention, partly because they associate with direct address to the man in the street. This is often coupled with the use of exclamation marks to increase the impression of forceful everyday speech rather than the more dispassionate medium of factual writing.

(7) *Onomatopoeia:* Newspaper language, to catch the attention, is often 'noisy' – if read aloud it has strong sound patterns such as alliteration, assonance, onomatopoeia. Although readers do not usually read newspapers aloud, many people literally hear a voice in the head as they read so that even silent reading can be said to have a sound impact on the reader.

(8) *Quotation:* direct speech, like the script of a play, gives the impression of events recorded as they happened.

(9) *Word picture:* 'blood bath', 'bombshell'. If quotation suggests the words of actors in a drama then word pictures create the set in which the action is played, completing the association with the world as a stage.

Tabloid newspapers use these devices to a much greater extent, a distinction which older children will probably be able to make for themselves by contrasting the same occurrence reported in both a tabloid and a broadsheet newspaper – though in the end they may still prefer the tabloid as more direct and vivid.

Sports Reporting: Cliché

Many of the above, particularly those concerning vocabulary choice, create a set of clichés which can be grounds for criticising such reporting style. In its defence, though, it has to be admitted that both the pressures and time constraints under which reporters write and the casual way in which newspapers are read encourage the use of cliché as a shorthand signposting of meaning. Sports reporting in particular has generated its own set of cliché terms, partly mindless, to avoid real analysis and partly to set off familiar chains of association, though avoidance of the more obvious cliché and the drive to sound dramatic has led to the invention of intriguing circumlocutions. For instance, in football the word 'kick' would be likely to occur most frequently as the most frequent of all actions on the field, but sports writers seeking to avoid the obvious have devised the following alternatives: drive, hammer, hit, lever, lift, loft, pass, push, release, stab, strike, tap, thread, thrust, touch. Football enthusiasts might enjoy making technical distinctions between such terms, and sports writing is rich ground for children to analyse.

It is also worth noting in relation to sports reporting that ball games are usually shaped by a time structure, i.e. goal in the first minute, followed by indecisive mid-field play, after half time, last-minute goal and so on. This makes it a structure easier for children to handle than other aspects of reporting.

Crime Reporting

Another way of highlighting the characteristics of a style is through parody, which exaggerates particular features so that the reader recognises it without fail. Andrew Rawnsley parodied the style of sensational crime reporting to make a political satire of the government's handling of the sale of the formerly publicly owned Rover Car Company. This is an extract:

QUESTIONERS FAIL TO CRACK 'MRS BIG' IN USED CAR FIDDLE

Mrs Margaret Thatcher, a 64-year-old Finchley woman, was brought in for questioning yesterday about the latest record crime figures. MPs said they were particularly anxious to talk to the woman about the shocking increase in car theft.

In one particularly notorious case, an entire car manufacturer went missing, along with £44 million of taxpayers' money.

The Rover company was eventually discovered – with a respray and its plates changed – in the hands of British Aerospace. They claimed not to have known the company was 'hot', saying that they purchased it in good faith, after it had been passed off to them as a straightforward privatisation job. (continued)

(© Guardian News Service, 1990)

The satire depends on what is called 'intertextuality' in literary criticism; that is, it relies on the reader recognising the style of another literary work, in this case the sensational style of the tabloid press, probing immorality and criminal practices among the rich and famous, seemingly deploring their escapades whilst at the same time revelling in the detail. Sensation is signalled by cliché words like 'shocking', 'notorious'. Crime in the used car trade is itself a stereotype, emphasised here by the use of some well-known trade jargon/slang – 'respray', 'plates', 'hot', 'job'. At the level of phrases, journalistic clichés like 'Mr Big' have lost impact, in that they cannot surprise by their originality as the pastiche writer here knows, but they are short, sharp and vernacular. In the longer phrase 'a straightforward privatisation job', tagging the slang 'job' onto a more serious term lowers the tone into that of the criminal underworld. As with all copy written by a journalist, I have been able to act as sub-editor and cut almost two-thirds of the paragraphs from the bottom, without making nonsense of the first part of the article, which gains its impact overall from the cumulative effect of supplementary detail.

EXPOSITION

Introduction

By exposition is meant extended writing, close in structure to the traditional school essay, which deals with factual topics in an interesting, readable way. In adult life the major source is what is known in journalism as 'the feature article' to be found extensively in newspapers and magazines. See the list in Appendix 1 of the subcategories of journalism, many of which are feature articles of one kind or another. Usually writing theory brackets all forms of informative writing together and no distinction is made between, for example, information brochures and feature articles. However, from the user's point of view the differences between such forms are very marked, not least because they emanate from distinctively different sources, serve different purposes and use different techniques. For instance, unlike information brochure writing, feature articles in newspapers and magazines are usually in a discursive style, and run to a substantial length; the text is not usually heavily supported by the visual. Importantly the writer's opinions and personality are allowed to come through, often very strongly. As the Informative shades towards the Persuasive, so the handling of information will be coloured by the writer's intention to persuade the reader to a certain viewpoint; as it shades towards the Evocative, so the writer attempts to create a picture in the mind of the reader. Usually in a feature article persuasion or evocation are secondary purposes, devices to hold the reader's attention; the primary purpose of the writer is to convey information.

Having said that, however, the term 'feature' is used to describe a wide range of writing; in newspapers and magazines common subjects are fashion, entertainment, gardening, motoring, travel. In specialist magazines on hobbies and interests, features can form the bulk of the content, in a variety of shapes and sizes: a profile of a personality, an interview, a 'best-buy' review, 'how to do it' account, an account of an event and so on.

The main substance of the content is factual information in the form of a continuous prose essay although there might be charts and diagrams or reference to photographs or illustrations alongside the text. Many teenagers read magazines, both general and specialist. They tend to be sex stereotyped, sports and computing magazines being targeted generally at boys whilst there are many general magazines whose features on fashion and stories of romantic encounters suggest they are for girls. Teenagers might also have encountered feature articles in newspapers, particularly on entertainment, fashion, profiles of sports personalities.

Structure

A choice needs to be made by the writer as to whether the reader is already familiar with the topic or not. That determines the amount of explanation of basic terms, equipment necessary and so forth. The first paragraph should explain why it is being written and give some background to the topic whether the article is intended for expert readers or novices.

The form is close to the traditional essay in having a structure of paragraphs of the pattern: introduction – development – conclusion. Alternative paragraph structures are described in Appendix 3.

The opening should attract attention, and some of the ways this can be done include:

(1) A question: 'Have you ever wanted to get away from it all?'.
(2) A scene: 'Crowds jostle round a shop window . . . .'
(3) A challenge: 'Big pike are always difficult to land.'
(4) A reward: 'I've been doing this all my life so I can make it easy for you.'
(5) A drama: 'Bursting out of the undergrowth . . . .'

The main body of the article will follow, divided into a series of paragraphs, the number depending on the total length and whether the writer feels the reader can cope with information in a few large steps or many small ones. Possible approaches include:

facts and figures
account of an event or process
dramatisation of a scene
personal experience recollected by the writer or interviewees
an anecdote illustrating the topic
opinions of the writer or an expert

The last paragraph will be some kind of conclusion. This might be a summary of main points; a personal reaction to the material (perhaps witty); a recommendation to the reader interested in knowing more.

A year 8 top band class were asked to write a feature article on a hobby or interest which they enjoyed and knew a lot about. The article was to be for a hobbies magazine for a non-specialist readership of their own age, the intention being to give information to a reader just starting the hobby. The title was open-ended, 'Getting started in . . .'. One boy wrote:

GETTING STARTED IN TRUCKS

Imagine the dusty outback of Australia. No noise except the birds and animals. The ground starts to shake and you hear the roar of an engine. Then suddenly, a Volvo F12 TURBO INTERCOOLER, a Roadtrain in fact, comes rolling through. You catch sight of the cab and the two trailers. The truck has gone and all that is left is the smell of the diesel and the dust from the wheels and you can hear the sound of the engine still in your ears.

Well, I don't know about you but I can imagine that scene very clearly. My hobby is TRUCKS! I read about them, write about them and draw them. There is a number of magazines on the market but I prefer Commercial Motor and Trucking International. These magazines are about £1.00 and are packed with sales, info and photos plus reviews of new trucks. My collection is growing all of the time. I have about 50 magazines and my oldest is from 1979.

I got started on TRUCKS because two of my uncles, Jeremy and Paul, drive trucks and so does my dad. My dad has been driving for about 18 years and when I was born, a little after in fact, I used to go on short journeys with him. Back then he drove a Renault Saviem but now he drives a VOLVO F12 TURBO INTERCOOLER, F reg. I have only been in it once, to Yarmouth to pick up a trailer, but hope to go in it again. It's very comfortable. He's got a phone, cooker and a decent radio cassette plus one of my favourites, the CB! When I grow up I hope to follow in his footsteps or tyre tracks!!

One or two summers ago I did some truck spotting! In four days I collected over 300 numbers, names and firms. I even started a small – very small – business. Selling pictures and postcards and badges I had made, with trucks on of course. I only charged a few pennies and it was more of a hobby, something to do at night. This was fun, while it lasted!!

I really enjoy my hobby and am building up a big collection of items. It's an easy hobby and I hope to keep it up for years to come!!! (complete text)

This is a convincing piece of writing for three reasons. Firstly the writing has authority because the writer includes detailed factual information, on types of truck and equipment, and names of trade magazines. Secondly this comes from personal knowledge and this first-person viewpoint allows him to communicate an infectious personal enthusiasm; the many exclamation marks are a sign of this enthusiasm. Thirdly he shapes the writing using rhetorical devices to catch the reader's attention; creating a dramatic scene as an opener, directly addressing the reader. The primary purpose of informing is here heavily influenced by the secondary purpose of persuading the reader to take up the hobby.

It is worth highlighting all the ingredients in the teaching process which brought about this piece:

(1) The writer has a personal interest which includes concrete hands-on experience and academic knowledge.
(2) He has read models of the target form, i.e. feature articles, on the subject and so knows how adult writers hold their readership.
(3) The teacher gave the class a guideline of the structure of a feature article and discussed with them ways of catching reader attention.
(4) The target audience was clearly specified, and rough drafts were read out to the class so that there was interim feedback to the writer to gauge success.

It will not always be possible to allow children to write on subjects so near to the heart and to their concrete experience as this; in his writing development this boy will need to learn how to write about much more remote subjects in a more dispassionate way. But here the enthusiasm for the subject has brought to the surface the boy's detailed knowledge of how feature writing works – how it catches and holds the attention of the reader – enabling him to craft a piece of writing so as to communicate factual information with feeling.

CRITICISM

Introduction

In adult life we are likely to encounter 'criticism' in a wide sense across a range of activities, though not under that title. Almost every newspaper and magazine has reviewers who write critical commentaries on many subjects. Most obvious in their relationship to traditional literary 'prac. crit.' are the arts critics who review new books, films and theatre productions. Beyond that obvious link, though, there are journalists who write for all kinds of magazines to review new equipment and services, describing faults and merits so as to give advice to readers on how best to spend their time and money. It is possible to extend the range even further to include those groups of journalists variously called commentators, correspondents, columnists or editors who write not news itself but commentary on events in specialist aspects of the news, particularly sport, politics and finance. So the range of criticism which we encounter outside the academic world can be extended to cover such diverse models as a four-page review of this month's 'Best Buy' in stereo systems, to a four-paragraph review of a local amateur dramatics production, to a four-column commentary on the current economic climate in Brazil. These very different styles and focuses have in common that each writer interweaves an objective account of the facts together with a subjective appraisal of their significance in order to guide the judgement of the reader. All types of criticism are likely to address three basic concerns: (1) a description in technical detail of the features of the product; (2) a comparison of these features with other products; (3) a summary of the pros and cons, justifying a recommendation to the reader – whether or not to buy/experience it/subscribe to a viewpoint.

These concerns often shape the overall plan of the writing into such a sequence, though concerns 1 and 2 may take up several paragraphs each and 3 only a few words. Some types of criticism will use the formats described in the field of Explanation earlier in this chapter: lists, highlighting and so on, with charts and illustrations. Others will use the form of the feature article described in the Exposition section. With the simple three-part structure here the form can fit almost any subject in the curriculum where an appraisal can be made of equipment or experiences: the best design for a windmill, the most effective growing medium for seeds, the most interesting sport for a particular interest group and so on. As such it could be used as an alternative to the standard format of the science report.

The Review

Traditionally in the secondary school curriculum the term 'criticism' has been associated with 'practical criticism', i.e. the analysis of the technicalities of a literary work – novel, play or poem. Written in the form of an essay, it has been used to focus children's attention on literature as construct, to promote their insight into the detail of set literature texts, rather than to give them an outlet for personal views. This gives higher priority to the head than to the heart, but recent developments in teaching literature have stressed personal response, leaving the pseudo-scientific approach of literary criticism to A level and beyond, substituting for the lit. crit. essay imaginative projection into the literature through such forms as diaries, plays and letters. The review, though, is a form which offers a compromise between the two. It is essentially informative but it allows the writer a personal viewpoint, freedom – once the objective facts have been established – to express a personal response.

The Reviewer

A reviewer is a highly influential writer, licensed to guide the tastes, perceptions and buying choices of the readership. New York theatre critics are said to have the power to close down a Broadway show after the first night. The reviewer is expected to have three attributes in particular: a rich background experience of the subject, precise opinions, and an authoritative voice; that is, to make a judgement and be able to say why, though often with tact so as not to upset the novelist or the cast of a play (particularly a local one). As in all aspects of journalism, the assumption is that the reader's interest must be held, and in case it is not, the most important information should be put at the beginning of the text.

The writer should make the distinction between fact and opinion very clear, so that the facts of what is being addressed are stated logically and unambiguously, whilst the opinion is a reasoned appraisal of those facts. One would expect a clear distinction, with no use of biased language or innuendo. In teaching this field to children a useful assignment is to take a published example and ask children to underline in blue all the statements which are objective fact, in red all statements which are subjective opinion, in yellow all reasons supporting the opinion.

The Reader

The practised reader will expect the reviewer to take sides. Any review which is blind to the faults or idiosyncrasies of what is reviewed will mislead the reader and is just as much an abuse of the form as a rave review which reflects a reviewer's very partisan personal taste. Particularly in the local press there is a tradition of relatively benign criticism, perhaps for the pragmatic reason that the paper cannot risk losing the goodwill of potential advertisers and patrons by savagely criticising their efforts. There is a distinction between praising and appraising. No matter which side of the good/bad line the reviewer takes in making a final judgement, there should be a notion of balance.

Arts reviewers, no matter whether they are reviewing books, plays, films or TV, write for two distinct readers at the same time. The first reader has not read the book (or seen the film) but would like an informed opinion on whether it is a worthwhile experience. For this reader, reviewers must not spoil the experience in advance by retelling key points of the plot, so must go about it another way, perhaps by describing their personal reactions to an emotional climax or twist ending, not the events themselves, so not giving the game away. Such a reader might enjoy comparisons with other books by the same author or in the same genre, having read them already. The second reader has read the book and, either loving it or hating it, wants to find out what someone else thinks and feels about it, preferably someone well informed. The two readers to some extent have conflicting interests but neither needs the detailed analysis of the text which you would expect in academic literary criticism.

Structure

Whichever of the two readers is the intended target, the style is usually direct and personal, the writer being permitted to address the reader with rhetorical questions such as 'Do you like a good cry?'. Although the writer is handling facts and making intellectual judgements, the style is a balance of the logical and the personal. Indeed, it is very common for a reviewer to develop a persona, openly stating very decided tastes and opinions. This can be a lot of fun for children, compared with the more remote impersonal style of the traditional school lit. crit. essay. Take this short example from *Books for Keeps*, a review periodical:

BADGER ON THE BARGE AND OTHER STORIES
Janni Howker, Fontana Lions, 0 00 672581 3, £1.95.

The greatest disappointment in reading these stories was coming to the end of each one. Watch out for Janni Howker. She writes with such sensitivity and such an awareness of the needs and relationships of young people that there must be more to come.

In each of the five stories a young person works through a difficulty by discovering a perspective in the loneliness of someone much older. 'Badger on the Barge' tells of Helen, coming to terms with the sudden death of her brother and with her parents' reactions. Through old Miss Brady's barge, Helen comes to realise her own worth and leads her parents forward to accept a future without their son.

Recognising the cruelty of racist jokes, the loneliness of the old, acceptance of death and the need for independence are dealt with in the other stories and worked out through blending the needs of the young and old.

The language is at times quite startlingly visual and the sense of being part of the story very strong. Excellent stories for sharing with the twelve to fifteen-year-old group. I look forward to more. (complete text)

The review begins by setting out the facts of title, author, publisher, ISBN number and price. Even though the style of the review is impersonal until the 'I' of the final sentence, the opening paragraph is mainly subjective opinion, with the writer taking on the role of authoritative guide of the reader's taste. The personal view is very forcefully expressed giving the writing a predominant voice. The second paragraph is completely factual, without appraisal or subjective impression, although it does require the writer to be skilled at perceiving the themes which link the collection. The technique of zooming in on the first story as an example emphasises the factual reliability of the writer, who briefly summarises the storyline. The third paragraph zooms out to indicate the specific themes of other stories. The final paragraph is more explicitly subjective in appraising a particular technical strength of the writing and recommending the book for a specific age range.

Writing a Review

The book jacket is probably children's first encounter with writing a review since the back cover text usually contains the interweaving of fact and opinion of the form. Blending text with illustration in the design of a book jacket is an attractive assignment which displays well and so is highly motivating. The form contains several components, which can be included or omitted to make it more or less complicated. Children will learn most by taking the jackets off library books to see how they are designed, and are usually surprised by the result when one is unfolded: the front cover is actually on the right-hand side not the left; all pictures and writing are on the same side of the sheet, with one side completely blank. If you read across a removed book jacket from the left, you will usually find something like this: (1) left infold – books by the same author, price; (2) rear cover – eye-catching quotes from the book or book reviews; (3) spine – title, author, publisher; (4)

front cover – illustration, over-printed with title, author, publisher; (5) right infold – plot synopsis or extract or eye-catching 'puff'.

It is just possible to replicate these sections by folding a single A4 sheet, but the sections are very small and it looks more authentic to cut a strip from an A3 sheet. Alternatively joining separate sheets together allows the work to be done as a series of separate tasks – spoil one and you do not spoil them all.

The usual classroom starting point for a book jacket is designing the front cover picture which illustrates some important moment of the story or theme of the book. This in itself calls for careful thought and selection, no matter how old the child; it involves recalling the detail of the book and encourages appreciation. A useful starting question might be 'What did you most enjoy about the book?' To this can be added the title and the author's name; the kind of lettering used and the positioning of the writing within the picture are important considerations. For developing the writing of criticism the important ingredients are the synopsis of the early stages of the plot, factual notes about the author and the 'come-on' to the potential reader.

Basic Pattern

Moving on to other forms of criticism such as the newspaper, TV, theatre or book review, a simplified three-part pattern to guide children is to: (1) describe in outline the facts about the plot, setting and characters of the film, play, book; (2) select one or two details which are most important and describe their pros and cons; (3) sum up giving an overall judgement or making a recommendation. Since it will have a marked effect on the resulting style, from the outset the writer needs to decide which of the following stances to take:

(1) To give a balanced view – the good points and the bad points equally so that readers make up their own minds.
(2) To be enthusiastic overall with very few negative comments so as to hook readers.
(3) To be negative overall so as to convince readers not to bother going further.

One 7-year-old wrote this, which is a review at its very simplest level:

> We went to the Book fair. Fungus the Bogeyman was there. I liked him best.

The TV guide in a newspaper is a simple model which in a few words gives an outline of the plot and sometimes a judgement on the quality of the programme.

Complex Pattern

Older children may be able to follow a more complex six-part structure which can be used for a review of any subject, across the curriculum:

(1) *Introduction:* catch the reader's attention with a question ('Do you enjoy. . .?' 'Have you ever noticed . . . ?'). Next give the name of what you are reviewing, briefly stating what it is for. If it is produced by a well-known company, remind the reader of other products.

(2) *Overview:* using the past tense, give a very brief summary of what the product can do or what the event was.

(3) *Focus:* zoom in on a particular detail. Say why it caught your attention and describe it.

(4) *Commentary:* zoom out from your look at one aspect to describe others more briefly. Give reasons why they are better or worse than the one you focused on.

(5) *Personal appraisal:* you will probably give clues about what you feel all through the review indirectly or in brief comments. In this paragraph you can say outright what you did and did not like about it. Try to avoid vague expressions such as 'It was alright' or the old cliché 'It was boring.'

(6) *Summary:* leave your reader with a final brief impression. In just a sentence or two, try to sum up the main qualities of what you are reviewing and whether it is, in whatever sense, worth buying.

Using that structure a year 9 boy (middle band) imitates the racy style of the local newspaper's film reviewer; short sentences, slang, abbreviations, exclamation marks:

THE NAKED GUN

A spoof to end all spoofs from the makers of *Airplane*. A hilarious video which you just can't take seriously. It has everything a normal gangster film has – drugs, shootouts, beautiful women (Priscilla Presley) – and one thing they don't have – GAGS!!

It starts off in Beirut with cop Frank (Steve Nelson) on a mission to spy on Gorbachev, Ayatollah Khomeini and other world leaders (this has nothing to do with the film) and he ends up beating them all up!

Some of the jokes are a bit too subtle and it's easy to miss them, there are so many. You'd have to see the film about three times to get them all! But who's complaining? I'd watch it five times anyway!

My favourite bit was when Frank was at a public interview and then went to the toilet, forgetting to take his microphone off! You can guess what happens next!

It's easy to keep track of unlike so many other spoofs where they are so busy getting the jokes in they forget the actual theme. It's basically about cop Frank trying to stop the bad guy killing the Queen, only it's hard to find evidence as he is programming other people to kill her! The ending is hilarious, though, because . . . well, you'll have to see it yourself!

Whatever you feel about that up-beat style, which imitates in writing the spoken style of disc jockeys, the young writer has followed the style of the model, has balanced information with opinion, and has expressed a personal enthusiasm as a kind of criticism.

Other Applications

It is the range of subjects to which criticism can be applied that gives the field so much potential across the complete school curriculum. Every subject could use the form of the review since it is not confined to the arts subjects, personal reading and the school play. Any kind of event – a school trip, the fête, improvised drama, sports day – can be used as the subject, with the basic structure of state the facts and give an appraisal. The comparative 'best buy' approach suits more scientific subjects, but is not more difficult for that reason since the text can be built around visual representation of data – charts, graphs, labelled diagrams. So subjects for this type of review can include equipment used in art, science, music, PE.

Propaganda

At the extreme end of the Informative scale the propaganda writer deliberately uses 'misinformation' to construct a text which is plausible in terms of the values of the society and time in which it is written and which appears to be within the Informative range when in reality it is Persuasive. I did not assign propaganda a separate field on the diagram of the model of Primary Purpose in Chapter 3 preferring to keep the model simple, for propaganda seems to me to be a special case, and not a common target for writing. However, in the argument for promoting resistant readers it is clearly highly significant and deserves attention. In examples of propaganda used in school, detection is usually straightforward when they are from a known historical context – First or Second World War or Iron Curtain rhetoric. At a distance from the heated emotional context which brought about such propaganda its mechanisms seem gross. The classic epithets of remote governments accusing western society as 'imperialist warmongers and their running dogs' seem grotesquely exaggerated by our own standards of propaganda and seem to be so obviously untrue as to need no sophistication in resistance. But it is easier to detect propaganda when it is from another society or another age; more difficult when it is contemporary and from our own society. Then the sympathies of the reader are less resistant, hence more easily seduced. In wartime it would be possible for government sources to declare that 'Last night 24 enemy bombers were destroyed without the loss of any of our aircraft; we are close to final victory.' The figures of 24 to nil might be untrue, likewise the inference of impending victory, but from the writer's point of view the means justifies the end of keeping up public morale, while the readership would so hope that the facts were true as to readily believe that the message was reliable information.

Our view of contemporary events, though, is less confident. We have been alerted by such writers as George Orwell to expect strident propaganda in the domains of warfare and extreme political systems. At the more subtle end of the bias scale it is less easy to detect its effects in the daily press. Which of the two following accounts of the same disturbance in central London is 'true'?

Example 1
On Saturday, a huge anti-poll tax demonstration in central London turned into an ugly riot, with a mob hurling missiles at policemen, breaking shop windows and looting on a large scale. Only firm policing contained the situation and prevented loss of life.

Example 2
On Saturday, a peaceful, orderly protest march became a violent mêlée when police charged terrified crowds with vans and horses. The force of the charge pushed some of those trapped through shop windows. Police over-reaction risked the serious injury, even the death of innocent bystanders.

The two passages have been constructed so as to show clearly the differing viewpoints of the respective writers and the techniques used to frame the information so that it reflects their underlying value bases. In the first passage the event is called a 'demonstration', a neutral term though it does suggest physical action, which coupled with the descriptor 'huge', neutral in itself, begins to suggest a pejorative association with a threat to law and order. When the demonstration becomes a 'mob', the final step is taken for a pejorative bias in the report of the event. The demonstrators' actions are ascribed to deliberate criminal intent, by contrast with police action described as 'firm', a term which is vague and not a fact, being a subjective judgement on the positive side of the scale. In the second passage the event is described as a 'march', a relatively neutral term, which is given a positive bias by the two descriptors 'peaceful' and 'orderly'. The march becomes a 'mêlée' (neutral) whose 'violence' (negative) is attributed to the police. The breaking of shop windows (negative) is authoritatively attributed to police action. That the police 'over-reacted' (negative) is an overt subjective judgement, though again authoritatively asserted, and given further negative loading by the (non-fact) speculation that further injury could have been caused.

To answer the question of which of the two passages is 'true' raises the philosophical issue of the nature of truth and whether impartiality and objectivity are possible outside the strictest kind of scientific enquiry. Such issues are at the highest levels of literacy development in schooling but it is important throughout to keep bias and misinformation on the agenda; if children are not to be exploited by print, we should encourage healthy scepticism in reader-writers from the earliest age.

Developing Skills

(1) Make resourcing a priority. The school and class libraries should be exciting places. Teach children to use all sections, not just fiction. Library systems favour books; where the models you are working with do not fit that format, use file boxes, ring binders and poster displays to build up a range of accessible real models as resources for children to use.

(2) No matter what the age of the child, it is an advantage to focus on one specific form at a time and to work in detail on that form. Development comes from the interaction between reading examples of a form and writing in imitation.

(3) Direct children's writing choice so that they cannot always avoid forms which they find more difficult. This is not to suggest that form is more important than content or that children should not write at times in free form or in a form of their own choosing; but conversely for them always to write in an unfocused form is not providing a balanced programme of development.

(4) Select models which have clear characteristics, even if this means writing your own for the purpose. These characteristics become your criteria for assessing children's attempts at the form and the results will suggest the next stages in the teaching programme.

(5) It is possible to find real forms suitable for any age/stage of development. In teaching forms of instruction, for instance, in

the earliest stages choose instructions for simple recipes, keeping pets, familiar games. In the middle range choose more advanced processes such as making models, sports techniques, *Which?* reports. In the advanced stage look at more extensive public information leaflets, technical manuals.

(6) Identify the characteristics of the form explicitly for children. With the youngest children this will mean simply pointing features out as you hold up a text such as a brochure during a class discussion. These characteristics can be reinforced individually as they work on their own texts. In addition, older children will be able to write texts using simple guidelines which the teacher has produced, to build on their intuitive knowledge of the form concerned. At a more advanced stage children will be able to analyse texts for themselves; this will be easier if the teacher writes specific questions to guide their attention, e.g. 'Who is the intended reader?' 'What does the writer believe?'

(7) After they have finished their writing, identify the characteristics of a form which children have found difficult and continue the teaching programme with these as the target.

(8) Teach use of reference books: dictionary, thesaurus, encyclopaedia, information books, instruction manuals. Informative writing requires precise language, and children should be able to find for themselves with minimum guidance the most exact terms for any purpose. Such books should always be readily available and habitually used.

(9) Teach the use of planning, so that children have an increasing range of planning strategies (see Chapter 4 for possibilities).

(10) Teach children how to read each other's work critically so that they become used to writing for a real audience and see the communication problems of their writing immediately demonstrated. If this is done at the planning stage, later problems can be avoided; then again after first draft, to check on the effectiveness of the writing; finally at proof-reading to reduce secretarial errors.

Promoting Critical Reading/Writing

(1) With all ages, wherever possible compare two or more examples of the same form. Ask children to: spot the differences; say which version they prefer; work out why they prefer it. Follow exactly the same process with their own writing. It may make the point more clearly if you write your own contrasting examples.

(2) At all stages encourage children to notice, comment on and criticise print, including school textbooks. Ask them what they

understand clearly, vaguely or not at all; to suggest alternative wording, structure, additional information. Link this with library research and comparison with other books on the same subject.

(3) Teach children how to analyse the content of what they read using boxes, charts, matrices (see Chapter 4) to set out the main ideas of the writer and how they are organised, i.e. the same techniques which they use to plan their own ideas before writing.

(4) Bias is of particular significance in the Informative range. Teach children how to analyse examples of informative writing for: fact/opinion; major fact/minor fact; objectivity/subjectivity. This is most easily approached by underlining the facts in one colour, the opinions in another, then putting a star alongside the most important details. Discussion of the facts by the whole class can show where a writer has made omissions, perhaps to bias a seemingly objective account. Contrast with another piece of writing on the same subject will show up bias the most clearly – as well as the relative merits of one technique compared with another.

(5) Spot the writer. Ask children to underline instances where the writer's personal experience or values come through in the writing. Is it a marked or unmarked feature? Whether to write from a personal viewpoint and to what extent is a basic choice to be decided at the planning stage.

(6) Encourage children to rewrite texts so as to add bias or to change its allegiance. Take a playful attitude towards writing; instead of redrafting which is just a rewrite, ask children to write a sample of the text in the third person, then a second in the first person, the final draft being their own preference. In the process they will have gained insight into their own material as well as into the effectiveness of technique.

(7) Older children may enjoy writing parodies of a particular form. The process of exaggerating characteristics makes their own knowledge apparent to them and demonstrates a resistance to the weaknesses and seductive strengths of the form. Read parodies to them and open up critical discussion, referring to the models being parodied.

7

PERSUASIVE WRITING

Introduction

In the United States television programmes of a new kind have recently emerged, seemingly informational, but so heavily sponsored that they have been called 'advertorials' or 'informercials'. These composite terms are a reminder that rigid categories are evasive, primary and secondary purposes being so blended on the writer's palette. The primary purpose may be persuasion but the force of that persuasion may come from the factual information contained in the text. As for the breadth and depth of that information, the writer must anticipate how familiar the reader is with the topic, which then determines the extent to which specialist terminology and register may be used and need to be explained. Hence Persuasive texts are unlikely to be information dense unless they are for a specialist readership, and such writing essentially seeks to give an interpretation of information rather than an objective account. Identifying the nature of that interpretation is the goal of resistant reading.

Reader Viewpoint

In all writing it is important to take the reader's point of view into account but persuasive writing is particularly reader-oriented. After all, the notion of persuasion implies that the writer anticipates resistance but intends to win the reader over. More than that, it is a central principle of this purpose and the main criterion by which success should be judged, that the writer intends the reader to take action as a result of the reading – either physical action (a purchase) or mental (a change of heart/mind). To effect that action is the force which drives the crafting process, for the language of persuasive texts is crafted to catch and hold the reader's attention from beginning to end, the action line frequently being held back until the close.

Completeness of structure through that holding of attention from first to last is a central principle across the range of Persuasive forms. That most frequently encountered and most intrusive use of persuasive writing, Advertising, is tightly constructed so as to persuade us to recognise a product, desire it and by the end of the writing, to want to rush out and 'buy one today.' In Argument the points of the argument may build up through accumulation, the most important point being held back till the final paragraph, even till the closing statement, to create dramatic impact and to leave the reader with a lasting impression. That is in contrast with major forms of the Informative where the reader is seen as interested in only part of the information offered, as in a newspaper article or encyclopaedia entry, which eliminates the need for 'hype' in the language or build up to a climactic ending in the structure.

Writer Viewpoint

To some extent the tone of a text is a matter of stylistic choice by the writer but it is partly determined by the relationship of the writer with (a) the subject and (b) the intended audience. Where the writer feels passionately about a subject, this force of conviction may be expressed through declamatory style and emotionally loaded terms. Where the audience is seen as potentially resistant, the writer may become more circumspect, use less emotive terms, and construct more logical steps in the argument. The range of persuasive tone can be represented as a spectrum from weak to strong: tentative – consultative – affirmative – evangelical.

(1) *Tentative* – a reduction of the forcefulness of the argument indicated by such phrases as 'A lot of people like chocolate but not everyone does', 'This would lead us to believe . . .', 'Probably nothing can be done, but we can live in hope.'

(2) *Consultative* – confiding in the reader through such phrases as 'Would you like this to happen to you?', 'You probably know the feeling.'

(3) *Affirmative* – indicated by positive statements and clear distinctions which make for clear-cut points, e.g. 'What happened was wrong and we intend to take the following steps to put it right.'

(4) *Evangelical* – indicated by extreme commitment to a point of view expressed in strongly emotional or heavily rhetorical terms, e.g. 'Never, never let anyone break ranks over this.' 'Christmas is too commercialised!'

No matter whether subject focus or audience focus is the priority, there is likely to be a predominant tone in a Persuasive text, though there may be an inserted tone change for contrastive effect, such as an impassioned ending to an otherwise rational argument.

ARGUMENT

The term 'argument' has been much discussed in recent years and has taken on a wide range of meanings. The term is used here in a narrow sense to refer to writing in which the writer seeks to persuade the reader by logical reasoning. The writer may be partisan, but expression is rational, rather than emotional. Used in this way the term argument is closer to the definition of the court of law and not at all in the popular sense of a heated dispute, which is more nearly represented by the field of 'Assertion' which follows.

Balanced Argument

The writer of a balanced argument persuades the reader to believe in a proposition by a chain of reasoning within a context of facts which may be open to interpretation. The writer selects a justification for that viewpoint from the available information like a barrister in a court of law selecting evidence to support either the prosecution or the defence, or like the impartial judge summing up the material facts to the jury.

The issue of objectivity is complex. Although he takes an impartial stance regarding available options, Tim Radford writing on the subject of global warming implies that he belongs to the pro-conservation lobby:

> There is more than one solution to the carbon dioxide problem, but only one that is sure to work: burn less carbon. This can be done by designing systems to use fuel more efficiently, or to tax or otherwise control fossil fuel use, or both.
>
> Scientists looking for more dramatic technical solutions have suggested treating carbon dioxide like any other waste and finding a way to bury it safely. One theory, examined recently in *Nature*, is to dump it in the sea. In theory, if carbon dioxide is pumped from power stations into the brine at depth, it should dissolve. According

to one model, 99 per cent of the gas should dissolve before the bubbles can rise 150 metres. Because the dissolved gas would then make the seawater around it more dense, it would sink and be carried along the ocean currents to even safer levels, there to be safe for perhaps 1,000 years.

It happens anyway. The oceans remove perhaps one-third of all man-made carbon dioxide by dissolving it at the sea's surface, and the sea already holds 65 times the quantity of carbon dioxide in the atmosphere. (continued)

(© Guardian News Service 1992)

The writer uses the first sentence to signpost his main theme; the tone is affirmative, setting out a clear range of options, which indicate to the reader how the reasoning to follow will be structured. The second paragraph focuses on one specific solution, quoting authorities for support (the rather nebulous 'scientists' but the specific journal *Nature*). The third paragraph is very brief, typical of journalistic style. It opens with a punchline for dramatic effect, then gives figures to support an overview of the solution. The article continues for six more paragraphs, alternately focusing in on detail and zooming out to place it in a wider context, using fact and authoritative theory to support the initial proposition.

The literary essay is just such a blend of exposition and interpretation. The writer is usually expected to give a factual account of the characteristics of a literary work using quotations as factual evidence. Either woven through this account or in sections the writer also gives a personal interpretation of the significance of the quotations and references. Unsure writers can either give far too much unsupported opinion (an emotional response) or too much factual evidence (re-telling the story) with insufficient interpretation. In either case consistent training in how to plan the ideational structure is one of the most positive steps teachers can take.

Partisan Argument

Where the writer wishes to take a side in the argument, both sides may be presented one after the other before the writer reaches a conclusion or the two viewpoints may be interwoven. After a spate of attacks by dogs on the general public and children in school playgrounds, there was a debate in Parliament over possible restrictions; increase in the licence fee, muzzling of dangerous dogs, banning of certain species. A year 9 middle band class were shown selected newspaper cuttings on the attacks, on the Parliamentary debate and on the keeping of dogs. During a class discussion ideas were put on the board in the form of a basic web chart (see Chapter 4). The class were then asked to plan an argument as if for a magazine or a feature article in a newspaper, taking up one side or other in the debate; either the pro- or the anti-dog lobby. Their plan used the 'window' format (see Chapter 4) where the page is divided into four, to hold the ideas of each of four paragraphs or sections, in this case: (1) an introduction describing what had led up to the Parliamentary debate; (2) the pro-dogs argument; (3) the anti-dogs argument; (4) in conclusion the writer's suggestions for the best solution to the problem. Most writers depart from their plan to some extent, hopefully for the better, but the following example by Deborah does reflect that plan:

KEEPING DOGS

Dogs are very much in the news at the moment because of the frequent attacks on many people. Why is this happening?

Dogs such as Rottweilers and Retrievers cause many of the attacks because of bad handling. These type of dogs are very frightening. That is why a fine must be made so that these attacks can be stopped. If you have got a dog, make sure you train it at an early age. For some of the dogs that have made these attacks, the only thing was for them to be put down or euthanasia. Make sure if you have a dog you take care of it.

There are many good reasons for keeping a dog. Some of the good reasons are, they are lovable pets to keep and take care of, and they are good if you like going for long walks everyday. But if you don't take them for walks and just leave them at home all day with no care or attention, they will get very bored and that is when they become aggressive and start to make attacks on people. Personally I like dogs because they can have great friendship with old and young people and they can make their owners very proud by doing and winning dog shows.

There are also many reasons against keeping dogs, like the mess they make on streets and in parks where young children might be playing which could cause illness. In my first paragraph I said that dogs were very much in the news at the moment mainly because of the attacks on people. Dogs like Rottweilers and Retrievers are the main culprit because they are big fierce dogs which need good handling from an early age. Just recently a 4-year-old girl was attacked by a Rottweiler and had over 200 stitches on her face let alone the rest of her body. I think the one thing I don't agree with is mixed pedigree dogs like Rottweiler and Pit Bull terrier. I think this is totally wrong and should be stopped. Sometimes the main reasons for dogs starting to attack people is boredom and cruelty.

In conclusion, I think what should be done is that dogs like Rottweilers and Retrievers and mixed dangerous pedigrees should be muzzled when out in public. And if they do attack, a heavy fine should be laid down to stop them. I am not for or against keeping dogs, but if they keep springing these attacks on people tougher sentences must be made.

The text opens with a clear overview statement to place the argument in context, and the rhetorical question which follows is intended to encourage an active response from the reader. The subsequent paragraphs each begin with a key sentence which signposts the paragraph's theme. This device helps the reader follow the ideational structure and it is a device which has been prompted by the 'windows' plan where each window was labelled. However, the content is rather more jumbled than the key sentence suggests in paragraphs 2 and 3; the ideas in the windows should have been more carefully checked for appropriateness when the plan was being finalised. In paragraph 4 there is a reference back to the opening, which is not necessary, though it does show the problem that children have in holding all the points of an argument in the head; the writer assumes that the reader has the same difficulty. The final paragraph successfully indicates where the writer stands on the issue and has the force of a 'take action' ending.

By contrast David in year 7 shows that he is at a much less advanced stage in his argument against smoking:

WHY PEOPLE SHOULDN'T SMOKE

There are many reasons why people shouldn't smoke. I think what drives young people to smoke is because they think it makes them look rugged and tough. People often try to tell you that it keeps them calm but I think they're just saying that to try and stop me nagging them about smoking. Smoking also affects your lungs because it makes your lungs clog up and you might not be able to breathe as well as you used to. Smoking does not only affect the person who smokes but annoys people around. Smoking can cause fires or explosions. People say a normal smoker loses about eight years of a normal life. These are some of the reasons why I would not smoke.

The argument has personal commitment, highlighted by the first-person viewpoint, and he puts forward a range of facts/opinions to support his proposition. Those are strengths in his text, but the order of his statements is seemingly arbitrary and the ending weakly repeats the opening, missing the opportunity of a punch-line which Persuasion so favours. Because the text is brief the lack of structure is not confusing to the reader, but if he is to develop further to write longer and more complex arguments, he must learn to plan the overall structure. If he had used a web chart the points which he uses in his essay would have stood out as the following key concepts: personal health risks, effects on others, physical dangers. Seeing that he had only three key concepts he might have thought of more, and then sub-concepts to add to the weight of evidence. He would then have had enough information to create paragraphs in a more substantial argument. As it stands the writing has very little of the persuasive about it; the writer is doing no more than setting out his own reasoning, without attempting to persuade a reader to his viewpoint. Again in the planning stage it would have helped him to have imagined a real person as the target reader whom he wanted to persuade to stop smoking. His argument could have been presented in the form of a letter or a campaign leaflet which might have more effectively motivated him and drawn him into the subject.

change the style, it's written to suit child.

Emotional Argument

Where the writer has a strongly partisan point of view there will be a tendency for the persuasive technique to move towards Assertion, which is described as a separate field in the next section. Professional writers can blend the colours of persuasion more subtly so that in spite of their strong feelings, the force of argument is projected through reason, with emotion in the background. Take for instance an information leaflet produced by The League Against Cruel Sports arguing the case against fox-hunting. Although in some parts the language of the leaflet is close to Assertion, this extract overlays the emotional with logical reasoning:

> Like all hunting with hounds, foxhunting is cruel by design. Hounds are bred not for speed that would produce a quick kill, but rather for their stamina. This gives the lengthy chase that is so attractive to the followers. Many riders view the hunt as an excuse to gallop over fields and crops from which they would otherwise be barred.
>
> Hunts kill some 13,000 foxes and their cubs annually. However this makes no difference to the overall fox population and is not intended to do so. Most farmers regard foxes as harmless and many welcome their ability to control genuine pests. Hunters spread the myth of the fox being a pest to justify the cruelty evident in their pastime. The League publicises the truth about foxes and provides information packs for schools and the general public. (continued)

Young writers who feel strongly committed to a subject write with passion, using a declamatory style which would seem inappropriate if what was wanted was a rational argument. 'I think that fox-hunting is wrong. We wouldn't like it if foxes killed us . . .' is the assertive opening of a year 4 boy's argument. For young writers to use the style of Assertion as their interpretation of argument is a natural stage in their development, and it is far better that they write with real conviction, hopefully at all times, learning gradually how to temper their expression appropriately, shifting the emphasis from the emotional force of their belief onto the force of evidence for that belief.

Where older children write emotionally it might be tempting for a teacher to react with a comment such as 'You should not let your feelings run away with you,' but since this is likely to kill off the personal commitment which the declamatory style shows, more positive motivation is preferable. Since the slip from Argument to Assertion is predictable, it can be forestalled if the work is monitored at the planning stage, to ensure that two kinds of information are balanced: (1) what I believe; (2) facts to support my beliefs. Where such monitoring was not possible in time, the writer should be congratulated for expressing personal commitment, and on the rhetorical techniques used, but if there is time for further work, ask the writer to read the text over through the eyes of an opponent and write the opponent's reply. This can be in a cameo form (such as a letter, memo, journal entry) for brevity, but it should use reasoned argument and evidence. This should be a creative way of distancing the writer's original viewpoint and of teaching discrimination between Assertion and Argument through the contrast.

Illustrated Argument

In all kinds of writing and talking we use anecdote of the type 'I knew a man once who . . . .' It comes naturally to us and by it we make the abstract concrete, using our experience as evidence as we comment on life's rich pattern and readjust our world picture. Within forms of Argument such illustrative anecdote can be either a component part or the main feature. As a component part within a text an anecdote is a story in cameo form. Deborah used one in paragraph 4 of her 'Keeping Dogs' argument above: 'Just recently a 4-year-old was attacked by a Rottweiler . . . .' As a main feature the Fables of Aesop are a well-known example, where the exploits of animals illustrate the foibles of humanity. Or again the seventeenth-century French writer Charles Perrault added a moral onto the end of his version of well-known folk tales so as to add instruction to delight. His version of

Little Red Riding Hood ends with a warning to all innocent young
girls to beware of the wolf in whatever guise he might appear. A
recent anti-drugs advertisement began:

> Carol used to go to a lot of parties, liked to hang out with the fast
> crowd . . .

and went on with a synopsis of a young life that went wrong to
illustrate the more abstract message of 'don't do drugs'.

Another kind of illustration commonly used as a component in
Argument but also in many other forms is a quotation, where the
words of a person are given in direct speech. This effectively dramatises specific views or experience because the person seems to be
actually speaking in the present tense within the text. Because human
beings have an insatiable curiosity about life and its consequences,
such anecdotes and dramatisations are very compelling when embedded in any writing, and very effective as a technique in the craft of
persuasion.

However, in the interests of developing resistant readers we need to
make children aware that anecdotal evidence is subjective and may be
hearsay, hence it is unreliable, in spite of its power of attraction over us.

ASSERTION

Assertive writing is to be found in the leaflets of protest campaigns,
political campaigns, the leader articles of newspapers, charters (and
bills of rights, constitutions), petitions, letters to the editor and letters
of protest and complaint.

In Assertion the writer expresses a viewpoint with conviction in
order to win the mind – but perhaps more significantly the heart – of
the reader. In the form at its most forceful the writer believes that the
point of view expressed is the one which must 'win', and the tone may
be aggressive, even combative rather than just assertive. The force of
the assertion may be lessened by concessions such as 'it may be' and
'perhaps' or the balance of 'on the other hand' and 'admittedly'. The
force of the assertion may be increased by emphatic declarations such
as 'it must be', 'without doubt'. Although the force of an assertion
will be strengthened by the use of factual evidence as in a logical
argument, this is likely to be framed in emotive language, with increased use of rhetorical devices such as rhetorical questions, repetition, declarative statements and an accumulation of concepts which
create a particular mood or mental picture.

The most obvious persuasive device to young writers in the field of
Assertion is that of emphatic declarations of personal belief – short

statements, explicit references to personal emotional reaction, and emphasis through underlining and exclamation marks as in 'I didn't like this book because it was really *boring*!!!' The forcefulness of assertion is driven by a passionate belief in the rightness of one's own cause, and such powerful motivation is an excellent starting point, though it can border on the inarticulate if not shaped through crafting. This can begin at an early stage. Viktoria in year 2 was so inspired by the 'Green World' project created by her teacher that she went on to draw up a petition:

> We the undersigned wish to protest about you starting to hunt whales again. We think it is terrible because some whales may become extinct. We think you should change your decision and go against whale hunting.
> Yours sincerely,
> Viktoria F. age 7

She wrote this on her own initiative and unaided except for that telling characteristic of the petition form 'we the undersigned' which her teacher suggested. Viktoria asked all the class to sign it and it was sent to the Norwegian, Icelandic and Japanese embassies.

Letter of Complaint

A letter written to a specific individual to complain or protest is probably the most frequent form of assertion made by adults in real life. We would all hope that children do not have such immediate reason in their lives for writing, but a year 9 project on Charles Dickens' *Oliver Twist* gave Ann the experience through imaginative projection to write this letter:

> To the Chairman of the Parish Council.
>
> Dear Sir,
> On visiting your workhouse last Tuesday I was appalled at the condition that the orphans live in. All the children I saw were dirty and miserable with nothing to do. They looked half starved and had been beaten. They need exercise and they didn't appear to have any. And where is religion these days? None of the children I talked to had any religion at all.
> The matron Mrs Mann tried to persuade me to drink but I went through a door into the main room which was in a terrible state, cold with damp walls and the ceiling falling apart.
> On opening another door I saw a coal cellar with four ragged children. This is a disgraceful way to punish children. The staff are lazy and careless. I caught one of them drinking in a corner.

In the middle of the day the food was one ladle of watery gruel which was not enough for them to keep alive.

I am sure you do not know about this but why have you not investigated this before? Try giving them love and care and maybe an education. I know they are orphans but they still have privileges. Even if your funds are limited, please do your best.

Yours sincerely,
A.H.
(complete text)

The force of this assertion comes in part from the detailed evidence which supports it, but also from the persona which the writer has created. The strongest clue to that comes from the rhetorical question-outburst 'And where is religion these days?' which suggests a writer of mature years with a strong sense of what is right. The tone of moral outrage throughout is probably driven by this projection into another person's viewpoint. Persuasive writing is more likely to be successful if its driving force comes from within, from belief in what you are writing about; the craft comes in moulding that drive into language which communicates effectively. Here there is a clear development of ideas and ordering of facts, ending with a positive suggestion for action, which is good psychology for the protester.

Tone

The letter of complaint is an interesting sub-set of the formal or business letter for which there are generally recognised conventions. The recipient of a formal letter is assumed to be someone not known personally to the writer, and probably a person in a position of authority. Tone is very difficult for young writers whose passions can make them rude, even abusive or threatening, to the detriment of their case, so they will predictably need instruction on the difference between aggression and assertion. Aggression would include verbal abuse, and threats of physical violence which is not likely to have the right effect. 'Formal' usually implies 'polite' and this is the best way to describe it to children, suggesting that they imagine they are writing to 'Someone like our Head teacher' which should suggest the appropriate tone by concrete example – though you could be in trouble if it doesn't. The notion of an essential politeness is more likely to lead to restraint, and a senior person in the firm is more likely to be influenced by reasoned argument. The appropriateness or otherwise of tone does not show in the planning stage, but it does show if you ask children to write 'samples' (described in Chapter 9), i.e. brief extracts before they write a full draft. They can try out the sample on a partner and ask the question 'Is that rude?'

Assertion, though, does have devices which aid the penetration of official inertia without resort to ranting:

(1) Persistence – 'I will write again if there is no action.'
(2) Awareness of successive stages of complaint – 'I will send a copy of this letter to your head office.'
(3) Insistence on positive, realistic action as a result of the complaint – 'I think in the circumstances a full refund would be reasonable.'
(4) Knowledge of the law and one's rights – 'The guarantee says that I am entitled to a new machine if the old one cannot be mended.'

Structure

As with all extended writing, distinct groups of related ideas make up the overall structure. There is no single pattern which suits all occasions but a useful general guideline might be:

(1) First paragraph – the writer introduces him/herself and explains the reason for the writing, namely to complain, and including the circumstances of purchase, how the defect was discovered.
(2) Second paragraph – the evidence to support the complaint – a photograph, the names of witnesses, description of the fault, photocopies of receipts of purchase.
(3) Subsequent paragraphs – additional information about the expectation of the goods purchased, references to consumer rights.
(4) Penultimate paragraph – suggestions as to what reasonable action might be acceptable from the firm: a refund, a credit note, alternative goods, an apology, compensation.
(5) Final paragraph – summary of what the writer expects the recipient to do next; hope that satisfactory relationship will result for future relationships (ending with positive psychology).

Charter

In recent times the charter has become a popular form, with government charters for citizens, patients, parents and so on. As an assertion of the rights of an individual in a particular context the form is related to constitutions and bills of rights which use the register of legal language and are thus not easy models to replicate with children. The current notion of a charter is more appropriate for the classroom because it implies 'plain English' and uses the simpler structures of the informative, such as a numbered list of points. The pattern is clear from the following extract from a 'Pupils' Charter' written by two year 8 boys:

(1) We should be able to say what we think in class and not what the teachers decide.
(2) We should choose which days we have which lessons.
(3) We should choose which nights we have homework.
(4) We should have one free lesson each week.
(5) We should choose which teachers we have.

This unemotional list of assertions is a charter at the simplest level, and could be replicated by the youngest writers, since each point is a single simple sentence on the pattern 'We should . . .'. However, the piece could be expanded into a more complex form; what we have here would then be a cameo, on which to base a second-level piece of writing, still assertive but calling for more crafting of the language. The clue as to how it should be developed lies in what to an outsider is its delightfully subversive propositions. They cry out for: (1) an expansion of the reasons behind the assertion; (2) a real purpose of persuading a specific readership: other pupils would be the most discrete audience whereas school staff or governors would be more political. So the writers could be asked to make their propositions (all or, say, the three most significant) the basis for a broadsheet open-letter to other pupils, to win their votes. They would need to add logical reasons for each proposition and use rhetorical techniques to persuade the readership into taking action.

Newspaper Leader

The leader writer is licensed to go beyond objective reporting of fact, beyond impartial commentary to the point of asserting a partisan viewpoint, indeed forcefully enough to influence reader opinion, to be a 'thunderer' to use the sobriquet of *The Times*. The following example is taken from a provincial newspaper, such papers often having the additional appeal as a model of taking a strong view on local issues which children may already know about:

SICK SOCIETY

One of the most perverse and distasteful symptoms of the violence in our society is the increasing number of assaults on hospital staff.

The sexual attack on a nurse at the West Norwich Hospital at the weekend comes days before the publication of a security review which is likely to call for the locking of doors. Now a local union official is urging restricted public access at night, photo-identity cards, panic buttons and the hiring of security staff.

Physical assault is the most publicised aspect of the general intimidation and abuse to which staff are subjected by a small, unpleasant night-time incursion. So long as efficiency and public confidence are uncompromised, guards, panic buttons and other previously undreamt of NHS facilities must now become part of hospital life.

Although the headline is a pun, it flags unqualified disapproval. The strong condemnation in the opening phrase 'perverse and distasteful' dramatises the writer's judgement, establishes an explicit value-base and shifts the tone up a notch from disapproval to indignation. In terms of its syntax the opening sentence is a balanced proposition, i.e. it has two halves which are interchangeable and could indeed be reversed, like an algebraic equation $A = B$, where one half is the equal of the other. Here A ('one of the most perverse and distasteful symptoms of violence') is an opinion on B which is a material fact ('assaults on hospital staff'). Because it is a balanced sentence, the material fact of the second part gives weight to the opinion of the first part, and therein lies the persuasive power of the structure; both halves have the status of proven fact. The rest of the article continues this colouring of fact with opinion.

Since none of us is likely to oppose the personal belief of the writer here, we do not 'mind' being so worked on; if we share the belief we are not likely even to notice the rhetoric. But it is essential for us as teachers to recognise that there is a value base present in the writing, strongly affecting the way the writer treats the subject – and intended to affect how the readership reacts. Where we do not share the value base of the writer we would want to resist, but children should also be taught to identify implicit as well as explicit value bases in texts with which they agree.

Unfortunately assertion is also too often found in news items on the front pages of the tabloid press, where the rhetorical devices of assertion are used to give a strong 'voice', so colouring (or discolouring) what one might expect to be impartial reporting of fact. A notorious example was the lead headline of The *Sun* on polling day of the 1992 General Election, 'If Kinnock wins today will the last person to leave Britain please turn out the lights.' Certainly a forceful assertion and certainly not objective news reporting, such powerful rhetoric in that and other partisan newspapers was considered by some political commentators to have played a significant part in the Labour Party's defeat at that election.

Although Assertion is closely related to Argument and to forms of the Informative, the distinction between them which this classification makes is important for the very reason that developing reader-writers risk being misled if they cannot firstly identify assertion, then read through it to disentangle fact from opinion, to evaluate the value base of the writer and if necessary to resist the assertions being made. Assertion is a powerful field, which can have a debit side; on the credit side, writing forcefully with conviction in a just cause can be the best writing for the best of all reasons, where in Milton's phrase 'the pen is mightier than the sword'.

APPEAL

Charitable organisations create texts which aim to simultaneously inform and persuade the public so as to raise funds and change attitudes in society. Children are likely to encounter such texts in a variety of media and they are likely to be interested in the content of texts which concern such issues as conservation, animal rights, the problems of the dispossessed. Since the organisations concerned are usually less concerned with the commercial concerns of selling a product than with using argument to arouse the sympathy of the reader by describing the facts of their cause, appeal texts usually have more written content than commercial advertising. As such they offer more material to work on, and avoid the psychology of adult fears, fantasies and urges which pervades commercial advertising. Their underlying values might also be more acceptable in the framework of education.

At the relatively unemotional end of the scale is this Greenpeace campaign leaflet:

GREENPEACE: AGAINST ALL ODDS

Against all odds, Greenpeace has brought the plight of the natural world to the attention of caring people. Terrible abuses to the environment, often carried out in remote places or far out to sea, have been headlined on television and in the press.

Greenpeace began with a protest voyage into a nuclear test zone. The test was disrupted. Today, the site at Amchitka in the Aleutian Islands is a bird sanctuary.

Then Greenpeace sent its tiny inflatable boats to protect the whales. They took up position between the harpoons and the fleeing whales. Today, commercial whaling is banned.

On the ice floes of Newfoundland, Greenpeace volunteers placed their bodies between the gaffs of the seal hunters and the helpless seal pups. The hunt was subsequently called off.

In the North Atlantic, Greenpeace drove its inflatables underneath falling barrels of radioactive waste. Now nuclear waste dumping at sea has been stopped.

In the North Sea, Greenpeace swimmers turned back dump ships carrying chemical wastes. New laws to protect the North Sea have been promised.

Peaceful direct action by Greenpeace has invoked the power of public opinion which in turn has forced changes in the law to protect wildlife and to stop the pollution of the natural world.

The basic structure of the piece is the classic essay pattern of an opening paragraph giving a general introduction to the topic, followed by several paragraphs which itemise the argument, and finally a conclusion which sums up the argument, with a punch-line.

The first paragraph introduces the topic, repeating the title which is a concise phrase, powerful because it is a dynamic image which associates the survival struggle of Greenpeace with the struggle for survival of the natural world.

The paragraphs which follow are on a simple repetitive pattern which makes the argument easy to follow. They are of two or three sentences, the first being an assertion in the form of a simple description of action taken, followed by a supplementary sentence or two describing the successful consequences. The final sentence is an assertive statement of the positive result of the action taken.

There is a strong element of time reference to strengthen the structure. The first paragraph begins with an assertion of the past record of the organisation; the chronology of their successes is developed in paragraph 2 ('Greenpeace began with . . .'); paragraph 3 continues onto the next stage of their work ('Then Greenpeace . . .'). The major structure shifts from a time sequence to a geographical web pattern, referring to a major zone of the world in each of the next three paragraphs. However, the time line is retained as a minor structure within each of paragraphs 2–5 as a 'before–after' contrast ('Greenpeace . . . boats/Today . . . banned'; 'placed their bodies . . . subsequently called off').

The final paragraph is a single sentence, the longest in the text, making a more generalised statement. The last part of the sentence 'to stop the pollution of the natural world' is the key message which underlies the whole text, the central principle of the movement. To hold it back until that final position creates a dramatic effect, a frequent technique in persuasive texts.

An important feature of the tone is the way the writer increases the status of the organisation by suggesting its heroic status, like David against Goliath. The title itself first suggests the heroic contrast 'Against all the odds', then other large–small contrasts follow: 'its tiny inflatable boats', 'placed their bodies between the gaffs', 'swimmers turned back dump ships.' This is subtly done but its cumulative effect has more impact than more explicit claims which might sound boastful and hence off-putting to the reader.

Viktoria in year 2 who wrote the petition quoted earlier in the Assertion section was very moved by the plight of whales but her teacher stressed the need to give facts and reasons for her strongly felt beliefs:

> Whales may become extinct because they are being hunted and caught. They are being used for lots of things like people are using their oil and their blubber for things. They are much happier in the wild so leave them alone.

Note particularly the action line which ends this Appeal, a sign that the writer has grasped a basic principle of writing with a persuasive purpose for an audience. Although her friend Gayle's writing is also a considerable achievement, her facts are not so well ordered and she does not make the appeal nature of the writing explicit:

> Whales live in the sea. If we don't stop killing the whales there will be no whales left in the sea. Whales are mammals and the whales eat plankton. Whales are being killed by us.

Shock Appeal

Not all Appeals use the calm voice of reason such as that of Greenpeace. In order to break through our defences many Appeals now use heavy shock tactics. If we can remain impartial for a moment on the rightness or otherwise of its cause, let us consider the techniques used in this example, an RSPCA advertisement in a broadsheet newspaper:

THE CONTINENTALS LOVE FRESHLY BUTCHERED HORSEMEAT. WHEN ARE WE GOING TO SUPPLY IT?

> Sadly, we're going to supply it after 1992.
>
> Because in 1992, it will once again become legal to transport live British horses to the continent for slaughter. (A practice that was effectively banned here over 30 years ago on the grounds of extreme cruelty.)
>
> If the trauma that some other animals suffer during live transport is anything to go by, the slaughterhouse could provide our horses with a merciful relief.
>
> Our horses could be herded in the transporters with electric cattle prods. They could be locked in the transporters to kick and trample each other for up to 24 hours. (continued)

The shock begins with the association of 'butchered . . . meat' with horses, an association which is not part of our culture in Britain. I am not sure of the emotional effect of the term 'continentals', which does not seem to carry heavy negative load, but in these days of partnership and international understanding the copywriter would presumably not want to seem prejudiced in other than this single issue. Throughout the text is heavily loaded with words which have emotional shock association: slaughter, trauma, electric prods, trample and so on. The passive voice predominates ('It will again become legal', 'They could be locked') which focuses on horses as the only identified life forms, victims of anonymous third parties. There are repeated patterns of syntax: 'Our horses could be', 'They could be'.

Although the crafting techniques are very clear, a judgement has to be made by teachers as to whether such strong material, designed to be disturbing, should be used in the classroom and with what age of child. For the author the end justifies the means, and such shock techniques are becoming more common in such contexts as accident prevention and the Aids campaign.

A year 9 class produced Appeal writing as a result of a project on the exploitation of animals. Jackie's text reproduced here was written on a word-processor, in two-column layout using several fonts and graphics. The single word heading 'WHY?' was afterwards partly coloured red as if blood were dripping from it:

WHY?

ANIMALS ARE PUT THROUGH HELL JUST FOR VANITY

Why should animals have to suffer unjust treatment just so some wrinkly old lady can look 21 again? Many of the cosmetics products tested on animals are inefficient and still cause some people to have skin disorders and rashes. In tests animals are subjected to having shampoo in their eyes for days whereas humans would only spend a few seconds with the same substance in *their* eyes before washing it out. Is this really necessary? Other times their fur is shaved off, the skin split open and lotion to test is put in to see the reaction on the animal. The lotion is left in the cut for 2–3 weeks and the excruciating pain caused can often kill. Can this treatment be justified? Animals are not going to use cosmetics so *why* should they be used for testing?

Let us hope we will soon see the end of this unnecessary suffering. (continued)

She finished by actually naming several companies, showing the kind of moral courage which I do not need to have in this text, and so I end the quote at that point, just before the end. She expresses her viewpoint uncompromisingly, without tact, since her target audience might include the 'old ladies' whom she attacks. She wishes to challenge reader complacency or wrong values, and she does this through a number of rhetorical devices: rhetorical questions to prompt active response; stark contrast with 'days' versus 'seconds'; italic font to emphasise 'their' and 'why'; emotional shock tactics with 'skin split open' and 'excruciating pain'. These are all techniques of Assertion, but she makes the text into an Appeal through the tone change which begins 'Let us hope'. She has gone a long way towards understanding the crafting techniques of the writer who wishes to persuade the reader by an Appeal.

ADVERTISEMENT

Because ours is a consumer society, highly dependent upon attracting customers to buy manufactured goods and services, advertising is a major field with many forms, across the full range of media; radio, television, journalism, billboards, direct mail. Newspapers usually contain several different kinds of advertising: classified, display, feature, announcements. The medium is so all-pervasive that it can be taken for granted that every child will have an extensive internalised repertoire of what advertising is and can do in several media, predominantly television but not exclusively so. Much of it is highly accessible – reaching out to the potential market is after all its priority – but it must be debatable whether or not all of it is usable with all ages of children, not least because of the psychological ploys it uses. Creating resistant or sceptical readers must be a highly desirable educational goal; anyone who has lived with young children as Christmas approaches will realise only too well how susceptible they are to the claims of advertisers.

Guidelines for child writers need to take account of a range of advertising forms which runs from the extended purple prose of travel trade brochures to the slogan catch-phrases of billboard posters. The basis, though, of all advertising and the starting point for teaching the field is that its first purpose is to persuade – even seduce – the reader into 'buying'. That distinctive purpose is highly influential on the shape of the writing, from the 'headline' which catches the attention of the reader to the 'strapline' which makes the reader want to 'rush out and buy one today.'

Creativity

The first principle of the modern advertising copywriter is to attract and hold the attention of the reader, who is envisaged as a potential customer. Although potential buyers may already be looking for information about a product and therefore read willingly, such willingness cannot be taken for granted. Instead the writer assumes that the reader needs to be persuaded to buy either by logic or more usually by appeal to powerful emotions and attractive associations.

Because theirs is highly crafted language, advertisers use many of the techniques of what was once the most crafted form of the spoken then the written language – poetry. Because speech evolved before writing, the earliest rhetorical devices were those of speech – the sound effect patterns of rhyme, rhythm, alliteration, assonance. Their purpose was to so pattern the sound of language as to make it easily memorable for the oral storyteller and ear-catching for the listener. With their aid bards could remember and recite legends, sagas and historical accounts which took hours even days to perform, whilst their listeners could remain enrapt, partly mesmerised partly stimulated, by repetitive compelling sound patterns. A class of the youngest children will be able to recall and recite lists of the slogans and catch-phrases of advertising in just such a way because the same techniques are used.

One interesting issue is the tension in heroic poetry between cliché and novelty. Some objects are referred to always in the same words, called a 'tag'; for instance, Homer refers always to the sea as 'the wine-dark sea' which becomes the established term presumably to reassure the listener with the familiar phrase. At the other extreme some terms are constantly varied, presumably to excite interest; for example, the extensive range of terms used to describe swords in the Anglo-Saxon poem *Beowulf*. Advertising similarly at one end of the scale creates familiar terms and catch-phrases which later become cliché, of the 'Beanz meanz Heinz' kind, while at the other there is a constant search for unusual uses of language. To ask children only to be original in creating adverts is to miss this essential tension between the familiar and the novel.

Additionally poetry from the earliest times used language to evoke vivid pictures in the mind, either by association (simile, symbol and metaphor) or through description and suggestion (imagery) so that listeners were drawn into creating a film-like evocation of what they heard in their own heads. It is this line of development, the visual, which is one of the most significant differences between advertising, poetry and all other forms, because in addition to word pictures with which advertising and a great many other forms abound, the literally visual is used wherever possible in advertising. Not just pictures of people, places and things but all aspects of the graphic: page layout, use of colour, print size and style. A detailed study of advertising involves co-operation between teachers of English, Art and Media – indeed advertising agencies employ people with highly specific skills in those fields working in collaboration.

Display Advertisement

A great deal of advertising has to be brief so as to concentrate its impact, which makes it easier to focus on fine detail. The display or block advertisement is a form with specific genre characteristics, making it a useful cameo for demonstrating the principles of advertisement more generally. The form is to be found in magazines or newspapers, and since it is more expensive than the more common 'line advertisement' of the 'Classified' columns it is usually the choice of professionals who are advertising services or products.

The form usually involves the following components:

Border and white space
Headline
Bodycopy
Illustration or visual
Logo
Strapline
Address block

(1) *Border and white space:* the text of a display advertisement is set inside a border around which a box is drawn to mark it off from other text in the newspaper or magazine. Both the black lines of the box and the 'white space' on either side of the lines are important in attracting the eye to the advertisement itself; it should not look cluttered or hemmed in on the page.

(2) *Headline:* a news headline is usually thought of as very short, but in an advertisement the headline may be longer, to a maximum of fifteen words. A longer headline is possible when it uses a series of sharp phrases which:

    (a) Speak directly to the potential buyer ('the prospect') and introduce his/her interest, e.g. 'First-time buyers'.

    (b) Mention the product favourably, e.g. 'Executive homes'.

    (c) Raise the curiosity of the prospect, e.g. 'Which would you prefer?'

    (d) Make the product sound newsworthy, e.g. 'Breakthrough in medical science'.

    (e) Catch attention with unusual language and word play, e.g. 'El Dorado delivers the dream'.

(3) *Bodycopy:* this is text placed below the headline which contains the main factual information. The tone may be one of 'hype' (short for hyperbole) describing forcefully or colourfully the qualities of the product. Hype is so marked a characteristic that children intuitively replicate it without prompting, having subconsciously absorbed so much of it in their time. The bodycopy may be very brief or extensive, depending on the amount of money spent, but no matter how extensive, it should:

(a) Speak to the individual (you, we, the modern woman) or target group, not to the general public.

(b) Be convincing that the product or service is of value or meets a need, e.g. 'Proved in extensive trials.'

(c) List as many advantages as concisely possible for the product or service, e.g. 'Safe, silent, economical.'

(4) *Strapline:* a dramatic final statement which makes the reader want to take action – to buy the goods. 'Don't delay – buy today'.

(5) *Graphic design:* a newspaper will usually have a graphics department specialising in the design of advertisements. A display ad will be designed as a whole, balancing graphics and copy to make the whole attractive and eye-catching. Type-face may be chosen to be appropriate to the product – as in computer products. Illustrations can be placed anywhere within the display space, and can be of a variety of kinds: cartoon, line-drawing, photograph. Colour may be used in some newspapers, in some of the key lettering or in a line-drawing, but less often in a photograph because of cost.

(6) *Logo:* the advertiser may be an established firm which already has a known trade mark or logo which the public might recognise. If so this will be featured in the display. The advantage of a logo is that it is a symbol, and symbols have the power to compress meaning. Ideally that meaning should be a range of favourable experiences or past associations with the firm and its products. It suggests that the advertiser is not a fly-by-night who is trying to con you.

(7) *Address block:* where the advertiser is advertising locally, the address of the premises is crucial. Just a phone number will certainly save space, and will be adequate provided the reader trusts this as assurance that the firm actually exists. A solid address in a known part of town creates greater feelings of security.

(8) *Overall* the advert must, as advertising agencies say, 'pull the trigger', i.e. make the reader want to buy. It must be unambiguous, leave no doubts, make the reader willing, even enthusiastic to buy.

Bodycopy: Information

Bona fide companies who believe in the products they offer for sale still have to catch and hold the attention of readers in a competitive market and induce them to buy the product. Simple statements of facts are not enough and there has to be a skilful blend of fact and image. Most advertisements are relatively short, and so do not offer a great deal of copy to study, but you will find some good longer examples in the weekend magazines of the popular press, such as the following:

ELIZABETH AT THE BALL

The enchantment of a young lady's first ball . . .
memorably evoked in an exquisite figure
of fine porcelain
individually crafted and painted by hand

The year is 1635. In the regal setting of a palace ballroom, the music begins. As the sparkling notes of a lute cast a spell of enchantment over the room . . . a young nobleman catches sight of the beautiful Elizabeth, making her debut in a romantic satin gown.

She is a vision of elegance in a peach satin gown, a masterpiece of the dressmaker's art, with panniered skirt and pastel silk puffed sleeves. A toss of her head in its plumed cavalier hat . . . a flutter of her ostrich feather fan . . . and his heart is hers to keep.

'Elizabeth at the Ball' has been created by Brooks & Bentley under the guidance of renowned fashion authority Vera Maxwell. Recognised as an expert on the history of fashion, her designs have won her the coveted Coty award and have been exhibited in many museums, including the Smithsonian Institution, Washington, D.C.

A hand-crafted work of art

'Elizabeth at the Ball' is completely historically authentic and accurate. This period costume figurine is a lovely recreation of the Baroque Era's lavish and romantic fashions and is crafted in the finest bisque porcelain. With even the most intricate of details – from her pleated Medici collar to the bows on her elaborately puffed sleeves and the separate feathers in her ostrich fan – captured to perfection.

Skilled craftsmen paint each piece by hand, creating a sculpture most subtly toned and textured – a work of *exceptional* beauty.

Available exclusively from Brooks and Bentley

To acquire this romantic and appealing work of art, it is not necessary to send any money now. Simply return the reservation form by. . . . If you prefer the convenience of ordering early, telephone anytime – 24 hours a day, 7 days a week – by calling. . . .

PLEDGE OF SATISFACTION

Brooks & Bentley takes pride in offering works of uncompromisingly high standards of quality, created with care and dedication by skilled craftsmen. Each issue comes with our assurance that it will meet your highest expectations. If you are not satisfied with your purchase for any reason, simply return it within one year for a replacement or full refund (including any postage you paid).

Most extended adverts are based on a specific 'angle' or basic idea which is supported by the images, selection of detail and the structure. The angle here is that the figurine is represented as alive, which is probably how collectors of figurines imagine them.

The strongly marked style has an immediate impact, intending as it does to sweep the reader along with the hyperbole of such concepts and phrases as: 'exquisite, renowned, expert, captured to perfection, exceptional beauty', appropriate here because the figurine is being marketed as a collectable work of art. In the same cause there is also a running theme of reference in a variety of ways to high quality manufacture: 'individually crafted, hand crafted, masterpiece, authentic and accurate, skilled craftsmen, subtly toned and textured'. Additionally the text contains a chain of descriptors which carry a high charge of emotional association: 'romantic, enchantment, vision of elegance, lovely recreation', presumably because the potential purchaser is seen as having a penchant for romance.

The all-important details of how to buy the advertised product pick up the same style in the phrase 'romantic and appealing work of art' but there is another psychological appeal added, or rather subtracted, namely that of resistance to pay, indicated in the notions of: 'simply, convenience, anytime'. It is a 'reservation form' not a form of payment, reinforced by 'send no money now'. It is pointless in the commercial world to produce expensive advertising copy which does not sell the product.

Children can identify these devices more clearly by first underlining them in the text, then listing them under specific headings (romance, craftsmanship, purchasing). Younger children might underline words they do not actually understand. You might try showing them the text without the appealing picture accompanying it, to see whether the words suggest a mental picture the same as the physical one, or whether all children form the same mental image from the text as each other.

We can also point out to young writers that the copy has a clear structure, in this case five parts:

(1) The headline, beginning with 'Elizabeth' down to 'painted by hand' which gives a cameo version of the whole text.

(2) The first two paragraphs of the bodycopy which are an evocation of a ball attended by an imagined real-life 'Elizabeth'. The first paragraph gives an impression of the total scene, the second zooms in on the detail of Elizabeth as if the figure were a real person moving.

(3) The third section first giving the credentials of the designer and then those of the figurine. The ideas of these two paragraphs are concluded in a final brief paragraph, closing with the punch line 'a work of exceptional beauty'.

(4) The factual details of how to buy the figurine, followed by the 'pledge of satisfaction'. The factual even legal detail requires a more prosaic style in this section though there is a back reference to the tone of the bodycopy in 'romantic and appealing work of art.'

(5) The pledge of satisfaction, which returns first to the elaborate style of the bodycopy but which in the final sentence takes on the style of a legal statement because it is an assurance of the legal rights of potential buyers.

This is an appealing model to use with children not least because of its basic angle, of describing the figure as being alive. This is an attractive idea to children because it is how they think (or perhaps thought in the past) about their own toys. I read the advert to a year 6 class who then on their own copies underlined words which they felt made it effective, listing words and phrases under specific headings (romance, craftsmanship, purchasing). We then talked about these words and phrases, about their meaning and associations. They then thought of a toy or model of their own to advertise using the angle of the toy being alive. The planning stage included: (1) listing the attractive features of the toy and its weaknesses which they might have to compensate for; (2) describing in a few phrases an appropriate setting in which it would come alive; (3) describing the toy moving; (4) expanding the list of attractive features into phrases which would attract attention. The sexism implicit in the results reproduced below reflects, I hope, their early conditioning in the home rather than anything they learned in the classroom, but typically the girls advertised soft toys and the boys went for Action-Man. James wrote:

THE ULTIMATE ARMY

They charge into the desert, sand blowing in their faces. A sound of guns and tanks cracks the silence. They duck the bullets flying overhead. Sounds of a retreating army. The Ultimate Army have won with triumph.

The Ultimate Army are hand-painted with army clothing and tin hats. They are in fighting positions and grasping war machines.

Available from all James Stores. Buy now and pay in September. The amazing Ultimate Army for the princely sum of £15.00. To order write to 5 Shepton Avenue, Cringleford, or if you prefer a quick order, phone 50602. NOW!

He has tried to use the exotic vocabulary of hyperbole like the model and hence the phrase 'won with triumph' which is rather odd but appealing. 'War machines' is usually applied to large vehicles rather than hand-weapons so that is not so successful. He has got the right tone with 'princely sum' but unfortunately for the buyer the phrase usually means 'very expensive' so it is the wrong psychology.

Emma's is far more sophisticated linguistically and psychologically:

PINK ELEPHANT

A child's first toy
An enchanted memory . . .
wrapped around a soft pink dream.

Imagine a new-born baby, a beautiful baby girl, soft and pink, cooing in her crib. A tiny hand makes a tiny fist in which to gain life itself. Imagine now the softest toy to hold and cuddle, a perfect toy for a perfect baby.

Pink Elephant has been brought especially to you by Beautiful Babies Limited.

Also limited are the number of these unique elephants made by hand for *your* beautiful baby.

For you to purchase this 'Beautiful' toy, send *no* money. Instead only six vouchers from any other Beautiful Babies Limited products (provided each item costs within the region of £20.00).

With your 6 vouchers, send a stamped addressed envelope to:
B.B. Ltd.
P.O. Box 12
London SW12
Or ring this number *anytime* for information: 081-625430

Thank you for your interest.
B.B. Ltd.

She begins with the direct address to the reader 'Imagine', and that direct address continues throughout. She has taken 'enchanted' from the model but made it into an evocative metaphor 'wrapped around a soft pink dream' appropriate for the context of baby clothes. 'Beautiful Babies' is a cliché but in the best sense of having a cliché's simplicity and comforting associations in addition to alliterative appeal. She has the basis of a chain of reference to exclusivity through 'limited' and 'unique', and to quality through 'perfect' and 'softest'. Like James she has misunderstood the marketing aspect, with which she is least familiar, since the buyer would have to go through all the motions of buying six products, spending £120.00 and sending off vouchers. She has, though, eased the pain of buying with 'send no money' and emphasising 'anytime' which shows she has begun to recognise some of the psychology/language of 'pulling the trigger'.

We should notice about this that Emma did not make the toy come alive but transferred the focus to a real baby, the intended recipient. From that I draw the moral that talented writers get away with breaking the rules. Even though it helps many children to have clear guidelines for writing, they must have freedom to follow up their own ideas if they think they are better; too tight a constraint can stifle creativity. It is a difficult balance for the teacher and the real test is whether the alternative piece of writing is effective. From this example of her work I think Emma is more likely to be an advertising copywriter than I am.

Early Finishers

Early finishers in this class then wrote a playscript in which a dissatisfied customer took the advertised product back to the shop to complain for some reason. This picked up the list of weaknesses of their product which they had listed in the planning stage, and the follow-up activity was for children to read between the lines of their own purple prose to the reality behind it, to encourage resistant reading of advertising copy. The same purpose would be served in a different form by a letter of complaint. Both of these activities would be what I have called 'cameos' in Chapter 4.

Humour

Humour is an important device in persuading people but it is very difficult to define and classify. It is the emotion which we show most clearly in our body language – smile, giggle, laughter – and it is one which affects other aspects of our behaviour very strongly – it makes us feel good about life. When children write for an audience they like that audience to show a marked reaction, and because the effect of successful humour is so markedly demonstrated physically by an audience, it has a strong appeal, in my experience particularly to boys. We do not give such obvious external clues of other emotions such as the classic pity and fear, and in a performance reading of children's work it can be difficult for writers of 'straight' pieces to follow a successful humorist.

Children's humour can be very different from that of adults and when they attempt it in their writing the results can make the teacher cringe. They often enjoy the slapstick action which is best expressed through films and cartoons of the Laurel and Hardy, Tom and Jerry kind, but this is very difficult to create in writing. So for younger children the safer kinds of humour are the puns and word plays beloved of advertising.

It is probably apocryphal but an early washing machine advert was said to read: 'Don't kill your wife with over-work. Let electricity do it!'

Humour in the form of parody is especially significant in fostering resistant reader/writers because it requires them to analyse and create simultaneously. Graham Rawle in an illustration for a Martin Bracewell article created a satirical effect by linking together catch-phrases from the different hi-tech products which you might find in a credit-card marketing brochure:

CUT IRONING TIME IN HALF

Ever missed a delivery or a caller through not hearing the doorbell? Now here's an ingenious solution: a deafening 100 db siren that clips onto your belt or golf bag which also gobbles up dust and dirt and is totally weatherproof. This amazing electronic spell checker will drive nails into plasterboard, brick or aggressive dogs. (continued)

(© Guardian News Service Ltd. 1990)

Resistance

Advertising raises ethical issues: Are advertisers' claims justifiable? Have we a right to privacy? Do advertisers play on our weaknesses? Do the means justify the end? An important part of our purpose in education should be to raise these questions and to give students the skills necessary to become critical readers of the field. If they know how advertising works, they will know how they are being worked on, so that they can resist if necessary. This should be a constructive scepticism, however; it is pointless to suggest that advertising is of itself unethical and an unworthy model for language development.

DESCRIPTION

Description is a component part of most forms of writing; the journalist describes the scene of the crime, the poet the winter landscape, the feature writer the latest fashion designs, the technical writer how a process works. Movement and stillness, setting and action, inner and outer reality, words attempt to fix these states of being. Indeed description is so all-pervasive that it is difficult to know where it begins and ends. For the purpose of categorisation there is a problem in defining this as a discrete field of writing, but within the Persuasive range distinct applications of description are to be found in feature writing on interests such as gardening, fashion, sport and travel. In travel writing description is more than a component; centring on people, places and action, it is a major characteristic of the form, and so in a book about real writing I take that as my justification for making Description a distinct field. For instance, the travel brochure uses description as hyperbole to sell holidays and so definitely belongs in the field of Advertisement, but the guidebook uses description to heighten appreciation which mutes the persuasive devices of marketing.

The Guidebook

Encounters with travel writing probably give most adults pleasure because the form is associated with holidays past, present or future. Similarly children find it an attractive context about which to write; models are easy to come by and you will find appropriate material for all ages of children. It can be linked to the direct experience not only of personal holidays but also school trips and guides to local attractions. The person who wrote such materials may be willing – even flattered – to talk to schools about crafting techniques.

One common way of organising the description in a guidebook is to take the reader on a tour of the attractions in the museum, town, zoo, devoting a descriptive section to each of the sights to be seen on the tour. For children's own writing, a map is one of the best forms of plan (see Chapter 4). The city guide which follows is based on the notion that the reader is actually walking a route as it is read but the viewpoint also zooms in and out on detail like a camera:

NORWICH MINI-GUIDE

A fine old city . . . view it from whatever side you will.

Norwich is a beautiful and ancient city with a long and historic tradition; today it is still a busy commercial and shopping centre, and a city where theatre, music and the arts flourish. From St. James Hill, above the city on Mousehold Heath, the buildings of old Norwich can be seen clustered around the Cathedral within the circle of the city walls and the river. The streets, alleys and many mediaeval churches and fine old buildings illustrate how prosperous and important Norwich has been for nearly a thousand years.

The story begins on Tombland, once the Saxon market place; two mediaeval gateways lead to the mainly Norman Cathedral in its peaceful surroundings in the Close. Nelson was a pupil at the school here, first established in the fifteenth century. A short walk leads to Pulls Ferry, the ancient Watergate to the Cathedral. (continued)

The travelogue begins with the city motto, a quotation from the novelist George Borrow, which is appropriately flattering for persuasive purposes. The major promotional theme is the town's history and the extent of its culture. References to the past therefore abound. In just the first paragraph we are bombarded with: ancient, historic, old (twice), mediaeval, a thousand years. Flattering epithets are a feature of the writing throughout, in addition to phrases loaded with appealing images, sure signs of persuasive writing, though compared with the possible hyperbole of the advertising world this is a dignified version.

Sensory Experience

In physical description much of the factuality of the text relies on the evidence of the writer's senses. How the writer interprets this evidence is a major factor in shaping the persuasive effect of the text, for the information can be described in objective detail or muted appreciation or purple prose hyperbole. Interpretation of sensory information is usually woven into the text and not immediately obvious, but happily for my purpose an American brochure extolling Colorado as a holiday region used the responses of the five senses as its structure:

REVIVE YOUR SENSES!
. . . with the South Central Colorado difference.

The day-to-day routines of life can tend to dull the human senses over time. Occasionally you need a recharge or an awakening of the senses in order to stay sharp and alert. You need an experience that is totally unique. One that excites the senses. You need to discover the difference offered by South Central Colorado. So let your senses go as you read along and become part of a land that will always stay with you.

SEE THE VARIETY
Your eyes are the first to notice a change. The majestic splendor of the Rockies grabs you as it appears on the horizon. Soon, you begin to notice details like deer grazing on the side of the road, the tremendous variety of flowers and trees, and the unique charm of the buildings in the towns you pass. Your eyes have truly come to life, soaking up the beauty, the culture and the wonder of it all.

SMELL THE DIFFERENCE

The next change is more subtle, you barely notice it at first, but suddenly the air is sweeter with the soft scent of pine. You can breathe deeply and smell the wholesome aroma of fresh-caught trout cooking over an open camp-fire. Or, go back in time as you smell the mustiness of an old mine while on a guided tour. Savor these unique scents and the experience will never fade from your mind. (and so on)

Although it is not intended as a direct marketing text, it does use the characteristics of Advertisement, by contrast with the Norwich mini-guide, and that is probably a comment on the difference between the language cultures of the two countries. Having studied that model a year 6 class wrote leaflets for attractions in their own region, and although they were asked to concentrate on sense impressions, the marketing purpose came through. Graham wrote:

KELLING HEATH
The caravan park of your dreams

The sound of the wind rustling in the trees greets you as you arrive. The smell of steam arrives as the steam train comes into the park's station. You see squirrels and a wide variety of birdlife in and outside the woods.

Taste our magnificent food. We have fish and chips and a range of healthy foods as well.

The adventure playground provides pleasure for children throughout the day and the bar gives entertainment at night.

He begins well with the sounds of 'wind rustling' and then the unexplained but evocative 'smell of steam', and again 'magnificent food', not a sense impression but an emotional reaction to one. However, 'a wide variety of birdlife' is too generalised to have any impact, and he would have been better to have imagined a scene on which the camera could have panned and zoomed, to include the squirrels. He could perhaps have studied menus to extend his cuisine vocabulary but he is beginning to build up images from the stark information of the site's attractions by using sense impressions.

In human beings taste and smell are not as well developed as the other senses, which is reflected in the limited ability of our language to discriminate where those senses are concerned. On the other hand our sight is particularly well developed; we are capable of making fine distinctions as to size, length, breadth, texture, colour, shape, movement, relationship with other objects. We can interpret human intention, motivation and character through our observation of dress, facial expression, body language, movement. Language is rich in visual vocabulary and techniques. We make fine distinctions by use of precise terminology which is further fine-tuned by the additional qualification of adjectives and adverbs. Re-creating a picture in the mind of the reader comes also through comparisons with other experiences using symbol, imagery, simile, metaphor. Indeed metaphor, a process of using concrete description of one thing to illustrate another, is said to be of major significance in the development of language, for instance the abstract concept of 'to understand' being a metaphor for the concrete action of 'standing under' which by implication comes to mean 'under the influence of' thence 'to comprehend.' We use colour in the term 'purple prose' to describe one extreme descriptive style. It is a compliment to call a piece of writing 'a graphic description' while more generally we speak with approval of 'colourful writing'. The importance of the visual in writing is not confined to descriptive forms, for we use the term 'viewpoint' as a metaphor to describe the values and attitudes which colour a writer's representation of experience.

Sound is not so well provided for as sight in language but a wide repertoire of sound experiences is available to us; particularly the human voice – tone, pitch, dialect, intonation – all of which present interesting challenges to the writer trying to replicate them. Through onomatopoeia we try to replicate in language the sounds around us. Sound associations are used extensively in poetry, which therefore provides rich language models.

Touch to some extent complements sight because we can see texture, such as the roughness of a piece of wood, though it is only through touch that we can feel its relative warmth compared with stone. We use many touch metaphors in our everyday speech. 'Soft in the head', 'a slippery character', 'a sharp tongue', 'a rough diamond'. We can feel the difference between the texture of different kinds of material in clothing. It would take very skilled use of language to pinpoint those textural differences, but through such contrived practical experiences linked with use of a thesaurus appropriate language can be explored.

Our senses of taste and smell are less well developed again and this affects the lexical range available to the writer. It explains the constraints on writers on wine and cookery who are caricatured as devising phrases like 'a pleasant little wine with a delicate nose and a full body'. Children, though, are very interested in food. Ask a class what books they remember most clearly from their childhood and then check how many contain descriptions of feasts of one kind or another at a significant point. The undeniably popular Roald Dahl even set two well-loved books inside food – *James and the Giant Peach* and

Charlie and the Chocolate Factory. Ted Hughes's robot in *The Iron Man*, a major source of project work in primary schools for many years, intriguingly has food fads. Images of children as food themselves haunt myths and folk tales. Although brief as models, the more inventive menus from contrasting sources such as American-style burger bars and haute cuisine restaurants can excite children's interest in the intriguing problem of describing the taste of food and drink.

One classroom strategy to increase sensory awareness is through its opposite, sensory deprivation. 'How would you find your way round your bedroom in the dark – what would you touch as you try to find the door?' Sources such as the blindness sequence at the beginning of John Wyndham's *Day of the Triffids* and Theodore Taylor's *The Cay* are classic models.

Another way is to use a changed perspective as the stimulus, seeing the familiar again in a novel way and stretching limited language resources to express that experience. For instance, seeing the world from the perspective of either a giant or an ant. The traditional model was *Gulliver's Travels* and the land of Lilliput, but reduced size is a classic theme which occurs in many books such as *Alice in Wonderland* and more recently in Lynne Reid Banks' *The Indian in the Cupboard*.

Emotion

The range of senses goes beyond the five generally acknowledged. We can sense hot and cold, we have a sense of balance (see Edgar Allan Poe's obsession with vertigo), and we have a repertoire of emotions which can express themselves in physical ways: fear prickling the back of the neck, making the knees go weak, the stomach churn, the head pound, vision blur.

An emotional scale in writing is particularly significant because the reader is given a strong clue as to how to respond to a text if the writer includes an emotional response to what is described, either explicitly, 'I felt sad for days afterwards', or suggesting an emotion implicitly, 'She skipped off down the road'. Children are generally very limited in their ability to express anything beyond the main points on the happy–sad scale. I seem to have read 'I felt sick' on so many occasions, to indicate any one of a wide range of extreme emotions, not just the after-effects of a roller-coaster ride. Clearly work with a thesaurus will extend their range of alternative terms, but such a short-hand tag as feeling sick to indicate a 'speechless' emotional state may be an indication of limited ability not only to express an emotional state but also perhaps to comprehend it. Limited expression may reflect limited experience as much as limited vocabulary. All the more reason for actual experience as well as the language which expresses it to be a focus in classroom drama, writing and discussion, if we are to help children to understand emotional states and to respond compassionately in their dealings with others.

Structure

As with all non-narrative forms, description offers no natural structure. In the creative writing era many teachers used pictures as a stimulus, but I always found the resulting writing formless. Consider it. When you look at a picture your eye can wander at will, in no predetermined order. There will probably be a central point which will catch the eye first; perhaps the composition suggests a priority: it may suggest a narrative, which is what children generally seek as a lifebelt. The piece of writing below shows the problem. In it William in year 5 is describing a picture in a history text illustrating a mediaeval fair:

> In the picture you can see lots of people. There is a lady selling apples and pears. A man is holding a sword. He has just wounded a person. There are two big wheels. Two people are allowed in each carriage. There are four carriages on each big wheel. There are swings and they also have 4 swings on one bar. Only one person is allowed on a swing. There are stray dogs walking and running in the fair. The fair looks quite big. It was probably on a market place. The flags are not waving about so probably it was not windy. There are two figures on a sort of tower. Underneath the tower there are two men pushing a wheel round and round. It looks like it is nearly the end of the fair because there are not a lot of people. The people look like they are having a good time on the rides.

The weakness of this piece lies in its lack of an overall structure. It begins with five observations about the big wheels, but like the eye the writer's viewpoint roams at random over the whole picture, returning in the end to the people on the rides. To construct order other than random impression calls for design in the planning stage. Pictures sometimes fit a four-part scheme of zooming in – background, middleground, foreground, close-up – or out, if the order is reversed. From the example here, though, a more obvious pattern would have been to cluster the observations: (1) setting – market place, tower, flags, big fair; (2) crowd scene – lady selling, man with sword, dogs; (3) rides – big wheel, swings, other wheel; (4) atmosphere – good time, end of fair.

Before taking on the assignment a good model to have looked at for this age range would have been Ruth Craft's *The Fair* which describes a painting by Breughel, section by section within a narrative structure. Importantly the writer there wrote as if she was inside the scene, not as a person looking from the outside at a picture, as the child above has done.

In the piece which follows James in year 5 has tried to capture the atmosphere of a modern fair through sense impressions. The structure is chronological, a walk being linear in both time and space. However, the random nature of the experience which he meets adds to the power of the sense impressions which make him dizzy – one of those sense impressions outside the usual range; he walks 'deliriously through a dream':

> The gavioli plays away to itself as crowds bustle along through the fairground. 'Did you win?' 'No' can be heard. There seems to be very warm air lingering about. Lights are shining, all different colours. I seem to walk deliriously through a dream. The candy floss stall and other things hum away like drones. Shrieks go up as the waltzer comes into sight. Aaagh! Shriekk! 'Mum can we go on the waltzer?' 'Yes, I suppose so.' All aboard and off we go on the waltzer, screaming with laughter and joy. Everything goes blurred as we go speeding off on our journey to nowhere. Lights go on and off, go dim and bright and joy reflects out of our eyes as we scream again. The only thing we see are the lights flashing on and off. Now we slow down, but are at top speed going round soon. Once again we slow down and stop. We get off dizzily and go to see other wonders of the fair.

Contrast the emotional power of James's writing with the cool objectivity of Michael, writing a different assignment in the same class project:

> On the ghost train you go along a tunnel-like building which is very dark except for individual lights which light up things like skeletons coming out of coffins. When the carriages start going you are plunged into darkness and there are things like ghosts and skeletons. Sometimes the carriages turn sharply away from the wall or a monster's mouth when you think that you are going to crash into it. At the end the train goes out of the tunnel through two big doors.

Again the structure is a linear chronology and an accurate description of features of the ghost train. The difference is that we do not have any of the subjective responses of the writer. He is not a participant in the scene and therefore does not describe his sense impressions, nor does he project into those of a third party. If we are to judge the two pieces of writing as successful within the field of Description, we cannot judge them by the same criteria.

Movement

Description is not, of course, confined to the scenic, as though the writer were a passenger on a train looking out through the carriage window or strolling through a fine city. In the passage which follows, a speed skier describes the sense impression of skiing at almost 130 miles per hour. Here the writer by direct address makes the reader 'you' into an actor not a spectator. The writing is highly coloured with personal emotions and sense impressions as the language tries to evoke the action, coupled with comparisons with other experiences which the reader might have had which will make the alien experience more real.

> You concentrate on what is happening. You pole off from the start, one good push. Skate. Flick the tip of your ski like the tip of a condor wing. Drop onto your knees with your instantly streamlined body, piercing the air like the missile you are, driving yourself, taut and relaxed.
>
> Vibrations begin in the tip of the ski. At first it's a subtle shimmy. Then it encompasses both skis and body. The vibration crescendo is reached at about 110 mph. Then begins the quiet side of speed skiing, with the roar of the wind just behind. Smooth. Deadly if the mind slips. The steepest part comes at 128 mph. The test, the flat that has been rushing up like a huge white mass.
>
> Wham! White-black eye roll – involuntary gut-throat grunt. Thighs meet calves. Sometimes bum meets snow and gets toasted. Stand up at 100 mph into a banking turn with heavy lean. Apply brakes. Time-space warp. Back to the top, quick. Do it again, maybe better, maybe faster.
>
> (Steve McKinney; from an article by John Samuel.
> © Guardian News Service Ltd. 1990)

Contrasting this passage with those analysed earlier suggests the range of writing styles to be found under 'description' as both a field in its own right and as a component of other forms. The Norwich guide describes a relatively static and leisurely cultural experience, to be savoured by the participant as a spectator; so the reader is a spectator of its long sentences, against the background of which the occasional low-key emotive phrases stand out effectively. Its structure is open-ended, for just as the tour could be extended, so could the text. The Colorado guide is more highly charged, a feast of the senses, the writer's psychology being to bring out the hedonist in the reader, whether the reader's pleasure be active or passive. Its structure is complete once each of the senses has been illustrated. In the skiing passage, though, the writer is describing something which is dynamic and dangerous, where events pass in a blur of speed; the writing is impressionistic, reduced to the most suggestive phrase, the key impressions for each stage of the descent, rejecting completed sentences in favour of a breathless series of images. Its structure is chronological; the writing ends once the action is complete.

Developing Skills

(1) The context in which children write should fully engage their emotional involvement. Even when they are dealing with less emotionally charged fields such as Argument, unless they have a full involvement with the subject their writing will be hollow, not just emotionally detached but insincere. Purpose is the driving force of writing.

(2) Increase children's sensory awareness through real experiences within the curriculum. William Blake described the poet's purpose as to 'cleanse the gates of perception' of the reader. Development of their descriptive skills is as much to do with developing their powers of perception as with developing their powers of expression.

(3) Because of the factual basis of many persuasive forms, writing involves using research skills: consulting reference books, interviewing people, sifting through information for the appropriate material. Projects should be timed and structured so that this is possible.

(4) Use as models real texts which are rich in persuasive features. A portfolio of examples, kept, for instance, in a clip file in plastic folders, allows children to examine and make comparisons between the range of options which real writers choose from to effect a persuasive purpose.

(5) Link new concrete experience with linguistic experience so as to broaden and fine-tune children's perception and discrimination. Train them to use a thesaurus.

(6) Make sure children consider their ideas in full, through talk, reading and experience then work them out in an appropriate plan before drafting.

(7) Emphasise the importance of reader psychology at the planning stage, when projection into the mind, interests and abilities of a target audience will have an effect on the writing to come.

(8) Encourage the writing of a brief sample of a text so that it can be tried out for its effect on a partner before a full draft is written (see Samples in Chapter 9).

Promoting Critical Reading/Writing

(1) Compare several examples of the same kind of persuasive text and note as many differences as possible. The contrast will highlight the angle or 'selling pitch' of the different writers.

(2) Underline the facts behind the claims of a persuasive text so as to identify what is not fact, and the emotional coloration of the language.

(3) Set out the main points of an argument or an assertion in tabular form; attempt to add to them and then to counter them with alternative points on the opposite side of the argument.

(4) Identify and underline the rhetorical devices of the writing – see Chapter 5 for information on such options as repetition, imagery, coloured language and so on.

(5) In discussion speculate about the deep intentions of the writer and encourage scepticism or more objectively a 'sense of enquiry' about the claims made.

(6) After children have written a persuasive text, have them follow up by writing another, perhaps in a different and shorter form, which takes the opposite point of view; perhaps changing texts with a friend and responding to the points which they make.

(7) Channel their natural sense of fun into writing parodies of persuasive texts, which exaggerate their characteristics while encouraging resistant reading and a 'sense of enquiry'.

8

EVOCATIVE WRITING

> The function of literature as art is to open us to dilemmas, to the hypothetical, to the range of possible worlds that texts can refer to.
>
> (Jerome Bruner, 1986)

Introduction

Narrative forms have traditionally been the substance of initial reading schemes, and thereafter of comprehension exercises to extend reading skills, but for teachers of English the study of literature is only partly related to the development of literacy. We have prized literature above all for the insight it offers into the human condition, into the thoughts and feelings of ourselves, others like us and not like us, for its celebration of the best of feeling expressed in the best of language. Do we need to justify that, living with the problems of the twentieth century: violence, crime, changing social order, family break-up? We hope that education will prepare children for life, but nowhere in the curriculum do we include the study of psychology – what makes people tick – or philosophy – the meaning of life, except through literature. Yet most of us who teach it will have met at some time people who assume that literature is synonymous with self-indulgence, with escape from the serious business of life.

The major fields of the Evocative – poetry, novel, drama – are no less 'real' than any other; if in doubt, analyse the content of a day's television programmes for stories and drama of all kinds, or the song lyrics of popular radio for non-stop poetry. The human species is obsessively interested in evocations of other lives. Nor are forms of the Evocative distinct and separate from 'real' writing since all forms can be interwoven. Take the clear example of Janet and Allan Ahlberg's *The Jolly Postman*, a rhyming narrative about a postman on his rounds which delightfully blends all kinds of writing, as the envelopes which he delivers are opened by the reader; formal and informal letters, junk mail, postcard, invitations. Through what is called 'intertextuality' the main text reminds us of other texts; the postman calls on a witch, recalling the story of Hansel and Gretel, but since he brings a catalogue of witch accessories we are reminded of all the junk mail we have encountered. In just such a way the current emphasis on 'authentic texts' can be taken as an extension of the traditional model rather than an opposing one, with real texts being inserted into the literary curriculum as if into envelopes. However, unlike the book, real forms like a quart into a pint pot will inevitably reduce the amount of literature that can be squeezed into the years of schooling. Over time there will be a shift in the ideological balance of the English curriculum which we will have to monitor closely.

In common across its range of influence the term Evocative proposes that the primary concern of the writer is to call into the mind of the reader an impression of the world, either in whole or in part. That world may be a fact or a fantasy, past, present or future; it may have a complex value system or none at all; it may be vastly detailed as in an epic novel or stereotyped as in an anecdote, or so suggested in a poem that readers complete the evocation for themselves. Through the medium of words on the page the writer attempts to engage all of our faculties, emotions and senses, so that we vicariously live the experience described, linking that experience in some way with our own. The effectiveness of that engagement is the criterion for assessing success, for evaluating the progress of the young writer and for deciding how to further development. Because the effectiveness of engagement depends so greatly upon the personal response of the reader as unique individual, the measurement of success is notoriously subjective and hence problematic.

Defining the Reader

Writers of Evocative forms are notoriously unclear about whom they are writing for, in marked contrast to writing for other purposes. The readership of a newspaper is seen by its writers as being in a hurry, straining to catch only the most significant information from a throwaway medium; the advertising copywriter tries to catch the attention of specific target groups by appealing to their particular hopes and fears. The reader of the Evocative is less well defined, but is assumed to have leisure, wishing to savour a text which deserves a careful reading and then a re-reading. This means that cliché is rejected for such shortcuts to meaning are unnecessary, even undesirable; both the meaning and its expression can be complex, intense, extensive and original. In all forms of writing the writer sets out to convey a specific meaning to the reader, but with complex evocative text the reader's personal experience and associations of language are likely to create alternative readings from that intended by the writer. Whereas in the Informative range the spaces between words can lead to unhelpful misunderstanding between writer and reader, in the Evocative such spaces allow the reader to give to the text as well as take from it, as a personal interpretation of the text is created in the mind.

The reader is envisaged as being involved, even completely immersed, in the created world of the writer, from beginning to end. Evocative writing then has a totality of shape. Above all, the text is considered to be an art form, having an aesthetic meaning in addition to the meaning of its subject. Poetry originated as an oral/aural medium and it is still helpful for the writer to think of the effects of sound and image on a listener. Likewise a script-writer must imagine how actors will express the written word when it is brought to life on stage, in speech and action. All forms of the Evocative are, however, considered here as written in the first instance. As such they are written to last. Although an advertisement may use poetic techniques to achieve a persuasive purpose, no one keeps adverts on a shelf to take down to re-read for enjoyment except perhaps the copywriter; few people will read a computer manual from cover to cover, but the reader of Evocative forms appreciates the significance of both the medium and the message, which throws a heavy burden of responsibility onto the crafting process.

POETRY

Of all the forms of writing described in this book, poetry is one which is seen as among the most problematic. I regularly meet teachers who do not read it to children or do not ask them to write it or both. In spite of its pre-eminence as a vehicle for creativity and freedom of personal expression, its density of form and meaning make it for many as unattainable as the enchanted Princess asleep in a castle surrounded by a forest of thorns. Ted Hughes (1969, p. 119) summed up the dilemma: 'the actual substance of (our experience of life), the material facts of it, embed themselves in us quite a long way from the world of words.'

The young Yorkshire poet Simon Armitage, interviewed in 1992 about his poetry collection *Kid*, commented, 'It's hard graft. For me a couplet is like swimming the Channel, it's difficult, and even the free-flowing pieces in the book have been worked on and redrafted and planed down.'

Yet by the same token of linguistic challenge poetry should remain a major field in writing development. Like the forest of thorns the problem is not as insurmountable as it might seem on first meeting, and we have three talismen to help us break the evil spell. Firstly poetry has been demythologised, its definition widened beyond the narrow traditional canon to include songs, greetings cards, advertising, newspaper headlines – forms of language which to a greater or lesser extent use the structures, cadences and sound effects of poetry. Examples are not hard to find because the techniques of poetry are so powerful and all-pervasive.

Secondly, in spite of spending cuts there are many attractive poetry anthologies now available and more coming out all the time, including poetry from across the world (see, for instance, Dhondy, 1990). They offer a wide range of alternative models and subjects for children's writing.

Thirdly there is now a very large body of writing on the subject of teaching poetry, containing highly practical ideas for the classroom. For primary see, for instance, Brownjohn (1980 and 1982), Corbett and Moses (1986), Pirrie (1987) and for secondary Benton (1990), and if I might be permitted an immodest plug, Hayhoe and Parker (1988). A tool like a rhyming dictionary (see, for instance, Fergusson 1985) now in a children's version will greatly help in the composing process.

Generating Material

It is not possible here to do other than indicate some of the main considerations in choosing material for poetry writing. As with all writing it is essential that the writer knows the subject before beginning to craft. It may be best to delay mentioning the word 'poetry' until the subject matter has been established, because as soon as they hear the word poetry many children begin to draft in rhyme, and where rhyme is in the driving seat meaning often goes out of the window. It may be more helpful to think of poetry as a crafting process rather than a set of specific forms – the word poet in its Greek origin meant 'a shaper'.

Poetry is most powerful when the writer has got inside the experience; as William Blake put it:

> To see a world in a grain of sand,
> And a heaven in a wild flower,
> Hold infinity in the palm of your hand,
> And eternity in an hour.

The first skill of the writing process is that of perception; perception both in the mind's eye, recalling past experience or imagining other worlds, and in seeing the world around through all the senses. In this way poetry is related to science for both poet and scientist look with wonder at the world through a microscope. Poetry is not isolated in the curriculum and not limited to exploring/expressing particular types of experience. It is as much the concern to describe a steaming rubbish dump as a host of golden daffodils, to celebrate vigorous action or quiet contemplation, to explore concrete events or abstract feelings.

Pastiche

Many ideas for poetry will come from published poetry and other writing which children can replicate exactly or use as a stimulus, depending on their confidence, skill and creativity. Children should be able to browse through poetry books, should hear poetry read often and be allowed to imitate, adapt, respond to that experience. They will find it helpful to imitate the simpler patterns of poetry which they read and like. Emma in a year 9 top band read a 'list poem' which begins 'Brown is . . .' and like a string of pearls links a chain of images in the repeated formula of rhyming couplets. Her pastiche begins:

FEAR IS . . .

> All alone by yourself
> A misty road, a dusty shelf
> Twisted sheets, a sweated brow
> The wind that makes a piercing row
> A loneliness that stirs at night
> And shifts away at sign of light.
> (continued)

Such a structure is enabling because it allows the writer to draw very widely upon personal experience.

Children will want to write about their own interests about which they have both a lot of interest and a lot of knowledge. Ralph in year 7 was a keen ornithologist, and his exact knowledge helped him to project into the life of an owl:

LIFE AS AN OWL

The silence of the quiet dusk
Is broken as I screech across the open moors,
My eyes sparkle as the sun rises above the horizon.
I sweep down onto a fear-stricken mouse
To enjoy a tasty meal.
(continued)

Poetry, like all Evocative fields, encourages empathy, an extremely valuable characteristic which can be harnessed to develop in children an appreciation of others' points of view and a balanced scale of values.

Finding a Shape

Poetry offers many alternative patterns, some with an ancient tradition, some more modern; and since originality is particularly prized, the poet is always free to create new forms. All poetry is pattern-conscious, and has in common that its pattern can be seen as a shape on the page, quite unlike prose. As a generalisation, prose is written as a continuous block flowing from margin to margin and from top left to bottom right of the page, but poetry is written line by line, not from margin to margin, which emphasises its density of meaning. In a figurative sense the process of reading poetry is interrupted not flowing.

The aim of the crafting process is to create of the finished text a sense of completeness in a shape which will often be harmonious certainly to the ear but often to the eye, whether that shape comes from free verse or the tight structure of the sonnet. Among the many available patterns there is only time here to consider a selection which are representative of what can be done in the classroom in the following forms: free verse, visual pattern, syllabic pattern, sound pattern.

Free Verse

Although the skill of the poet's craft is in making the meaning fit the form, the form must serve the meaning and not stifle it. For that reason above all free verse is attractive, in setting up fewest preconditions for patterning. The freedom of free verse lies above all in its freedom from a set rhyme scheme, though it also lies in being able to make occasional use for special effect of many of the crafting devices described in Chapter 5. For instance although the meaning of free verse is not poured into the mould of a rhyme scheme, rhyme may be used for occasional ear-catching effect in, say, the closing two lines –

as Shakespeare used it to signal the end of an act to the audience in his otherwise unrhymed plays. Similarly occasional use can be made of the sound effects of rhythm, alliteration and assonance; of the visual effects of simile and metaphor; of the structural pattern of regular line length through use of the same number of syllables per line.

One distinctive patterning device of free verse is its use of flexible line length to emphasise meaning. This tends to be contrastive, so that after a series of long lines will come a line containing a single word – 'Fire!' – and the placing of the single word on the line emphasises it both in reading aloud and reading silently. It will help children beginning to write such poetry to understand that they can set out their ideas 'one thought per line' as they begin drafting; it is only then a short step to setting out the meaning line by line for maximum impact on the reader/listener.

Hannah in year 3 shows in two poems that she has understood how a dramatic effect can be achieved by such placing of words on the line:

> Out in the sun run run
> Go out of the sun and run run
> Back in the sun stop stop
> and sit down.

> Plod in and out of puddles
> Using your wellie boots
> Diddle and daddle
> Lazily about
> Early in the morning.

There is a close link with narrative structure in her poem as each line takes us on to a new element in the action, but it is not a story. She is letting us appreciate with her delightful moments of the life of an eight-year-old. Kevin six years older in year 9 is capable of exploring one image over several lines without the need for chronological structure, increasing the density of meaning through personification, as he imagines his stereo system to be a life-form:

STEREO

> Stereo shouting loudly,
> Trembling with vibration.
> Electricity flows through its veins,
> Revolving in continuous circles,
> Energetically working at its
> Occupation.

He has shaped each pair of lines to be of a similar length, and perhaps there is a deliberate rhyme in 'vibration/occupation'.

Snapshots

Hannah's poems above are single 'snapshots' of a life, and so they are very short. Free verse can be given an extended structure through a series of such snapshots, a technique which promotes visual imagery. A year 6 class had been doing a project on the Victorians for some time and finally they wrote poems on village life, imagining that they played a part in the working life of the community. The teacher's plan was to focus their imagination through four images as prompts around which they would shape the poem: (1) your place of work; (2) yourself in context; (3) tools of the trade; (4) a snatch of conversation.

Children chose for themselves what they would like to have been in those times. Then as they listened, pencils in hand, the teacher quietly talked to them about each of the four images while they wrote down their ideas as quickly as they could, without talking so that their response was completely individual. The first prompt was on the theme 'What does your place of work look like?' The Milkmaid (Emily) wrote the phrases 'Cows mooing, hooves clicking and clacking on the cobbled surface.' The second prompt was along the lines of 'What does it feel like as you arrive for work in the morning or as you leave at night?' The Blacksmith (Angela) wrote: 'My hair is sweaty and greasy, my eyes are smarting with dust, my nose is red and hot, my mouth is as dry as a bone, my ears are pounding.' The third prompt was 'See yourself at work; what tools do you use, what skills do you need. Where do you keep your tools?' The Fishmonger (Lee) wrote: 'He guts them, he cuts them, he fillets them and cleans them. He weighs them on a scale.' The final snapshot was to be a snatch of conversation – to bring drama into the scene and to prompt them to the insight that work involves interaction between people. The Architect's (Emma's) rough notes were crafted into:

> The whispered hum of genteel conversation.
> Work given
> Work accepted,
> A handshake,
> A promise,
> A contract sealed.
> Heads are bowed to bid farewell.

The prompts suggest an area in which ideas might be found, not the ideas themselves. Each poem in the class was totally different, and it is extremely important to stress that, for it is very difficult indeed to restrict children's individual response. The crafting process ensures that, after the basic ideas have been generated and the idea of snap-

shots absorbed, children are free to make the evocation their own.
Take for instance Susan's poem:

A BAKER'S POEM

Red hot flames sparkle as the sun shines through.
Heat warms the dough as the steam rises
Off the top of the smooth crisp surface.
The bread slides into the paper bag.
'Fresh bread!' I call, 'Fresh bread!'
The door opens.
One shilling slides across the counter.
I give back tuppence and set back to work with my wooden cutters.
The flour spreads on to my apron.
The smell of bread ready to eat,
So tempting . . .
drifts through the room,
As the sunlight streams through the window.

She has obviously had personal experience of the smell of fresh bread
(there is a baker's shop in the village) and that is a theme running
through the poem. The unfinished line 'So tempting . . .' cleverly
makes a gap for the reader's own taste buds to fill. She has not
followed the order of the prompts nor has she included a conversation, though the 'street call' dramatises the scene. She has also noticed
that sunlight bleaches the colour of a fire, which today's children
probably have less experience of; it has so struck her that she uses the
image to shape the beginning and end of the poem.

Displayed on the wall the whole set of poems created an album of
word pictures evoking a village community of a hundred years ago.

Acrostic

The acrostic is a very approachable development of the one-thought-
per-line format. The technique is very simple; the initial letters of a
word are set out down the page, one letter per line, and these letters
begin the first word of the line. It can be the name of a place, person,
object, action or abstract quality. For example, if 'green' were chosen:

Great trees on
River banks
Enchant the
Evening as
Night descends.

The writer here has also chosen to even out the line length to three
syllables, an optional additional pattern.

It is possible to create an amusing effect, as with 'Ant':

> A small creature
> No don't stand there!
> Too late.

Visual Patterns

As with free verse the main attraction of visual patterns is that once the ideas are in place the words can be crafted for as long as the writer chooses; since there is no predetermined pattern the ideas would be acceptable with no shaping of sound or image or they can be crafted to a high degree if the writer chooses.

Concrete Poetry

This form was probably so named because the words are arranged on the page in a physical shape which represents the concrete object described by the words. It is closely related to a picture and the visual gives it an immediacy of impact and a strong appeal to young children for whom it is an excellent starting point in writing poetry. Examples are to be found in many anthologies, but Wes Magee (1989) has made a collection which will provide many useful models.

There are two possible approaches. The first is to draw an outline shape of the object, say a pig, and to fill it with descriptive words and phrases. For instance Clive in year 3 wrote about a pig inside a cut-out pig shape:

> A pig is round and fat and short. It has four very short legs. The pig is dirty and makes a lot of noise. It grunts and it snorts all day long. And rolls about in the mud. He makes a lot of mess although he does not mind. A pig smells a lot but he is very very kind.

Written out as it is here without the shape emphasises that his text is essentially prosaic; however, key phrases were keyed into the shape: 'all day long' was written along the curly tail, and the four legs contained the ending 'but he' 'is very' 'very' 'kind'. The crafting process of the poem began with the writer forming a mental picture of the subject, then selecting telling detail about it and then crafting, albeit slightly, that detail into the poem's shape.

The second approach is to make the outline out of the words rather than as a cut-out; for instance the word 'firework' placed pointing up the page, and out of it fountaining words like 'sparkle, golden rain, lightning flash'. The poem can then be decorated with colours and makes an attractive display.

Syllabic Pattern

Line length as the determining pattern is more demanding than free form but the Haiku has become very popular in schools because it is a very brief and condensed form which makes the material to be crafted more manageable in scale. The pattern of the traditional Japanese haiku is: line 1 = 5 syllables; line 2 = 7 syllables; line 3 = 5 syllables. It is intended as a contrast of two word-pictures, usually of a natural scene, each of the first two lines containing a distinct image, the third line deepening their significance.

John in a year 8 bottom band wrote a page of haiku about his family as 'snapshots' for a photograph album, including the following:

DAD:

Medium height, bald
Big nose, black hair going white
Drives a big lorry

In Japanese courtly circles a Haiku would be given as a gift to an esteemed friend. In response the friend might write two additional lines of seven syllables each to present back to the originator. Incorporating the Haiku the whole now makes a new form called a Tanka. An artistic way to promote collaborative writing!

Diamante

The diamante is a syllabic form which makes a diamond pattern on the page. It can be on any subject, best suiting two opposing concepts: love/hate, cat/dog, war/peace. Concept 1 takes the first three and a half lines, and concept 2 the second three and a half.

```
                concept 1
            adjective   adjective
              -ing  -ing  -ing
synonym   synonym : synonym   synonym
              -ing  -ing  -ing
            adjective   adjective
                concept 2
```

The power of the form comes from the sharp contrasts it makes and the quickening of the second half as it counts down to the revelation of the contrasting concept. The structure is quite tight but children find it relatively easy to fill in the slots once they have understood the basic idea. Michelle in a top band year 9 wrote:

LOVE
hearts   flowers
smiling   laughing   watching
courtship   marriage : divorce   separation
crying   sighing   moving
tears   poison
HATE

Sound Patterns

Sound patterns which can be used to structure a poem traditionally include rhyme, rhythm and alliteration. Other sound devices which are not used to structure poetry are assonance, where the pattern is found in the internal letters of words, and onomatopoeia, where the sound of the word (bang, crash, rustle) captures the sound of the thing described.

Rhythm as a structure is perhaps best known through 'blank verse', Shakespeare's favoured form, which is a ten-syllable line (a pentameter) where every second syllable is stressed (iambic stress) as in 'If music be the food of love, play on'. In performance the stress of natural speech is given preference over the rigid off/on stress pattern of the iamb; in general stress patterns are problematic in English. The classic patterns of Latin poetry reflected a language which generated many polysyllabic words; the stress patterns of spondee, trochee, iamb and dactyl describing the stress patterns of normal Latin speech. Such systems do not fit the relatively monosyllabic English language so comfortably. It may be that we will become more aware of rhythm as a pattern through West Indian poetry which is now developing very fast and is highly rhythmic, though the rhythm patterns are often added by the poet as performer rather than being obvious from the written word.

Alliteration, where the initial sound of a word in the first half of a line matches the initial sound of a word in the second half, was the pattern used in Anglo-Saxon verse. It is much less demanding than rhyme since only the initial letter of words has the same sound rather than the whole word or final syllable of rhyme. A year 7 class had been doing a project on animals which included looking at a mediaeval Bestiary. Paul used alliteration as the structure for this collection of animal images:

> Hawks hover over cliffs so high to hunt their prey.
> Leopards lie waiting in forest land to catch their food.
> Lizards lubbing over deserts hot lie in the sun.
> (continued)

The best known pattern of all, however, is rhyme, though there is usually an added challenge in that much rhyming poetry also has a syllabic pattern in the form of a regular line length so that the language is doubly shaped. Because rhyme and rhythm are so widely used to structure nursery rhymes, children often take the word 'poetry' to mean that heavy patterning, even though it is very difficult for them to replicate. Making sound links within a rhythmic pattern can severely limit the meaning; the more limited the vocabulary the fewer options the writer has for matching intended meaning with required sound. Two things will help in particular; firstly a rhyming dictionary. Secondly using an important skill of crafting, namely juggling the words in the line like pieces in a puzzle so that a less critical word moves into the rhyming slot. Where two or more words are options for the rhyming slot the chances of both meaning and rhyme being satisfied are greatly increased.

Couplets

Hilaire Belloc's *Cautionary Tales* have a clear rhyme scheme, simple vocabulary and humorous plot which make them appealing models for children. For instance 'Jim, who ran away from his nurse and was eaten by a lion':

> There was a boy whose name was Jim.
> His friends were very good to him.
> They gave him Tea and Cakes and Jam
> And slices of delicious Ham.
> (continued)

Amy and Claire in a top band year 8 class collaborated to write a scatological version of this couplet pattern:

> There was a revolting girl called Claire
> Who picked her nose but did not care.
> Others told her she should not
> And she moaned 'I like it a lot.'
>
> Her mother told her that one day
> Her finger would get stuck and stay.
> 'I wish you'd listen to me Claire.'
> But she replied, 'I do not care!'
>
> Then one day it finally came true
> While she was sitting on the 'loo
> She inserted her finger up her nose
> While singing loudly 'Up it goes!'

She tried to pull her finger out,
She found it stuck and she did shout
'Help my finger is stuck up my nose
All my mother's warning now shows.'

So with this poem please take heed.
Do not go eating chicken feed.
So listen to your mother's voice.
Remember that you have a choice.

Limerick

The limerick is well-known largely because it is an excellent container for rudeness, enhanced by its strong rhythm and fixed rhyme scheme, especially its final rhyme which acts as a punch-line. Although it is demanding, children like puzzles, riddles and word games, and some forms of poetry link readily to such interest. Additionally children like having fun with language and love the limerick's humorous effect. Sajad in year 7 wrote:

There was a young boy called Paul
who was the laziest boy of them all.
He woke in the night
In a terrible fright
Having done fifty sums on the wall.
(All wrong an' all!)

Sajad has not only understood the rhythm and rhyme patterns of the form, he has wittily added an irregular line after what should be the last one for an extra humorous effect.

Performance

A poem is intended to be an art form, the crafting of meaning in words creating an aesthetic effect. Children's poetry is usually brief, which is all the more reason why it should be a target for teaching careful crafting and the most attractive presentation. In responding it is more encouraging for the teacher to look for flashes of insight and occasional effective uses of crafting techniques, rather than for completeness of form. Children may rarely produce a poem where there is total harmony of form and meaning but much more often surprise with the depth and originality of parts of their writing.

As with all forms, writing for a real audience will increase the incentive to craft, and possibilities include poem posters, greetings card, personal and class anthologies, school magazine. Poetry can also be integrated with art of all kinds to make an exciting display, promoting appreciation of language in its public readership. Poetry was originally intended for oral performance and it will help children in drafting if they say key phrases out loud, allowing the ear to be the judge of the best effect. Poetry can be performed in its own right as a celebration of the spoken word or integrated with music, for class, school or wider audiences informally or in 'eisteddfods' and school assemblies.

STORY

Although only a single item in the overall map of writing as I have described it, story is a major field in itself, both in school and in the world outside. Beyond schooling we do not lay great claims for ours as a society of compulsive readers, but there are signs that fiction reading still continues in spite of television. Blockbuster novels attract huge sales; public libraries still retain a large section for fiction; literary prizes, such as the Booker, command media attention; book club offers arrive with the junk mail. Ted Hughes (1969, p. 87) illustrated the influence of story on our thinking processes:

> When you cross a road you hesitate and make sure everything is clear. You do this because a little story has run along in your head and shown you a car coming, screeching its brakes, swerving to miss you, bouncing off the far wall, probably turning over three times and bursting its doors and spilling out people, collie dogs, etc. . . . quite a hectic little tale, and it goes through your head in a flash so quickly and lightly that you are hardly aware of it.

Story is of course much more familiar in the oral mode; jokes and anecdotes make up a large part of social exchange in playground and home. Adults relate incidents in their lives in a way which partly reflects literary conventions. There will be some kind of scene setting, with 'telling' detail; there will be quotations of what people taking part said; there will be a build up of tension. Above all there will be a structure which holds it all together, the logic of the chronologic linking a sequence of events. This pattern is common to almost all stories, from fairy tale to adult novel. It probably explains why the form is so attractive to us for it allows us to develop extended communication with others, and to structure the events of our lives in a way which has shape and significance. For this reason Barbara Hardy (1977) suggested that narrative is a 'primary act of mind'.

Hannah in year 3 shows the effect of the oral anecdote in the conversational tone of her story; the context is imagined, being outside her own experience:

BALLOON

I must be mad. I'm in the middle of a field taking off in a hot air balloon. I feel dizzy up here. 'Quick the steering has gone. We're going to crash in a forest.' Blood is flying everywhere. Me and Helen are still alive but Russell might be dead. Helen said, 'We'll have to carry him back to hospital.' 'Yuk!' 'Well we're at the hospital. What shall we do now?' 'Go in,' said Helen. 'Oh no, how is he?' 'Dead,' said the Doctor.

Helen and Russell are two best friends of the writer, whose intention here is to vicariously control their actions. The writing has the basic ingredients of a story; it has a main character who is the narrator, subordinate characters whose fortunes are interlinked, two settings (balloon and hospital), characters who interact in dialogue, and a sad ending. On the other hand it is unlike a written story in that the writer is a recordist of events as they happen, which is closer to the role of the journalist, particularly radio-journalist. Although there are two settings, they are signposted rather than described. There is no intrinsic motivation for the action; the characters have been transported from their usual setting and are acted upon by events. Most out of place though is the emotional tone, or lack of it, and a lack of real empathy into the events described; the two girls are well enough to carry the boy to hospital, but there is no insight into the difficulties this might cause, and the 'Well, we're at the hospital' is typical of children's drama where the imagined scene is explicitly stated to the audience. It is, though, pointless to criticise by such adult literary standards; at this age 'children's story' is a form of its own, more significant as a means of reflecting and shaping the child's developing picture of the world than her concept of literary forms.

Another story by Hannah whilst still in year 3 shows that she is recognising story beyond the intuitive level as a crafted form:

Once there was a leaf. It was a very grumpy leaf. It was a very windy day and the leaf was holding on to the tree with all his strength and then oh no not again said the leaf as he got swirled around and up side down. He flew over the city and towns and all the time he was grumbly saying I wish I was never a leaf always flying round. He landed on a pond. I hate water said the leaf and I think he's still there.

The tag 'once' both indicates that the writing belongs to the genre of story and establishes a time-frame which is completed by the ending 'still there'. The words story and history are related, and this is the life history of a leaf. Although a leaf is an inanimate object, personification is quite usual in the stories young children read and write. The leaf is given a 'character' ('a very grumpy leaf') which is reinforced in the action so that the characterisation becomes the main focus of the story. The plot is a chain of episodic events with a resolution, leaving the leaf finally a fixed position.

Six years older, Gemma in a year 9 middle band is able to consciously use the conventions of the romantic short story, probably from out-of-school magazine reading. She sets up a stereotypical context but distances it with a clever twist which shows that she is using it as a literary device to craft an effect on the reader:

REBECCA . . . AND ROBERT

The music played softly behind us, the lights dimmed to romantic levels. The dance floor was empty except for us. His strong arms wrapped around my waist. I let my head rest on his shoulder. He smelt of expensive cologne and denim.

He slipped his hand under my chin and tilted my face towards his. Slowly his moved closer, I could feel his breath softly on my cheek, his lips touched mine . . .

'REBECCA LEWIS, HAVE YOU BEEN LISTENING TO A WORD OF WHAT I'VE SAID?' boomed the familiar voice of Mrs Trinkett. (continued)

Both she and Hannah are probably helped by the first-person viewpoint to get inside the imagined, fictional experience, to see it and feel it. By contrast Wayne in the same year 9 class uses a third-person viewpoint and the result is a factual account rather than an evocation:

There was a boy called Neil who was killed in Norwich about five years ago in a wood near the city. He was killed by two men who were never caught. Then last year some people decided to build a plot of houses in this wood and over the next year some strange things started to happen, like a works car moving from one side of the building site to the other. Holes the size of buses appeared where a house was being made. Then one day the homes were finished and the families started moving in one by one. (continued)

Although written down, in form this resembles an oral anecdote, just the bare bones of a story; in literary terms we would call it a synopsis. Although it was handed in as complete, it is really still at the level of a plan, albeit a promising one, for either a gripping short story or a 'novel' in chapters. What the writer needs to do with this version is to develop the characters by asking questions of his imagination; who was Neil and what was he like when alive? Who were the two murderers and what motivated them? How did the workmen on the site react to the strange events? What did one of the families moving in expect and find? He needs to select specific events from the synopsis to build up like scenes in a play, dramatising the action with direct speech.

To help such children with their writing we need to show them the techniques of authors who craft carefully to produce a specific effect on the reader. Take for example the suspense which Robert Louis Stevenson creates in this extract from Chapter 3 of *Treasure Island*, seen through the eyes of the young central figure, Jim Hawkins:

So things passed until, the day after the funeral, and about three o'clock of a bitter, foggy, frosty afternoon, I was standing at the door for a moment, full of sad thoughts about my father, when I saw someone drawing slowly near along the road. He was plainly blind, for he tapped before him with a stick, and wore a huge old tattered sea-cloak with a hood, that made him appear positively deformed. I never saw in my life a more dreadful looking figure. He stopped a little from the inn, and, raising his voice in an odd sing-song, addressed the air in front of him:-

'Will any kind friend inform a poor blind man, who has lost the precious sight of his eyes in the gracious defence of his native country, England, and God bless King George! – where or in what part of this country he may now be?'

'You are at the "Admiral Benbow", Black Hill Cove, my good man,' said I.

'I hear a voice,' said he – 'a young voice. Will you give me your hand, my kind, young friend, and lead me in?'

I held out my hand, and the horrible, soft-spoken, eyeless creature gripped it in a moment like a vice. I was so much startled that I struggled to withdraw; but the blind man pulled me close up to him with a single action of his arm.

'Now, boy,' he said, 'take me in to the captain.'

'Sir,' said I, 'upon my word I dare not.'

'Oh,' he sneered, 'that's it! Take me in straight or I'll break your arm.'

And he gave it, as he spoke, a wrench that made me cry out.

'Sir,' said I, 'it is for yourself I mean. The captain is not what he used to be. He sits with a drawn cutlass. Another gentleman' –

'Come, now, march,' interrupted he; and I never heard a voice so cruel, and cold, and ugly as that blind man's. It cowed me more than the pain; and I began to obey him at once, walking straight in at the door and towards the parlour, where our sick old buccaneer was sitting, dazed with rum. The blind man clung close to me, holding me in one iron fist, and leaning almost more of his weight on me than I could carry. 'Lead me straight up to him, and when

I'm in view, cry out, "Here's a friend for you, Bill." If you don't, I'll do this;' and with that he gave me a twitch that I thought would have made me faint. Between this and that, I was so utterly terrified of the blind beggar that I forgot my terror of the captain, and as I opened the parlour door, cried out the words he had ordered in a trembling voice.

The poor captain raised his eyes, and at one look the rum went out of him, and left him staring sober.

The passage is particularly acute in sensory perceptions. Much of its effect is created by building up one set of descriptions which are then sharply contrasted with their opposites. The passage begins with a visual description of the scene which matches the mood of narrator. This 'pathetic fallacy' arouses the reader's tender feelings towards the boy, and so by contrast increases the impact of the harsh treatment he then receives from the unknown blind-man, later revealed to be called Pew. Pew walks towards the viewpoint of the narrator as if towards a camera lens, so that we see him in increasing detail from a long shot then to a medium close-up and then in close-up. This 'camera lens' technique is very useful for children not only because so much of their literary experience is based on film and TV, but also because it prompts them to see in the mind's eye, a very important skill for evocative writing.

The sensory description then shifts to sound, and it is illuminating to underline the sound effects which run through the passage: the tapping of the blind man's stick, his sing-song voice, the abrupt change of tone, the variety of tones of voice in the interactions which follow up to the 'trembling voice' of the terrified boy; the voice of Pew which begins as sing-song and soft-spoken, becomes sneering and ends as cold, cruel and ugly. There is drama not only in the sense of dramatic tension but also in that the action is projected by what people say; the author is placing more emphasis on 'showing' what is happening rather than on 'telling', i.e. recounting the events as past history. Children like Wayne more readily use telling because they interpret storytelling as the recounting of a synopsis of events. But showing is much more powerful as an evocation because it recreates the action before our eyes – and our ears, as we hear what people say as they say it.

Stevenson then focuses on feeling, particularly that of violent movement and physical pain, coming first of all with the sudden shock of Pew's grip when, seeing through the eyes of the narrator, the reader had expected frailty. Of all the many contrasts in the passage, it is the violence of physical movement and its significance which is predominant. Again the impact is emphasised by a chain of images, not shifting but this time accumulating: 'gripped like a vice', 'single action', 'wrench', 'iron fist', 'more of his weight', 'twitch'. Throughout all of this the reader's emotional response is led by that of the boy which begins full of sad thoughts, moves to feeling pity, followed by being startled, then cowed, faint and finally utterly terrified.

The passage ends with a two-line cameo which is a master-stroke of crafting because it re-enacts the movement of the whole passage as the emotional response of the captain is engaged; an unemotional first glance, the realisation of its significance and finally overwhelming terror.

Themes

When discussing with children what to write it is sometimes possible to suggest a theme as a starting point because a theme such as 'lost and found' can signal not only the topic but also where the story is going so suggesting the overall structure in a few words. For instance: Success through clever deception – Puss in Boots; Child ignored/misdirected – Hansel and Gretel.

Genres

An alternative approach is to start through a specific genre: crime, fantasy, horror, realism, romance, science fiction, western. For adult creative writers, the new idea, the fresh perspective is everything. They try constantly to extend the frontiers of art, and any hint of cliché is anathema. For children this need not be the case; almost everything they write is for the first time, and their constantly changing world and perspective means that cliché is almost a meaningless concept. After all in their choice of private reading many children like the formulaic, where character and plot follow predictable tracks; the literary prizes are not the ones which become popular reading. So it is helpful to show them the characteristics of different story genres, no matter how clichéd they seem to us with our adult experience. Where children have understood but do not want to be seriously involved they will exaggerate and parody; their creativity will come through as inspiration directs.

Protherough (in Hayhoe and Parker, 1990) found that a class of 11-year-olds could identify in discussion the typical features or 'markers' of the genre of fairy story:

(1) Formulaic – 'once upon a time', 'lived happily ever after'
(2) Linguistic – archaic registers like 'sought her hand in marriage'

(3) Situational – marriage-choice, tests and quests, riddle solving
(4) Locational – palaces, hovels, forests, far-off lands
(5) Conventional – character (kings and queens, old beggars, wicked witches, beautiful princesses)
(6) Animals – horses, dragons and other monsters, frogs, birds
(7) Objects – jewels, mirrors, spinning wheels, caskets, swords

As an example for older children, consider the stereotypical characteristics of the western:

Western

(1) Characters: good guy and buddy, bad guy and gang; schoolma'am, saloon girl, rancher's daughter; travelling salesman (carpetbagger); charismatic outlaw, crooked sheriff.
(2) Settings: frontier town – main street with board-walk, saloon, bank, store, livery stable, barber's shop; mining camp in the mountains; ranch on the prairie; cavalry post; Indian camp.
(3) Plot lines: good versus evil – cattle rustling, bank robbery, stage hold-up, intimidation of smallholders, gold rush, claim jumping.
(4) Crises: the insult, the gunfight, horseback chase, stagecoach hold-up, train derailment.
(5) Alternative viewpoints: the little woman, the Indian, the innocent farmer, the tenderfoot, the old-timer, the horse, the dog.

Plot

The plot is the string which holds the story together and on which the pearls of action are threaded, but it too easily becomes a tyranny for children. They think of stories in terms of action because action is concrete and the most obvious thing to be seen from the outside. They also watch a lot of television stories which are almost totally a series of actions, since the camera sees the outside and it takes a skilful film-maker to go beyond that into human motivation and character interaction. So children's stories are often just a series of bare unembellished actions, rather like Jack the Giant Killer who strides off down the road each morning to meet the giant of the day, a plot structure called 'episodic'. A typical story of that kind might begin 'A man was walking down a street and he saw some bank robbers rushing out of a bank . . .' and it might continue with a car chase, the gang surrounded, the arrest, the jail sentence. The chronology of the plot is often what is called 'bed to bed' since getting up and going to bed are the time framework for the events of the story. Linear plot, though, in adult forms tends to have stages, and children will develop a greater appreciation of longer story forms once they have grasped the implication of these stages:

(1) *Exposition* – the reader's attention must be caught and held, and answers given to the who, what, when, where questions. The exposition must balance telling and showing, i.e. static description and action which brings characters to life, arousing curiosity as to what might happen to them.

(2) *Complication* – an event or change of fortune breaks into the scene set in the first stage and so starts the plot moving. This stage will take up a major part of the narrative, perhaps with more complications added so increasing the pressure on the characters.

(3) *Crisis* – a moment of difficulty or danger for the main characters, exciting the reader's intense interest.

(4) *Reflection* – a calm after the storm for retrospection, introspection, speculation. Often this is associated with food and feasting in children's books.

(5) *Climax* – as characters are put under pressure of events so the tension for the reader increases until a final moment of high drama.

(6) *Resolution* – the complicated events are resolved one way or the other; the reader feels great happiness if the resolution is satisfactory, and sad if it is not.

The stage of reflection is the one most neglected by young writers. We expect art to have meaning; that the story will concern more than a series of arbitrary occurrences to a set of unremarkable people. Unless there is reflection, story is in danger of remaining on the level of the jokes we tell each other: 'A man went into a pub and he bought two pints of bitter and he said to the barman . . .'. Reflection carries the meaning or significance of the story and it can be evoked either by the author, in the continuous commentary which is interwoven in storytelling, or by a narrator who is created within the story, or by any of the characters. It might take the shape of 'thoughts in the head', i.e. monologue, or dialogue with another character or as highlighting commentary by the author/narrator.

Time-Line

It is rare for the time-line to be unclear in a children's book, so a provocative example is the picture book *Granpa* by John Burningham who through pictures and brief text evokes the relationship between a girl and her grandfather as a series of separate images, ending with the suggestion through the symbol of an empty chair that the old man has died. As the pages turn the focus is not on the passing of time, because there is no narrative sequence; it is only in the final images and in retrospect that time proves to have been significant. Although the book will be classified and shelved in a library as suitable for young children, it is fascinating for all ages.

As children get older they will find alternatives to linear narrative in their reading and will enjoy experimenting with such sophistications as: (1) flashback (action in the past); (2) prefiguring (action in the future); (3) meanwhile (action in parallel time); (4) sub-plot (minor event in parallel time); (5) suspense (delayed revelation).

These are more than just embellishments, crafting for crafting's sake, since they are all intended to have an effect on the reader; exploring the complexity of more than one action at a time, or exploring irony, deepening the study of a character, increasing tension so heightening projection into a character's plight.

Plot Shapes

In almost all stories it is the sense of overwhelming curiosity about what is going to happen which keeps us reading on – far into the night or on a railway platform, oblivious to what is going on around us. The technique of storyboarding (see Chapter 4) is a very useful way of setting out visually the overall shape of the story structure, in terms of significant action. There are distinctive plot patterns such as:

(1) *The Quest* – as for example J. R. R. Tolkien's *The Hobbit* where the central character goes on a journey from home through dangers to undertake a mission, returning safely at the end. The return home has a strong emotional appeal because it is safe, all problems are resolved and the resolution is clearly marked. Planning is helped by use of the visual such as maps.

(2) *Herringbone* – as for example in *Huckleberry Finn* where the voyage down the Mississippi on a raft is the spine of the text from which the central characters go on side adventures. It can also be a cluster of stories around a central narrative, like Chaucer's *Canterbury Tales*.

(3) *Stepping stones* – the episodic plot as in the traditional folk-tale of Jack the Giant Killer where Jack gets up each day, travels a little further and meets another giant. Such adventures can be added on indefinitely as there is no natural ending, and as such it is a useful pattern for a class assignment where each group writes a different episode.

(4) *Waves* – where the plot has a series of crises which the central figure overcomes, with time for reflection before the next, as in

Jane Austen's *Emma*. Although most plots have tension rising to a climax to some extent, the significant feature here is the time for reflection after each crisis, which is more thought-provoking for older writers.

Recently a new model has appeared in the form of the 'fighting fantasy adventure game' book which allows the reader multiple plot choices, as in a computer game. In the opening pages the reader is introduced to a central character in a situation usually fraught with danger hence with many decisions to be made. The reader is given a series of choices, 'What should the hero do now?' and having made a choice, is directed to a different page or paragraph number, to continue the narrative until the next choice is to be made. Such a book is made up of many alternative plots in a branching structure, any one of which consists of only a few of the available pages in the book. Such a book is best planned using a flow-chart, described in Chapter 4. In many ways such adventure books are an undesirable model, largely because the format is only suitable for the most action-packed, mindless-violence kind of plot. But as a form to imitate it has advantages; it is highly motivating for just those writers who need strong motivation, and it needs careful planning – in marked contrast to the usual spontaneous writing of linear narrative.

Characterisation

The models of story which we give to young children usually have almost no development of character in them. Fairy stories are an extreme example. We learn nothing of the miller's son who inherits a cat in *Puss in Boots*; he has no character and is a pawn to fortune and external forces like all other fairytale protagonists. Evil characters, the witches, trolls and giants are likewise unexplained being external forces which pre-exist. It is their character to be evil without hope of redemption or reform. Teachers will not generally be happy about this fatalistic view of the universe which such undeveloped characterisation implies. We have to tell children repeatedly to mistrust strangers, and that people who mean them harm will not necessarily be dressed in black and riding a broomstick, but because children enjoy action-packed stories with shallow characterisation, it is essential that any contrast is gently done and is not disparaging since the aim is to bridge two cultures, not force children's culture underground. They must be gently led to enjoy more reflective stories which deepen their understanding of people, the world, and relationships.

To increase the amount of time the child spends projecting into the lives of characters, we can deepen perception by asking prompt questions such as:

(1) *History* – Who is the character and what is his/her background? (Early years, family, formative experiences.)
(2) *Appearance* – What does s/he look like? (Shabbily dressed, rugged good looks.)
(3) *Personality* – Is s/he brave, foolhardy, honest?
(4) *Talents* – what can s/he do which helps the action?
(5) *Significance* – what of the above detail is most or least significant?

Insight will also be developed by such strategies as:

(1) Drawing a picture of each character – or a wanted poster or a passport or identity card.
(2) Compiling a profile in the form of written notes for each character, following such prompts as above.
(3) Discussing types of character – prompted by a theme the class is following (e.g. heroes and heroines/survival) or a book they have been reading.
(4) Taking minor characters out of a story the class is reading and developing stories about them.
(5) Writing a class story. This reduces the creative load on the individual, who then writes all or part of the story, comparing that later with other people's versions.
(6) Revisiting well-known plots such as Hansel and Gretel which do not have developed characters, and rewriting the story with fuller character description and explanation of motive. Because the plot is already fixed, plot focus does not trap the writer into simply recounting a series of unelaborated actions.

To develop the last point further, there have in recent years been many 'modern' versions of traditional tales, for instance Storr's *Clever Polly and the Stupid Wolf*, Scieszka's *The True Story of the Three Little Pigs* and Corbalis's *The Wrestling Princess*. Revisiting stories they encountered at a much younger age helps children see patterns more clearly and in more confidence. Such versions are models for older children in re-writing a given story from a different point of view and by imitating that approach children can build on and extend their earlier reading/writing.

Description

There is clearly a direct relationship between Description as an option within story and as a field within the Persuasive range where it is more fully commented on in Chapter 7. The description of place in a story can be merely to create a context, or it can be an essential part of the meaning. In either case, description should always use significant detail which adds to the story, and not be just a brief to a stage set designer. Such significant detail can be symbolic, part of the meaning of the story, for instance where the weather complements the mood of a character to create the effect called 'pathetic fallacy'. It is important also to remember the power of suggestion, that the active reader is creating a scene in the head on the basis of suggestion and does not need a catalogue. A text can have 'gaps'.

Historical fiction highlights the importance of descriptive detail; from the first line there are problems to be solved or avoided. Take for instance a female character granted an audience with Queen Elizabeth I. As she walks towards the Queen will her feet sink into deep pile carpet or rustle through rushes or echo on stone flags? Will she use 'thee/thou' address in speaking? The genre gives the chance for accurate historical research into character, setting and plot. Given the emphasis on empathy in modern history teaching this might be a valuable extension to the history curriculum.

Action

Although action is usually described in the past tense, it is best visualised by the writer as happening like a stage play. Using dialogue helps that sense of immediacy, as for instance this brief speech in the short story of Caroline in a year 9 middle band:

> The door creaked open and a tall black figure stood there. The black figure pointed a finger at me and I started to move towards the door of the castle. Now I was inside the castle, it was cold and dark. Pictures on the wall, they look as though they were watching me. Winding stairs going up far. The floors were made of stone and I could feel the cold coming through my shoes. The black figure said 'I am Dracula' and then I felt a cold sharp pain go up my nail. I pushed Dracula away and I had knock him out. I grabbed a knife and plunged it into Dracula's heart.

Her writing highlights the significance of suspense, an effect on the reader which can be crafted in a number of ways. Here the effect is achieved by the withholding of essential information until late in the text, and the withholding is made more natural-seeming because the action is seen through the eyes of a first-person narrator who does not know what will happen next. The writer first sets up a context which the reader recognises as menacing from past literary experience. The context becomes more threatening as the protagonist becomes trapped inside it, and so for the reader there is a building expectation of action which will threaten the protagonist. A writer always controls what the reader is or is not told, and the information about the host's deadly identity is held back until late in the text. Here the effect on the reader relies largely on previous literary experiences, the action being only perfunctorily described. The writer needs to look at descriptions of fight scenes and vigorous action in other works, although encouragement to review the scene and to imagine it in more detail would probably bring out ability already present. In a longer work suspense could be maintained by such devices as a cliff-hanging chapter ending, a 'meanwhile' episode, an unexpected twist in the plot, a misleading clue. Children enjoy rehearsing such stereotypes even though there is no originality about it from an adult point of view.

Writer Viewpoint

Viewpoint can either be neutral, like a camera recording the scene, or coloured as in a portrait which will favour or disfavour certain features to give an overall interpretation. First-person viewpoint makes the writer or narrator an eyewitness, who uses all the senses to evoke the physical sensations of the scene, and action. A narrator allows the writer to use first-person viewpoint and from a different value-base, which is useful for developing sensitivity towards others. The most extreme kind of first-person viewpoint is the 'stream of consciousness' technique which tries to capture the effect of the mind of the writer spontaneously recording and responding to experience as it happens, rather than narrating it as if it had happened in the past.

Third-person viewpoint gives the writer omniscience, hence more control over events, and the freedom to let the reader into the inner secrets of the characters. Where children interpret story as history, though, it can lead to writing which is too detached, too matter-of-fact. The omniscient narrator can eavesdrop on all conversations, go behind locked doors, see into all hearts and minds; it is a pity to limit its role to that of objective recorder of events.

Multiple viewpoint suits story written in chapters or sections, the advantage of the technique being to explore an experience more deeply by seeing it from several points of view. Robert Cormier's *I Am the Cheese* uses multiple viewpoint very effectively to mislead the reader into what is actually occurring in his psychological thriller written for teenagers.

Why do we ask children to write stories in school, not just at primary level but throughout? At the lowest level stories are literacy fodder – material to practise basic reading and writing skills upon. On a higher plane David Jackson (1983) points out that in story (and he refers particularly to what he calls 'gossip tales') people can impose 'a satisfying pattern upon the disconnected impressions of actual experience' (*Encounters with Books*, p. 8). He calls fiction a game which creates out of our jumbled impressions a mosaic, a significant pattern, 'a coherent unity of beginnings, middles and endings' (*ibid.*, p. 9). Absorbed as we are in the jumbled detail of our daily lives, fiction can trace possible meanings in life which relate to our own actions, relationships, values and beliefs. At the same time it can satisfy our own insatiable human curiosity about other lives, other possibilities; lives we could have led if our own circumstances had been different. Like James Thurber's Walter Mitty we can all in fantasy live out other lives, more dynamic than our own, more heroic, or more anything that we choose.

DRAMA

Introduction

In a playscript characters interact through dialogue to create a narrative, in the process revealing their inner thoughts, feelings and motives, assisted by monologue. Children often find it difficult to grasp the difference between story 'telling' and drama 'showing'. As a first stage in demonstrating the difference between telling and showing, some teachers use comics, which are a midway point between story and playscript. The cartoons give a physical representation of the characters and their action, as if they are actors on the stage but the words they say are in written form; the bubbles coming from characters' mouths contain the speech, while dotted bubbles are the convention for thought. The 'telling' or narrative commentary is often handled by a line or two of text underneath each cartoon picture. The look of the character is given, so the reader cannot create a personal image of that, only of the sound of the voice.

As part of the process of learning to craft in the medium, children have to realise that within drama, telling can be handled only in a limited number of ways:

(1) *Character list* (dramatis personae) – which describes the characters, personality and relationship with others.
(2) *Stage directions* – which guide the actors in how to speak and move, the set designer in how to create the setting, the costume designer in how they should look.

(3) *A narrator* – who gives background information and a commen-
    tary on the action.

In the novel the writer has complete control over the total picture
evoked and the product is intended to be read. The written form is
only the first stage for drama; its intended expression is an oral performance, for listeners/onlookers rather than for readers. A reader can
certainly make a personal version of a novelist's evocation, but that is
not likely to show in the form of the writing. A script is not only
intended to be interpreted by other people – director, actors, designers
of costume and set – it is structured with just those people in mind.
Stage directions are not heard by the audience; they become embedded in the way the lines are spoken, the natural-seeming actions of the
actors within a set, all interacting with and interpreting the writer's
script to create the illusion, the evocation of significant moments of
the lives of its characters.

As an example of the differences between the novel and the drama,
I have converted into a playscript the scene from *Treasure Island*
previously quoted in the Story section. So as to include as much of the
original as possible (using 370 words as against 488 in the original) I
have used a Narrator. That is not really necessary since the physical
presence of the actors, guided by the stage directions, would suggest
to an audience most of what the novelist had to evoke in words alone.
I could have used a separate Narrator but preferred the Brechtian
technique of a character stepping out of role to comment on the
action. This way, through telling rather than showing, I hope that the
effect which Pew has on the captain will be more emphatic, since in
the original the captain says nothing and makes no decisive movement, which is strong in a novel but would be weak in a drama.

JIM – NARRATOR: One day I was standing outside the Inn full of
sad thoughts about my father when I saw a stranger tapping his
way along the road, a poor blind man, a dreadful sight but which
touched my heart.

PEW: (in a sing-song voice) Will any kind friend inform a poor
blind man, who has lost the precious sight of his eyes in the
gracious defence of his native country, England, and God bless
King George! – where or in what part of this country he may now
be?

JIM: You are at the 'Admiral Benbow', Black Hill Cove, my good
man.

PEW: I hear a voice – a young voice. Will you give me your hand,
my kind, young friend, and lead me in?

(Jim holds out his hand and Pew feels for it, gently at first. He finds it, then in a flash seizes him by the wrist, and with effortless strength pulls him close thrusting Jim's arm up his back. Jim is powerless.)

PEW: (Snarling) Now, boy, take me in to the captain.

JIM: (With difficulty) Sir, upon my word I dare not.

PEW: (Sneering) Oh that's it! Take me in straight or I'll break your arm.

(He jerks Jim's arm further up his back making him gasp with pain.)

PEW: Lead me straight up to him, and when I'm in view, cry out, 'Here's a friend for you, Bill.' If you don't, I'll do this!

(He gives Jim's arm a wrench which makes him cry out. They turn towards the Inn door, then freeze. Jim turns his face to the audience.)

JIM – NARRATOR: Holding me with a grip of steel he forced me to the parlour door. So terrified was I of the blind man that I forgot my terror of the captain and called out the words he had said.

JIM: (in a weak, trembling voice) Here's a friend for you, Bill!

(Still clutching Jim, Pew turns his upper body towards the audience, into the spotlight. His hood falls away to reveal his face, teeth bared in a grimace of triumph.)

JIM – NARRATOR: (quietly) The poor captain raised his eyes, and at one look the rum went out of him, and left him staring sober.

The ease with which this scene in a novel can be adapted into a play demonstrates how dramatic Stevenson's technique is, in three senses: the scene is a moment of tension in a compelling plot, expressed through verbal interaction, charged with strong emotion.

Models

Because of television most of us, children and adults alike, encounter playscripts every day of the week. It is not just the popular genres of soap operas, situation comedy, police and hospital dramas which are scripted but also serious television such as news, current affairs, and documentaries, which use scripts far more than we viewers realise. But although we encounter scripts so frequently and across a wide range of genres, our awareness of the written form of the script is generally intuitive, because all scripts are intended to be heard rather than read. The skill of the scriptwriter is in capturing spoken language in writing which sounds natural in its context, and which the skill of the actor or presenter can turn back into speech.

Some reading schemes have widened the range of texts to include playscripts; children becoming independent as readers very much enjoy reading in a support group without a teacher, each taking a part in the play. Because the genre leads to oral performance children can be motivated to repeat the reading, rehearsing until it becomes polished enough to perform for the class.

Probably the first way in which the majority of children encounter speech in written form is within narrative fiction, where into the past tense of narration is inserted the present tense of characters speaking to each other. Its effect is to make the text seem real, actual, taking place before the reader's eyes. It has a powerful evocative impact. Such inserted drama is also widely used in other forms, for instance in news reporting, where a transcript of what a real person actually says as if in the present is inserted into a report of events in the past. In a playscript, though, it comes into its own, for actors on a stage or in a film speak the written words of the writer's characters in the immediate present as the reader/viewer looks on.

Story-Line

A story should have what professional writers call a 'controlling idea' or 'spine'. Writers for popular TV estimate that 75 per cent of the impact comes from the story-line and only 25 per cent from the literary components such as mood, description and dialogue; 75 per cent of the story-line's impact comes from the last act climax. A whodunit is likely to have a pattern such as this:

(1) *Exposition* – to establish the main characters in a situation; the dialogue must answer the 'who, what, when, where?' questions.
(2) *Complication* – something happens to threaten the pattern of the situation; the main characters may suffer one or more reversals. Human beings are conservative, so a story may begin conservatively, but then action no. 2 puts the character at risk.
(3) *Climax* – the impact of the drama depends on the climax, where the main characters are under pressure. Everything before must lead up to the climax which should wring the audience's emotions.
(4) *Resolution* – the audience likes all loose ends to be tied up; the classic murder mystery ends with the denouement in the drawing room. The key to endings is to give the audience what they want but not the way they expected it.

These four ingredients should not be seen as acts but phases of the play's movement; usually moments of high tension come right in the closing moments of an act to leave the audience cliff-hanging in anticipation – hence act 1 is likely to end with a sudden reversal of fortune which is then developed in act 2. The climax might arrive in the first half of the last act, and the resolution in the last half. In the course of any scene there should be a change of direction – in the circumstances of characters, in the direction of the plot, in the emotional climate and the values being explored. Children may well know intuitively of the build up of tension in the plot through watching soaps on television; so as to keep an audience viewing night after night the writer must keep up a series of crises, each episode ending with some unresolved interaction or problem. A plot synopsis, described in Chapter 4, will help children see wider plot possibilities than generating ideas during drafting.

Action

Inexperienced scriptwriters may have trouble seeing action in the head when they write a script. Typically they will write a character saying something like 'I am going to knock on this door. Oh it is opening' which clearly duplicates the physical moves of the actors who later interpret the script in performance. This is perhaps because children are most familiar with the conventions of story-novel in which dramatisation (i.e. direct speech) plays only a small part whilst the detailed description and commentary of the author is continuous and all important. They also watch action-packed film and television, where the camera follows the actors in every little move. Children have to learn the convention that in the theatre a great deal of large-scale action must happen off-stage; that it is suggested to the audience's imagination by the dialogue, by the reactions to news reports brought in by other characters. You can see the problem in this climactic scene from a plot-focused horror play written by Ruth in year 6:

THE MAD AXE-MAN

(Scene 6. In the woods)

BELINDA: Blake, Blake, over here. He's coming nearer.
(They hold each other tight.)
His axe is covered with dripping blood. Blake, he's going to kill us.

MAD AXE-MAN: I'm coming to get you, Belinda.

BELINDA: Blake, why does he want me? What have I done?

BLAKE: I don't know, Belinda.

BELINDA: Blake, Blake.
(She faints. Out of nowhere Conor appears.)

BLAKE: Who are you?

CONOR: Doesn't matter. We haven't much time. Quick, follow me.
(continued)

In terms of reaction, rather than action, the character of Belinda has a lot of potential for portraying extreme emotion, the substance of melodrama. Ruth has used the 'deus ex machina' technique to save her heroine, a classic way out of plot difficulties ('with one bound our hero was free' is the well-known parody). That problem could easily have been solved at the planning stage and more convincing action would have been within Ruth's ability.

Character

More difficult for her, though, is character portrayal. The short snatches of dialogue are typical of the young writer, who is not yet using dialogue to explore character and motivation. Almost everything that is said describes an action which an audience would be able to see. She could probably have been helped in the planning stage, though it will take a long time for her to develop real skill in this major characteristic of drama. She has used two girls as 'normal' as herself as the central characters, and that has not helped her. She probably sees herself as normal in the sense of having no distinguishing features – a problem also for the reluctant diarist – hence with no dramatic potential in the character. If in her planning she had drawn up a profile of, say, 'plucky 11-year-old, keen on martial arts' she would have had a character who could be more than a victim. If the robot-like 'mad axe-man' had been given a tragic past, and the friend had been able to charm the birds off the trees, then the drama could have been a revelation of character through speech and not a recounting of the action.

Drama depends totally for its effect on its characters; everything the audience hears comes from the mouths of characters without an author's purple prose to comment and explain. So drama will be more successful when its characters are interesting, memorable and meaningful. Young writers often think that in their own experience they have not met that kind of person; usually personal experience is rich ground for writing but drama is probably an exception. A scene based on 'An argument at the breakfast table' is probably too 'normal' – they do not see the dramatic potential in it, so as an alternative characters can be 'borrowed' from books, films, TV programmes – even events in the newspaper. Young children might write about toys or animals which because of their distinctive shapes can be given distinctive characters suggested through the way they speak and act. Professional writers call the interaction between two characters in a scene 'a beat', a term which suggests the kind of vigorous to and fro which draws audiences into the experience. Strongly contrasted characters are most likely to provoke such interaction.

The way characters speak can express personality, social status, emotional state and motivation. Who someone is and how they are reacting can be expressed by stage directions to the actor, or more subtly through the way the character's speech is written:

Regional roots – 'Ee wor reet mardy.'
Social class – 'Oh gosh, I'm most awfully sorry.'
Emotional scale – 'Get *OUT*!'
Hesitation – 'Well, er . . . I'm not – sure . . . no, nnnnnot sure. Could it be . . . ?'
Idiosyncrasies – a distinctive way of speaking, repeated so that the audience identifies it with the character, like Gollum's repeated 's' sounds in J. R. R. Tolkien's *The Hobbit*.

Children should be encouraged to listen to ways of talking in real life and on film/television and to discuss in school what they have heard. It is particularly helpful to identify in novels as well as in plays how writers signify such features as personality, stress, tone, regional accent.

Writing plays for 'radio', i.e. for tape-recording is a good way of focusing children's attention on just the sound of voices, on tone, accent, stress. The medium has its own conventions; a narrator will speak softly close to the microphone, a fade out and fade in of sound suggesting change of time and scene.

Monologue

Drama is usually conceptualised by children as being an interaction between at least two characters. We can get round this if we introduce them to the idea of monologue. Shakespeare used soliloquy to get round the problem of projecting the inner thoughts of the character; it is not 'realistic' for a character like Iago to step forward to tell an audience what he intends to do and to explain his motives in doing so, but drama must break out of social realism to go deeper into psychological realism.

Since we will all admit to having a kind of voice in our head talking over what we are seeing, doing and worrying about, even the very youngest children can understand monologue. It is the same process as any first-person viewpoint writing, and so is related to the diary and aspects of storywriting, where a narrator can reveal inner thoughts and feelings.

There are perhaps four possible approaches; firstly the 'stream of consciousness' where sense impressions drive the thoughts, recollections and associations of the character; secondly the kind of confessional 'this is who I am' as in Richard Scriven's poem 'The Marrog' suitable for junior children; thirdly the autobiography where a character reviews his or her life; fourthly the dramatic moment in the life where the monologue reveals the speaker's reality as in Robert Browning's poem 'My Last Duchess' for older children.

Setting

In planning children should decide how many scenes the play will have and where these are to be set. A lot of changes of scene are difficult to manage in stage plays if movement of scenery is involved so children have to understand the discipline of restricted location. They are used to the 'indiscipline' of film and television which have frequent scene changes. Experiential planning through practical drama is an excellent way of exploring staging problems with them before the writing begins, and focusing them on developing each scene to its fullest potential instead of flicking from one location to another in pursuit of plot interest.

Stage directions include information about where the scene is set, so that scenery can be designed to give the desired effect; they also describe the dress of characters where necessary and the kind of props necessary on stage for verisimilitude or actual use by characters. It will help children as part of the planning stage before writing to draw: (1) sketches of scenes – as either a ground plan or an artist's impression; (2) sketches of characters – in pictures, labelled diagram or pen sketch.

Narrator

Children find a narrator a very convenient device to put across to an audience the details of characters' movement across time and space. When they are inexperienced the use of a narrator will be reassuring, but as they develop they should be asked to think carefully about what the narrator adds, and to see if they can rewrite the material into the mouths or actions of on-stage characters. On the other hand there are exciting uses of a narrator; for instance the scene-setting in Dylan Thomas's famous radio play *Under Milk Wood* or the complex use in the stage play of Charles Dickens's *Nicholas Nickleby* where the narrator very flexibly plays a part in the action, stepping aside to give the audience a linking commentary on the complex plot.

Sources of Material

In searching for real-life material for drama, newspaper stories in the human interest class offer open-ended material: the classic 'man bites dog' suggests at least one character and a build-up to a compelling situation. Story reading is a valuable source because the essential outline of plot, setting and characters is already worked out, and possibly some of the key interactions with clues as to how the characters speak. In addition to novels suitable material can be found in myths, folk and fairy tales, which emphasise plot rather than subtle character study. Some poetry is also suitable; James Reeves' poem 'The Hippocrump' for instance suggests an archetypal village, perhaps in Africa or long ago. Through improvisation the village can be developed into a community in which children play a particular role (priest, hunter, healer, artist, potter) in work and in relationship with others (young, old, parent, child, brother). Other kinds of writing can be included within the play – songs and chants, rules, a history of the village, and myths of the tribe.

Other ready-made contexts can be found in television (and radio) soap operas, many of which children will know well. From them children will also have absorbed the essential principle of a cliff-hanger ending to each episode – and the cliff-hanger is useful because it permits children to write individual scenes which have a satisfyingly dramatic moment, without the necessity to write a complete play.

Puppets and masks are very valuable because they can speak for the puppeteer who may be too shy to perform as an actor. For young children fairy tale characters like the Three Little Pigs or Little Red Riding Hood offer a ready-made plot and characters with strongly marked characteristics which bring the scriptwriting task within their range. For much older children the same material can be revisited through modernised versions like Roald Dahl's *Revolting Rhymes*. Construction skills can be kept to the minimum; at the simplest level soft toys held from behind or cut-out pictures on a stick in a cardboard box stage like a Victorian children's theatre. The range of craftwork runs from the simplest decorated wooden spoon or sock to foam rubber gremlins and goblins, spin-offs from cult films. Between them the class may have many puppets and masks of various kinds at home, and the dressing-up box too may suggest characters.

Scripts for performance can also motivate writing in other forms than the Evocative, as for instance this script, a form of criticism, by a top band year 10 group for a programme they video-recorded called *The Good Book Show*:

> SUE: Hello, good evening and welcome to *The Good Book Show!* Tonight we present to you a discussion between Agatha Christie and Lynne Reid Banks.
>
> NAT: They will be battling against each other with words – hopefully that is where it will stop.
> (continued)

They have used several authentic touches: the two-presenter convention popular in many media magazine programmes; the triple welcome, an idiosyncrasy originally developed by David Frost; the signposting of drama to come, typical of media psychology.

Performance

Children will perhaps more often write scenes and complete plays primarily to be read as literature, not dramatised by actors on a stage or before a camera. Theatre though is a concrete medium; the actors, set and action all exist as concrete realities while the script is an abstraction, and children find it a great deal easier to write scripts if they act out their ideas as part of the planning and drafting process, creating and revising in response to actual experience.

Elsewhere I have suggested that writing for a real audience ought also to contain a dimension of deadlines and performance pressure. Putting on a performance for an audience necessarily involves putting pressure on the performers, and working backwards it should also put a positive pressure on the writers who are working to deadlines to finish the script in time. Anyone who has worked with children under such pressures will know the great pleasure and satisfaction it can give them – and to the audience who watches, wanting them to do well.

BIOGRAPHY

The term biography is used here in as wide a sense as possible, to include all forms of personal and 'life' writing. First of all I mean to include autobiography, since writing about oneself and one's personal experiences is a major focus of writing throughout schooling and particularly for younger children. From the notion of autobiography it is a small step to include the diary and journal (as in the 'Reading Journal') both of which have become significant forms for promoting a personal response to literature. Of a more literary kind the field includes the memoir, and more morbidly the obituary and the epitaph. At the opposite end of the scale of formality are included the personal letter (including the letter to an agony aunt) and even the postcard, because such forms are firmly centred on the life of the writer, and again highly significant not only in writing development but in the lives of our pupils beyond school. This wide definition of Biography is placed within the Evocative because although influenced by the Informative purpose, the writer's primary purpose is to evoke in the mind of the reader an impression of the whole or a part of a life.

It is unlikely that in school children will write a biography as the term is understood by the librarian and bookseller. As a form for children it is best approached not as a continuous prose account but as an opportunity for a writing collage; passages of recollections, impressions, evocations written as poetry, anecdote, description, dialogue, together with sketches, photographs and scrap-book souvenirs. In that format even very young or less able children can collate an extensive text, of a length and complexity which would be beyond them if it were in continuous prose format. In the field then forms range from the most informal and non-literary level, written mainly for oneself as audience, to the literary genre of 'biography' at the formal end of the spectrum and that is how the representative examples which follow are organised.

News

It is common practice in the early stages of writing for children to write their 'news' on Monday morning, in the knowledge that they will have had some personal experience over the weekend which the class and teacher will not know about, which gives them a genuine audience as well as content within their experience. On only their second encounter with a word-processor one able five-year-old in a reception class wrote the following with a friend, without any adult present, as his 'news' of the weekend:

> I went out with Lize and richard i saw a island and i pict a bite of blossom
> I got a dnsoor book and then I drawed dnsoors and then i drawed a wooly mammf then i pot it on my wool.

and although the text was left at that, it could easily have been edited to read: 'I went out with Liz and Richard. I saw an island (in the river) and I picked a bit of blossom. I got a dinosaur book and then I drew dinosaurs and then I drew a woolly mammoth and then I put it on my wall.' As it stands this piece, a remarkable achievement, could be classified as serving an Informative rather than an Evocative purpose. It has all the objectivity of a scientific report, recounting only the facts, albeit a selection of highlights. As this writer develops he will learn to make the text more evocative through the use perhaps of a narrative structure which carries the reader along, describing the physical detail of the scene so that the reader can see it in the head, expressing his reactions in terms of sense impressions, thoughts, feelings and emotions as his inner self responds to the external events, so that the reader empathises with his experience.

Postcard

The humble postcard offers a useful approach to just such development. It may be one of the most universally encountered of all forms of writing in the adult social calendar, but it has a bad name because of the joke stereotyped message 'Wish you were here,' a pathetic cliché with which writers apologise for the inadequacy of their command of language to convey any of the detail, impressions, feeling of their holiday. By the same token it is a valuable cameo form because its size physically determines the number of words that can be crammed in, so that it becomes a challenge to say all that you want to say in the space available. This then affects the style, and constructing a postcard on the blackboard with a class can be a good chance to highlight précis skills and to model personal writing in a crafted form.

Since this is a personal not a published form, completed examples will be hard to find, but you can write a working model for the purpose. It might be linked to an imaginative context such as designing a holiday centre in some exotic location, or to a project on the language of holiday brochures. Guidelines for the content might include:

(1) Selected details of travel, food, accommodation, weather.
(2) Personal reactions to the holiday resort.
(3) Exciting, strange, funny occurrences to date.
(4) Comment on the postcard picture; where it is, what it was like, how your first-hand experience was different from the picture.
(5) What sense impressions you get from around you as you write.
(6) What you are going to do next or tomorrow.
(7) What the reader would like about the holiday.

A skilled writer can write 100 words on a standard postcard – and if you set such a word length as a target you also create the need for neat handwriting. Amber in a low band year 8 wrote 112 words in the space. She has a strong sense of audience and of dramatic first-person style, close to speech, and the ability to compress her meaning in 'telegraphese':

Dear Zoe,
Met a lovely girl called Julie. Went out till 4.00 a.m. Went to this brilliant night-club! Silverman was on. Next day went to pool – load of drunks passing a very expensive wine around shouting uhh uhh uhh! Went on bull – fell off bull – only mechanical bull so I wasn't hurt badly. Went to dinner. The lemonade is called Revolta but tastes nice. Went round Benidorm at 1.00 a.m. last night – Saturday night out! Met nice boy. Tell you about him when I get home! Bye bye. Glad you're not here (not really) P.S. Had a disco first night here – great fun and won talent contest.
Luv, Amber.

Diary

Although the diary as a published form can be as extensive as a novel or even an encyclopaedia, its length is achieved by repetition of the basic pattern of a day-by-day bed-to-bed account, i.e. a linear chronology. The published form is generally a multiplication of that basic cameo, which is very useful in the mixed-ability classroom where the least able can complete a single day's worth, while the most able can continue for as long as interest and challenge hold. A major attraction of the diary is that it is a uniquely subjective vehicle which emphasises the writer's 'voice' in recounting fact, impression and belief concerning personal experience in a spontaneous narrative. It is the personality of the writer in revealing a pattern of interwoven interests which makes it a literary form. Because of its intimate personal nature, it has few genre characteristics though that is a strong characteristic in itself. This makes it an uncomplicated classroom form for children, added to which its bed-to-bed structure is probably the easiest of all structures to handle.

In a true diary there is no anticipated audience except the writer's own future self, so later readers are given the privilege of peeping into the intimate life of the writer. Classic models are the diaries of Samuel Pepys, Ann Frank and Captain Scott. Fictional versions are also popular, such as *The Diary of a Church Mouse* by Graham Oakley (1987) and *Diary of a Nobody* by George Grossmith (1975). More recently Sue Townsend's *The Secret Diary of Adrian Mole* (1985) has swept all before it in terms of popularity. In my area the famous literary diary is that of the eighteenth century Parson Woodforde (Beresford, 1978) who always made a feature of the food of the day:

> We had for dinner to day one fowl boiled and Piggs face, a Couple
> of Rabbitts smothered in Onions, a Piece of rost Beef and some
> Grape Tarts . . . I went out with my Man this morning tracing
> Hares, we found one fine one which the dogs killed. At Cribbage
> this Evening with Nancy won 0.2.0. She was very sulky and sullen
> on losing it, tho' not paid. She did not scarce open her Mouth all
> the Even' after . . . Miss Mary Donne is a very genteel, pretty young
> Lady and very agreeable with a most pleasing Voice abt. 21 Yrs.
> very tasty and very fashionable in dress . . . the Frost severer than
> ever in the night as it even froze the Chamber Pots under the Beds.

As a genuine vehicle for personal expression its appeal may be limited;
many children believe that their own lives are 'boring – nothing ever
happens to me', probably by contrast with television and fictional
adventure in which action-packed plot predominates. They need to be
given confidence in their own material, and led into the form through
detailed observation of their own lives, through experiential planning
– discussion, reading of poetry about everyday things, a day or two to
jot notes so they begin to see themselves as diarists before they begin
to write. They may appreciate clear guidance on subject matter and
style likely to be interesting to a reader. What the writer had for lunch
is not likely to be interesting unless the style makes it so with mouth-
watering description or witty irony. The art of the diarist lies in the
power of observation thereby arousing the reader's curiosity; the ability to be a spectator of recent experience in which one was a participant; to describe, explain, dramatise, commentate, speculate on such
aspects of one's personal life as: food, pets, clothing, outings, seasons
and weather, local, national and world affairs, personal triumphs and
disasters, friends, enemies and other relationships, who am I, what
will become of me.

However, the classroom is not a private place; there is almost no
form of writing within the school context which can genuinely be
called 'personal'. From a child's point of view the classroom is full of
snoopers and busy-bodies, teachers worst of all. Everything is at risk
of becoming public – 'Listen everybody, Stephen's written ever such a
moving piece about his dog dying. Read it out to the class. You don't
mind do you?' We should have every sympathy with children who do
not want to expose their innermost selves to public scrutiny, to use
their personal life as writing fodder. Whilst I think teachers can be of
the greatest help to children, in guiding them to understand their
thoughts and feelings so that they build up a positive world picture,
we must examine our motives and practices very carefully before we
ask children to be 'honest, sincere, write-it-from-the-heart'. Where
they do it, it shows remarkable trust and should be taken as a great

compliment to the sincerity of the teacher with whom the writing is shared.

Less contentiously we frequently use the diary form in education for a specific purpose, such as recording the events of a special day or projecting into the life of another person such as a character in fiction. It allows reserved children to distance their own selves or to project them through the mask of another life in history or fiction. Paul in a year 8 bottom band class became interested in Robinson Crusoe because of a comprehension passage on a work-sheet and volunteered to write several entries of an imaginary diary:

> It has been a long day on my solitary island. I saw a ship today. I waved to it but with no avail. I caught a small fish which filled me up to a T. I still think there is someone on my island, for instance I went to my small boat but it was gone. I am as scared as ever in my little hut. There are no more fish for me tonight so I think I shall retire for tonight.

Such a diary can be a cameo plan for a longer form particularly story or literary biography.

Log

A log is a variation on the diary, generally applied to more scientific subject matter, from a laboratory experiment to an expedition, real or imaginary. A ship's log is usually extremely concise, concentrating on facts of the course followed, miles covered, weather and so on. As such it is not a very promising model to follow, although across the curriculum there are many justifications for the form; for younger children a personal style ('I watched one of the eggs hatch out') with subjective impressions and emotions will make the form more attractive, and it can act as a useful stage in the development of scientific writing.

Journal

Many teachers find the Reading Log or Personal Journal a helpful technique for promoting children's personal response to their reading. The idea is that each child has a small exercise book or better still a hard-backed pocket book which can easily be carried around outside class. Children are free to write down personal reactions which occur in and amongst either private reading or set text reading in class. What is written down might include questions about what is happening and why, speculation about what might happen next in the book, personal judgements, thoughts and feelings provoked, poetry and creative writing stimulated during the reading, and so on. The relative formlessness of the journal is what facilitates this free response, and the possession of a book for the purpose means that many children will be drawn, through the writing process with teacher encouragement, into genuine dialogue with their reading. It is a matter of choice for the teacher whether or not to read and reply to all the journals, in writing or tutorial, at frequent intervals or at specific stages. Teacher response should be informal, i.e. the work is not assessed or negatively criticised, so as to encourage a genuine, felt response.

Biography

The term biography can be translated as 'a picture of a life'; or better still 'portrait' because although the content is partly historical fact, the biographer or autobiographer attempts to create an evocation of one person's life and times, dramatising with artistic licence the most significant moments. Some examples of the form have punningly been called 'faction' indicating a blend of fiction with fact or vice versa. Political memoirs are a related form and older children might find an approachable introduction in the *Yes Minister* and *Yes, Prime Minister* books by Jonathan Lynn and Anthony Jay (1986) based on the television series of the same name; they also use a wide variety of forms of writing, such as memos, in addition to narrative.

A brief form of biography more familiar to children is the 'profile' of a famous person – film star, pop star, sporting personality – in magazines and comics. The form is easy to replicate and can be structured as an interview, where the questions paragraph the information and the tone can be colloquial. In planning other forms, charts such as the family tree will show relationships, a time-line will help to prompt the memory for major moments in the writer's life. Photographs, souvenirs from holidays, etc. and personal treasures will all act as experiential plans and prompts.

Although in the classroom there is little time for children to write the extended form which we would recognise as Biography, it can be built up through a series of cameo pieces which are then combined to make chapters or sections in the whole work. There is a predictable set of memorable moments which everyone can be guaranteed to have had – first day at school, being ill, lost and found, favourite games. By focusing on such incidents the teacher can give guidelines on making the writing vivid – dramatisation through imagined dialogue, word pictures, recreated sense impressions. After such a collage of cameo writing, Julie in year 9 began her biography like this:

IT LOOKED SO VIOLENT AND DANGEROUS

First Day
In September 1980 I started school. I went to the Waveney First
School in Belton. I remember arriving at school with my mum. I
was half excited, half nervous. When we reached the main gate, I
caught sight of the 3rd and 4th year playground. They looked so
huge, violent and dangerous to me! We had to cross the playground
so I started to cry. At this my mum grabbed me by the wrist and led
me to the side entrance. (continued)

Looking back across such a span of time, more than half her life, the
experience is distanced and Julie is able to see herself at a weak
moment in safety, enjoying the nostalgia of reminiscence in a delightful piece of writing. Through separate cameos the piece continues on
first school experiences for twelve pages, under sections entitled 'The
classroom', 'The teacher', 'The lessons', 'The playground'. It is followed by three long poems called 'Morning break', 'Oh yes, I remember her well' and 'I remember', each decorated in the margin with
little sketches and embellishments. The collection is stapled together
to make a book, with a cover and an end page. The arresting title on
the front cover is a quotation from the first piece.

An approach which is less personal and suitable for group writing is
the biography of a community, made up of reminiscences of local
people linked with a commentary and historical facts. This can be a
challenging project, involving writing questionnaires, using tape-
recorders and making transcripts, collecting old photographs, maps,
visiting local landmarks to make descriptive notes. The final document
can contain quotations of the actual words of people recorded and
transcribed, 'then and now' descriptions of places, and 'notice this'
about photographs, all linked with a commentary. Possible structures
could be chronological or based on a walk around the community,
following the structure of the town guide, described in Chapter 7.

Developing Skills

(1) As part of the reading programme of the class use all forms of the
    Evocative and make connections/comparisons across the range.
(2) Use brief biographies, such as information sheets from publishers
    like the Puffin Authors series and those in encyclopaedias as well
    as complete books, to make children aware of authorship.
(3) Discuss the overall structure of long texts with the class. Can
    it be represented as a graph on the board, with patterns of
    anticipation-climax-reflection-resolution?

(4) In addition to studying whole texts, at times focus on the significant parts of several texts for comparison: beginnings, endings, scene setting, the chase scene, dialogue, character description and so on.

(5) Teach alternative chronologies beyond linear narrative: flashback, flashforward, meanwhile, sub-plot.

(6) Seek out the viewpoint of the author in the text, and distinguish between the author and the narrator. Is a first-person narrator the author? Is the author omniscient?

(7) Seek out 'reliable' and 'unreliable' character judgements.

(8) Review texts after reading; what changes have occurred in the reader's attitude, belief, knowledge?

(9) Identify the parts which have moved the reader in some way. Reread those passages to identify how the writer's craft achieved that effect.

(10) Heighten appreciation through performances of plays, poems and story which have been rehearsed and polished. Record the performances on cassette and CCTV to enjoy again and share with other audiences.

(11) Use writing to develop sympathy and empathy for the circumstances and values of others.

Promoting Critical Reading/Writing

(1) Read different versions of the same text for comparison: a Grimm Brothers' version of a folk tale with a Perrault; a traditional version with a modern retelling such as Scieszka (1989) *The True Story of the Three Little Pigs*, Corbalis (1986) *The Wrestling Princess* and comic strip versions of Shakespeare.

(2) Study popular (even poor) literature in comparison with the best so that children develop a sense of perspective.

(3) Encourage browsing. If a classroom has a library of books including poetry, children will be able to browse freely and often. Early-finishers can browse in the class poetry collection until the end of the lesson, or as a reward for good work a group might prepare a collection to read to the class.

(4) Cloze procedure: delete a pattern of words from a poem and ask children to discuss what words best fit the sound and sense. You might list the missing words below the text to reduce the level of difficulty, but it is a more open-ended discussion if there is completely free choice. The task focuses attention, makes children read between the lines and at best gives them courage to criticise by suggesting alternatives to the words of the poet.

(5) Author's Notebook: take the basic idea of a text (poem or section of a story) and write it down as the kind of notes the author might have made on which to base the text. Give these notes – but not the original text – to the class as the stimulus for writing their own. Only show them the original published text when they have finished their own; then they will already be inside the experience of the published text, having lived it for themselves in some way; they are more likely to be confident enough to criticise the published poem or story from a standpoint of equal writers.

(6) To help children appreciate the crafting process, have them keep plans and first drafts to review later; display the alternative versions and talk with the class about the revisions they have made.

(7) To develop their sense of themselves as writers, keep collections of their writing. Hold anthology lessons, put anthologies in the library, encourage them to look back on their work later in the year.

(8) Look for examples of evocative techniques in other kinds of writing, particularly such powerful attention-grabbers as headlines, advertising slogans and political catch-phrases which use visual imagery and such sound effects as alliteration, rhyme, onomatopoeia. List them, explain how they work and what is their intended effect.

(9) Give children a Reading Journal in which to write their honest reactions, not just once they have completed a book but their spontaneous feelings during their reading.

(10) Seek out the values of an author. Highlight and discuss examples of explicit or implicit values in reading matter: sexism, racism, ageism.

(11) Consider the morality of revelation as expressed in biography, diary, personality profile, investigative journalism, which in some way 'peep over the fence into the back-garden' of other people's lives. Is there a right to privacy and what are its limits?

9

INTO ACTION

Ignorant people think the scribe's profession is an easy one. Three fingers are engaged in writing, the two eyes in looking; your tongue pronounces the words and the whole body toils.

(Eighth-century scribe)

Just as for this poor scribe of long ago, for at least some of the time writing can be a torment for today's children. The classroom becomes a prison unless we make it something better, and to help us we have many years' experience of 'creative writing' and a wealth of exciting projects known to appeal to children in specific age groups. Added to that in recent times a set of procedures for teaching writing has been developed to break the writing task into a series of steps, whereby children can achieve more, with more confidence. At the heart of this classification of the 'writing process' is the concept of the classroom as a 'community of writers' – including the teacher who writes alongside the children sharing common problems and solutions with them. Many teachers are shy about sharing their writing, but it is worth the risk because of the interest children take, which makes success almost guaranteed. It is really the only way to model the writing process across a range of forms as you sketch out ideas, plan, draft, redraft and proof-read your own work as well as talking with them about their own. The stage beyond is to invite a professional writer to be 'in residence', holding writing workshops in the schools. Although this must be more of a special event and cannot substitute for the teacher also being a writer, it is a powerful stimulus, and the regional arts council may give a grant towards the writer's fee.

Pre-Writing Stage

A Reason to Write

There are so many possible reasons to write that we can do no more here than generalise. In our schools at present teachers have a great deal of freedom to decide what the classroom should become, and although all children find some textbook exercises interesting some of the time, we now generally agree that the best writing comes from more engaging contexts. In Chapter 2 we considered the factors which generate a writing programme, and there is only space here to broadly review possibilities.

Through our own imagination we can enter into other worlds without leaving the classroom, stimulating the imagination through reading books (factual and fictional), looking at photographs and fine art, watching television and film, creating drama, talking about our past experiences, present fears and future hopes, using stimulus from all the subjects in the curriculum. Writing can be a series of pieces connected by an extended theme, such as the world of work built around a factory simulation or a project on space where the classroom becomes a space-ship. It can be a series of separate pieces, which are linked because they explore the characteristics of a single form.

In the school at large we can write for and about events in the calendar: sports day, nativity play, fund-raising events. Children can write for real audiences such as younger or older classes, the head and governors, parents, a visiting speaker. Even traditional academic writing tasks can be reoriented and revived by being given a real purpose. The traditional book review, for instance, can be pinned onto the bulletin board or displayed in the library as a source of advice to potential readers of the book. The advantage of choosing immediate contexts for writing is that they provide familiar concrete experience, which is less demanding, so freeing the writer to give more attention to the language. We might, though, have to ask children to look at the familiar more closely in case they have taken it for granted and do not really see it.

We can leave the classroom and visit the street and shops outside to interview people and record what they say, or get on a bus to visit a museum, a concert, a farm. The advantage of new contexts is their fresh stimulus, though the language objectives need to be established with the children beforehand to focus attention during the 'distractions' of a powerful new experience.

There are many books to help teachers set up language-centred contexts; see for instance Parker and Hayhoe (1989) *Voyages*, or Ellis and Friel (1991) *Inspirations for Writing*. Whatever context we choose, within it the teacher needs to have an agenda which concerns language development, for the writing programme needs continually to stretch children's ability outwards and upwards; outwards to include a widening range of forms and upwards to increase their sophistication and accuracy of use.

Preparation

Where children take an active part in the choice of the context and the targets for writing they are more likely to be motivated because they have part ownership. This will not always be possible but even where the programme has to be totally designed by the teacher the trick in motivating children is to leave them space to choose, without losing sight of their upwards and outwards language development. The most obvious compromise is for the teacher to determine the target form but allow the child control over content. Where on the other hand the content must be selected beforehand, children will often suggest the kinds of writing which the teacher could predict, for instance writing their own fantasy quest stories after reading J. R. R. Tolkien's *The Hobbit*. Sometimes the teacher will have an idea, such as holding a mock political campaign, and will need to 'sell' the idea to the class.

Talking and reading are essential parts of the writing process. Sometimes their part will be informal and unplanned contributions to the lesson, when for instance children want to tell the class about a TV programme relevant to the topic. At other times reading and talking will be more formally framed: a library research project to give background information which is formally reported back to the class, the researchers referring to written notes. Where the class is trained in the 'conferencing' procedure described below, talk about the writing process will take place at all stages as writers discuss progress with a partner.

Agenda

Setting the context so as to draw children in involves negotiation, the teacher framing what children want to do in the context of what they need to learn next. Once the context is set, it generates a sense of purpose if children know where a lesson series is going. It is helpful if they can refer to an agenda which shows what they will be doing over the next few weeks; this might be displayed on a bulletin board in the form of a web chart, a flow diagram or a list of activities. An agenda should not require too many pieces of finished written work for assessment; a great deal of writing will be preparatory, and it is more effective for assessed pieces to be spaced out at intervals, so that a learning process leads up to them.

Children should be encouraged to make the project their own by bringing in material for display, telling the class what they know or have found out. If alongside the agenda there are suggestions for reading, library research, pictures, magazine articles, and points to think about, children are given a sense that the classroom is an interesting and busy place where everyone has a job to do. The worst classroom scenario is where everyone has to wait for the slowest to catch up or wait for the teacher to give the next order, and where no one knows what the writing is for or where it will go next.

Time Factors

If we are to be truly writing for real purposes, the agenda should include real deadlines, which are applied; that is the universal reality of the working world and we have a duty to make it a factor in school life too. In my experience the quality of the product does not increase in direct proportion to the time allowed. Although time limits put pressure on people and pressure is generally thought of as a negative, there is a flip side in that pressure usually has the very desirable effects of increasing concentration and motivation. Children greatly enjoy having worked hard when there is a concrete result to show for it, something they wanted to do. The pleasure may come only after pain, and the teacher may have to be very insistent to get them through that pain barrier.

Even within classes streamed for ability it is predictable that children will not work at the same pace, so the agenda needs to include additional projects for those making the fastest progress, or alternatives for those who need different work. Such an agenda with branching options gives children independence, since they do not need the teacher to be free before they are told what to do next. They can think and plan ahead if they choose, which is an important freedom for high ability and well motivated children. If they can check off on a class list beside the agenda what they have completed, that will give the teacher a quick check on class progress; not just the class teacher but everyone else. Slow children often do not know how slow they are, and the desire to keep up can act as a stimulus. Such an agenda needs advance planning but it can free the teacher for other tasks such as giving more individual attention.

Choosing the Medium

Very neat children may resist playing with their text as they compose because they do not like making a mess of the page. Most children dislike re-drafting and rarely do more than correct secretarial errors. Word-processing (WP) is a tremendous advantage because both secretarial and compositional changes can be made at any time without the need for extensive re-writing of all text including that with which the author is satisfied. WP is highly motivating and facilitates collaborative composition since three children can see the screen easily. Text can be created, stored and later revised, by someone else if necessary. The printer allows children with poor handwriting to produce impressive results, and with desk-top publishing software schools can publish material of professional standard. However, many people find the physicality of the old-fashioned technology much more satisfying. We should never lose sight of the personal nature of creativity; some people may be liberated by micro-processors, others stultified, finding true expression only with paper, pen and felt-tips.

Models

Children need to see examples of real writing which will excite their interest, so that they then want to explore them to see how they work and then replicate their effects in their own writing. The best source for such models across the complete range of real forms is to make your own collection. As you will know from experience many forms of real writing are easy to come by; they drop on the mat daily, unsolicited, they are thrust into your hand as you walk down the street – some of the most bizarre and thus provocative in the classroom arrive like that. Keep instructions for equipment you buy, pick up information leaflets, send away for guides and information packs, note down phrases you see and paragraphs you read, scan holiday brochures, campaign leaflets and so on with scissors at the ready. At first do not discriminate, but just collect. I keep my own collection in clear plastic envelopes in a clip file which I can flip through quickly to select the right example for teaching.

Children can learn a great deal by browsing through many examples, for instance holiday brochures, to pick up significant characteristics of the form. You might select two or three examples which have differing approaches so as to teach by contrast. Where direct teaching is favoured a single example may be preferable, to show the form's characteristics clearly and concisely. Sometimes the only satisfactory model is one you write yourself. Not only can you make the main principles stand out, you can explain at first hand how you crafted the writing for a particular effect. Your creativity will be exercised again later once children have started their own writing when as you go round the class helping them you give impromptu versions of possible options.

Once you have planned to target a specific form of writing, a likely sequence of teaching is:

(1) Ask your class – whatever their age – what they know about the target form. Have they written it before? What conventions and options do they know of?

(2) Write the characteristics they suggest on the board for everyone to see. If you write ideas on the board in the random order in which they offer them, demonstrate afterwards how to re-order their points into a prioritised list.

(3) Show them a model of the target form – one that has clearly marked characteristics, suitable for their interest and skill level. Ask them to identify its characteristics ('How does the writer try to persuade us to buy?'). Pair and group discussion is supportive here and it helps if they can underline key phrases and write notes on the text itself.

(4) Add their new observations to the list on the board. Compare the two and then build on that list, explaining appropriate terminology and extending their knowledge of crafting techniques.

(5) Use their analytical knowledge in a creative application – writing their own version of the target form – working through the stages of preparation, planning, drafting, proof-reading, publishing described in this chapter (see summary in Appendix 4).

(6) Remind the class of the characteristics of the target model when you describe the task – then use these characteristics as the basis for assessing their writing when it is finished.

Looking closely at the real model also involves looking at its presentation: variety, number and significance of type-faces, layout, use of colour and illustration. Getting the presentation of a visually attractive text just right is the best motivation for handwriting development, and far better than out-of-context practice of handwriting style.

Planning

A full range of planning strategies is described in Chapter 4. Of this range of plans, many can be visually attractive in themselves, and certainly plans and planning should be discussed, not discarded after this stage. It adds an interesting dimension to finished work on display if the plan and first draft are displayed with the finished text as one piece, mounted together on an A3 backing sheet.

The planning stage gives early evidence of a child's language needs, so this is when a great deal of valuable, and perhaps the most valuable, teaching can go on. It is the first chance for the new learning to be absorbed through being put immediately into practice. If the teacher only teaches in reaction to errors in the final draft, the child will be much less likely to absorb the new information because it is too late to apply it. In any case it is a notorious fact that children do not register the corrections that teachers write on the finished page – they may not read them at all – and teachers really are too busy to waste effort in teaching after the event.

Children will only take planning seriously, and learn its value over the years of schooling if all teachers clearly signify that planning is essential for all writing except that which is intended to be spontaneous and first impression. This means recognising that all forms of prior experience, reading and discussion are part of planning as well as the marks on a page which would normally be considered to be a plan. It means that when children are becoming independent writers, the teacher should make time for and monitor a written planning stage. Then when the final draft is completed, the review of the work should include a comparison of plan with finished product.

Drafting Stage

Writing Samples

In spite of the current theory of successive drafting embodied in the National Curriculum there is major difficulty in persuading children of the advantages of redrafting, and a further difficulty in persuading them to make significant changes from one draft to another. The problem is threefold. Firstly rewriting is physically arduous and mind-numbingly tedious if the whole text is being transposed only to neaten it up with minor revisions. Secondly handwriting tends to fill the page, so that where major revision would be desirable, there is no space on the page for complicated directions to guide the revision to be written in. Thirdly young writers do not seem to have the grasp of the total text or the experience of linguistic options to be able to generate alternative versions which differ significantly from their original. To these three drafting problems there are four solutions or at least partial solutions:

Firstly WP makes a major contribution to solving the first two since editing is so flexible, though the third problem, of 'seeing' the whole text, is arguably made worse when the screen does not reveal the whole of a long text. However, it is likely that as use of WP increases the theory of successive drafting will become less problematic. Secondly if the procedures in the planning stage described above and in Chapter 4 are carried out thoroughly there should be less need for major redrafting. Thirdly the peer-conferencing procedures described below support the drafting as it progresses instead of retrospective criticism once a draft has been completed.

Finally it is very helpful for young writers after the planning stage but before attempting a complete draft to write a *sample* piece, that is to say a small but significant part of the intended text. In this way they can experiment on a small scale, without the major commitment of a full first draft. They can play creatively with language, trying to find a suitable 'voice' for the text. They can try out its effect on a writing partner, and make revisions without the need for a major rewrite. Even better is the writing of two samples, alternative versions of the same idea: for instance an incident in a story seen from third-person viewpoint and then the same incident seen in the first person, or a detailed description of a setting compared with a starkly unelaborated version. The section of the intended text chosen for the sample piece should be a significant one within the plan, exploring the kinds of decisions described in Chapter 5. On some occasions it will be possible for the sample to be a cameo, i.e. a piece of writing complete in itself which becomes absorbed in a larger project, and suitable forms for this are listed in Chapter 4.

Conferencing

According to Butturff and Sommers (1980), teachers seemingly 'find it difficult to respond to student writing unless they can respond to it as a final draft' with the result that in talking to children about their work teachers focus on problems of mechanics, usage and style rather than on the effectiveness of communication. This gives children the impression that errors are more important than meaning-related concerns. This observation was supported by Schwartz's (1984) study in which children were asked to select the one passage of several which teachers would prefer; one that was correct but lifeless or one that was colourful and creative but flawed mechanically. Children chose the first, assuming that grammatical errors would be more significant to the teacher than content. To counter this tendency Donald Graves (1983) among others focused on the process of writing rather than the product and developed strategies to guide the teacher in interacting with children throughout the various stages up to final production. A key concept in the 'process writing' approach is that of 'conferencing', i.e. focused talk between teacher and child or child and supportive peer. Guidelines for the conferencing procedure are:

Teacher Action

(1) Listen carefully and let the child lead.
(2) Respond to the subject content of the writing first, as positively as possible, asking yourself:
   (a) Is the writer sure of the topic?
   (b) Has the writing a clear focus?
   (c) Has any evidence been left out which would strengthen the argument?
   (d) Is the language persuasive?
   (e) Does the writer make you want to read on?
(3) Ask enabling questions such as:
   (a) Why did you choose this subject to write about?
   (b) What is it about?
   (c) How far have you got?
   (d) What can I help you with?
   (e) What part do you like best?
   (f) Which part are you not happy with?
   (g) What is the most important thing you are trying to say?
   (h) Can you think of a different way to say the same thing?
   (i) What do you intend to do next?
(4) Respond to one problem at a time, guiding the child's decision-making rather than giving orders.
(5) Keep response short, simple and positive so that confidence is built up.
(6) Make unobtrusive suggestions such as:
   (a) What could you do to make it better?
   (b) Have you given enough detail?
   (c) Can you help me understand that part?

Child Action

(1) Close eyes and picture what the writing is to be about.
(2) Keep referring back to your plan and amend it if you make changes whilst writing.
(3) Delete old ideas as they are replaced by new ones.
(4) Read parts out aloud to your partner and ask how effective they are.
(5) Compare the finished writing with the original plan.

(6) Underline the most important word/phrase/sentence.
(7) Circle the best bits.
(8) Read it aloud again slowly.

Drafting: Solo

There cannot be many people whose writing is improved by noisy surroundings. Many young people like loud music as a background, but that is less intrusive than other people speaking directly to you expecting an answer or people moving around the room. Such conditions may be the norm in many schools, but we have to distinguish between physical conditions which support and those which interfere with concentration. Children need to learn eventually to work on their own for substantial periods at the fullest concentration, and this is a skill acquired over the years of schooling. No matter whether all outside is quiet or noisy, in the private world inside the head there will be a bustle of activity, as the writer sees images in the mind's eye and tries to capture them in words, sounding them out with an inner voice for their effect.

Some movement and talk will be necessary. Information books may need to be taken from shelves and skimmed through. Where dictionary use slows down the writing overmuch it may be better to leave that until first draft stage, but that other essential reference book, the thesaurus, is best consulted here, when the writer is trying to capture experience in exactly the right word. It is a wonderful aid to vocabulary extension and refinement in that it offers a wealth of shades of meaning around key concepts, and so essential a tool that how to use it should be taught or revised at the beginning of each school year. Episodes of intense silent writing may be punctuated by talk to report on progress and discuss problems, to try out samples on a partner, to consult the teacher, even to stretch the mental legs. Some aspects of talk during writing are described under 'conferencing' above.

In classrooms where the division between collaborative and solo work is blurred, i.e. where it is not clear whether talk or silence is preferred, then the targets for achievement should be very clear; lack of concentration will pull down achievement, but to an extent which cannot be measured.

Drafting: Collaborative

Writing can be collaborative, interwoven with talk between groups or the whole class and teacher. In considering strategies in the teaching of response to literature, Stanley Fish (1980) described classrooms as 'interpretive communities' which offer mutual support in developing literary judgement. The same justification can be extended to writing, where the same opportunities exist for interaction between equals for sharing experiences, for planning a composite writing task, composing, editing and providing a final audience which is sympathetic and constructively critical.

Redrafting and Editing

It may seem like heresy to say so in the light of present official policy, but it may well be that a single draft after a meticulous planning stage will be sufficient to reach a good standard in many circumstances. The point was made earlier that children in general dislike redrafting. The process is at its most arduous when the text is simply being copied with minimal changes from one piece of paper onto another, but children are much more willing to write further drafts if they are given the right motivation, and there are two obvious sources for this. Firstly if the work is to be published for instance in a wall display, they will not want there to be any errors, and so after writing corrections on the draft they will write out a best version, practising handwriting as they do so. Secondly if the final draft is to imitate the layout of a real model they will redraft in order to include ideas on layout excluded from the first draft. This means that firstly the teacher must give clear guidance on what should be included and what excluded in a first draft, so that further drafting is more than just copying out in neat. Secondly both teacher and children must be tolerant of genuinely experimental writing at the first draft stage: crossings out, direction arrows to show insertions and major moves of text, irregular handwriting, spelling errors and so on. This suggests that it would be helpful to write double spaced and in a rough book or on a separate sheet of paper.

Proof-Reading

As for proof-reading drafts, the main principle is that children should learn to be as autonomous as possible. Although their own proof-reading will never be one hundred per cent effective, it should be a thorough attempt to filter out the most basic errors. That way they will learn from their mistakes, but if the teacher makes corrections for them after the writing is finished they may notice nothing but the final grade and comment. Consistent training and firm standards will pay dividends in freeing the teacher for work more useful than error-spotting. If planning has been done thoroughly and children have tried out samples and drafts on partners in conference, editing should be limited to proof-reading for surface-level (secretarial) errors of spelling, punctuation and syntax.

Full stops and commas are difficult for children to check accurately for themselves but reading the text slowly to a partner can show up where punctuation is needed. The listening partner can be alerted to listen for missing question marks, which the intonation of the reader might indicate, for ideas which run together when they should be separated by a full stop, and for lists of items which should be separated by commas. As for apostrophes, a poster on the wall listing the most frequently used ones will again save the teacher time: 'I'm, we've, can't, they're' are the cause of highly predictable recurrent errors.

Young writers are bound to have a more limited range of correct spellings than adults, but checking each and every doubtful word can severely disrupt their flow of ideas during planning and sample writing. The discussion stage of planning may be a good time to write key spellings on the board, showing at the same time how the word is built up from a root by addition of prefixes and suffixes. Draw their attention to the visual image of the word, other words inside it and other words which have the same spelling pattern. The strategy for learning the spelling of new words is embodied in the National Curriculum protocol:

Look – look carefully at the word, trying to see patterns in the letters; see other words in it, and component parts such as prefixes and suffixes and associate it with other words.
Cover – form a mental picture of the word then cover it completely.
Remember – look carefully at the mental picture in your head.
Write – write down the word as you see it in your head. (Younger writers might be allowed one or more quick peeks.)
Check – uncover the word and check the spelling letter by letter with the target word. If there is a mistake, repeat the process.

Children quickly learn that the easiest way to check a spelling is to ask someone, particularly the teacher. This, however, is a lazy habit which makes them dependent on other people. We need to make them independent and adept at using essential resources. So, make sure that dictionaries are out on desks and being used at the proof-reading stage. Most poor spellers either cannot use a dictionary or are very slow at it. Keep showing them how to use the head-word above each column and make a game out of finding specific word-meanings at speed.

Post-Writing Stage

Publication

In these days when schools actively recruit their pupils there are many very real opportunities for publication. The school may have the old-style school magazine, but in addition a newspaper, brochure, year-book, perhaps produced with assistance from a local newspaper or publisher and perhaps with commercial sponsorship. All of these might offer outlets for selected children's writing. Children might also write for the new intake of their peers or for the governors and parents to report on a special project. School events such as fêtes and plays are opportunity for publicity, programmes and correspondence. The school population is an ever-present audience for displays, readings, assembly performances and reports. Possible audiences are listed in Appendix 1.

That writing should serve a real purpose and reach a real audience is the driving force behind the present theory of writing development. It is therefore essential that the audience for the written work should be discussed and agreed with the class at the planning stage. There is no advantage in taking the decision to 'publish' only after the drafting has taken place, since the knowledge that one is writing for a real audience motivates the writer and stimulates crafting at all stages.

Display

Making the finished product available for others in the school to see is the most usual form of publication. In primary schools we have a strong tradition of display on all available walls in classrooms and corridors, a glorious celebration of children's creativity and teachers' dedication. Conditions can be more difficult in secondary schools, though it is possible that there is a vicious circle underlying the sequence of low self-image, lack of background stimulus and lack of respect for displayed work. To break such a circle means that creating respect for displayed work should be a high priority beginning with display in more secure areas such as the library, foyer, main corridor.

For those not familiar with display techniques, the work gains in impact if different shapes and colours of paper are used both for the writing and for the backing paper on which the work is mounted. Children may write on standard shaped paper first which is then cut out with scissors afterwards; any shape is better than a rectangle of file paper which is not completely filled with writing. The case is most obvious with concrete poetry where the sense suggests an outline shape; you may have come across the classic of the 'poet-tree' where poems about trees are cut into leaf shapes and mounted on a poster cut out or painted like a tree. A ghastly pun, but young children enjoy it for all that.

File Paper

How often have you been into a classroom – someone else's of course – and found under the desks sheets of children's writing, crumpled, torn, overprinted with the dusty footprints of young feet eager to get out of the door? Or found inside a child's desk a shuffled pile of papers, all shapes and sizes? If children notice, as I think they are bound to do subconsciously over their years of schooling, what message does such scrap paper give to developing writers about the long-term value of writing? Certainly children realise that much school writing is a means towards learning rather than an end in itself, but if we believe that the best writing comes from contexts which have meaning for the child, then that writing should remain meaningful long after it is written. Children are more likely to come to see themselves as real writers when they can revisit their past achievements, seeing hopefully an accumulation of success.

This is impossible if the writing that they do is on file paper which becomes dog-eared in the bottom of a sports bag; or is covered in red inked corrections; or is locked away in an anonymous exercise book. Even after display it is important that it should be given back to the child, who has a place to keep it safe. We need to take care over this, though children are naturally and understandably careless. They have probably been unintentionally conditioned to consider school writing to be dead once it has done its job of securing a grade. Although exercise books have gone out of fashion, they suggest a much more positive image than the careless paper-chase, and can be personalised with a decorated cover, contents page, separate sections, an index. Stationers supply a variety of types, including one which has a blank page facing a lined page, very useful when showing young children how to make a plan (blank page) and apply it in their writing (lined page).

We must actively guide children into seeing themselves as writers, by ensuring that they build up a writing portfolio in such formats as:

Exercise book.
Class magazine.
Personal journal – possibly a hard-back, pocket-sized notebook.
File – loose-leaf collection or selection of one's best writing, with self-
    chosen resource materials.

Folder – appropriately decorated, with contents page, illustrations, section/chapter dividers, index.
Hand-stitched book – for one child or a group.

The psychological benefit from such a portfolio is especially important for less able children, whose work is often unattractive because they lack psychomotor skills and as they well know it has not been highly thought of by teachers. If the accumulating product of their effort is a scruffy set of paper, over the years the discouraging effect can be imagined. It is important then for a positive self-image to be built up; for them to be helped at the planning stage, for corrections to be made with them at first draft stage which means that their work can be published for a wider audience without stigma, and for the final draft to join a collection which is as visually attractive as possible. Whereas the portfolios of others in the class will include extended texts, they may have cameos as an alternative, polished in the rough draft stage so that it compares favourably with the extended pieces of others while being far more encouraging than unfinished work. The look and accuracy of their work can be improved on special occasions if they dictate it to a more skilful writer. Otherwise WP hides the crafting process and the stigma of endless corrections, making their lack of presentation skills insignificant, which is highly motivating for writers with years of experience of being labelled a failure.

Books

As children are able to write more it can be highly motivating for them to set about writing a complete 'book', either on their own or as a syndicate with each group producing a chapter. Books can not only take the form of novellas but also anthologies of stories, poetry, class newspapers and magazines, collections of different kinds of writing, information books on projects across the curriculum. See Evans and Moore (1985) for information on how to make books of all kinds with primary age children.

Desk-Top Publishing

With the new 'desk-top publishing' software the final product can now include multiple fonts and printed graphics within the text, and the whole production can be handled within the school to professional standard. This is highly motivating for some children who will give up hours of free time to become involved in writing, which no other motivation would have done. Letters to the outside world, reports on projects undertaken – all kinds of official and semi-official documents need no third person intervention. Schools can send discs through the post to one another, or via a modem directly as electronic mail. A standard printer can produce multiple copies, perhaps updating information in subsequent editions. The production process can simulate real life, with a work-station in the corner of the classroom waiting for real decision-making.

Review

Once the writing has been finally drafted and published it will be highly significant for the writer to know what the readership thought of it, and how effective the writing was. This means in the classroom giving time and opportunity for children to give feedback to each other about their work. If all the stages of the writing process have been carried out, the finished work should contain few technical errors, so that the attention of the readership should be on the content of the writing and the effects of the crafting. Children need to be trained in how to react to writing, particularly in how to think positively, focusing on what the writer has done best. Some children have great difficulty in doing that, instead finding the negative by implication with 'Why didn't you . . . ?' The only significant effect that such criticism has on the writer is to de-motivate and lower self-image; it is too late for the work to be improved. So at the outset of a review lesson remind the class of the conferencing questions and insist on that open-ended approach. In the early stages of training you may have to take a brief comment on only the good features and nothing else, not moving on to tactful suggestions for more effective writing until the class can handle it.

In school situations the teacher may also be an examiner, on some occasions at least, and so the review stage may include formal assessment. If assessment is to be formative, helping the child to improve, then it should be clearly based on the guidelines for the task established initially. A single mark for the whole work gives only a vague indication of achievement and is the least helpful approach. Several marks give far more specific information, and the following categories are likely to be relevant in the majority of cases: (1) content; (2) vocabulary and style; (3) syntax and cohesion; (4) effectiveness (interest and impact on the reader); (5) presentation.

Positive written comments which show that the teacher is also an interested reader can be highly motivating. For example 'I liked the part where . . .' can usually be applied in all situations and should certainly be more creative for the teacher than thinking up another way of saying 'Satisfactory'. If the teacher comment begins with an appreciation of the content then where they are necessary negative comments and those aimed at technical errors are more likely to be accepted by the writer.

Reflection

To see themselves as writers, children need to be able to review their 'collected works', to see development by comparing their present with their past achievements, to appreciate writing as a craft by having a body of substantial achievement. We must recognise that the writer is also an audience; during the writing process the writer is the text's first audience and will hear the text in the head as well as see it emerging on the page. As crafting takes place, though, the writer is too close to the text to see it in perspective, and becoming a writer involves using the distancing effect of time; reviewing and reflecting on one's work at a later date.

Once work has been safeguarded in ways described above under Publication, we need next to build in times for a class to celebrate its achievements: at the conclusion of the week, of the project, of the term, of the year. An anthology lesson can be a very powerful builder of morale and group cohesion. To set this up, the teacher when assessing each child's work puts a mark in the margin beside the 'highlights' (or 'best bits') and keeps a record of whose work it was and what piece is involved. That record is then made into a running order so that in the lesson the teacher can give a linking commentary, calling on individual children to read their 'highlights', giving everyone a chance to read aloud, while the anthology reviews the writing task. The emphasis is on positive achievement, in which everyone has a chance to share. At the end of the year the event might be more of an 'Eisteddfod', for which children choose their best work, rehearse a reading for performing for the class, the whole school or any appropriate audience.

More formally children can make an occasional written review of their progress, highlighting what they enjoyed and felt they did well. More informally, perhaps at the end of the year, they can share with their writing partner, remembering the challenges they have tackled. If we give them the chance to browse, to read to each other and to celebrate their writing at significant moments in the year, children will rediscover their past selves and recognise their developing skills.

Towards Independence

(1) Planning – teach a variety of planning strategies so that children will be able to choose the one which best suits their way of thinking or the specific writing in hand.

(2) Make self-monitoring a working routine: planning, using thesaurus and reference books, proof-reading.

(3) Encourage an interest in words, extending their vocabulary into more precise shades of meaning and technical registers.

(4) Encourage critical awareness of syntax – different ways and order of saying the same thing but for a different effect.

(5) Extend their range of forms by focusing on specific targets, using clear models and suggesting guidelines.

(6) Encourage the writing of sample pieces – short, alternative versions of important moments in the intended writing – before they start a complete first draft.

(7) Teach them how to use peer criticism of samples and drafts.

(8) Encourage redrafting which makes the impact of the writing more forceful, going beyond merely correcting errors.

(9) Set up a variety of real audiences as part of the writing programme.

(10) Encourage children to see themselves as writers by discussing their own writing processes with them, a little and often.

(11) Review writing achievement in class discussion and tutorials with groups, pairs, individuals.

Finally after so many words on the theory and practice of writing a Chinese proverb seems fitting:

Easy to know, hard to do.

Appendix 1
THE WRITING GENERATOR

acknowledgement
advertisement
affidavit
announcement
article
autobiography
ballad
biography
blurb
brief (legal)
broadsheet
brochure
caption
cartoon
catalogue
certificate
charter
confession
constitution
critique
crossword
curriculum
curriculum vitae
definition
dialogue
diary

directory
edict
editorial (leader)
epitaph
essay
eulogy
feature (article)
forecast
form
gloss
graffiti
greetings card
guide
headline
horoscope
instruction
invitation
journal
label
letter (see subdivisions below)
libel
list
log
lyric
magazine
manifesto

manual
memo
menu
minutes
monologue
news (see subdivisions below)
notes
notice
novel
obituary
pamphlet
paraphrase
parody
pastiche
petition
placard
play
poem
postcard
poster
prayer
précis
proclamation
prospectus
questionnaire
recipe
record

reference
regulation
report
résumé
review
rule
schedule
script
sermon
sketch
slogan
song
sonnet
specification (job)
spell
statement
story
summary
syllabus
synopsis
telex
testimonial
testimony
travelogue
weather forecast
will

Letters: 20 Purposes

acknowledgement
advice
apology
application
complaint
congratulations
farewell
inquiry
invitation
news

order
pen pal
poison pen
protest
recommendation
resignation
sympathy
thanks
to editor
warning

Journalism: 24 Sub-categories

arts review (music, theatre, film)
business news
cartoons
classified advertising
competition (e.g. crossword)
crime news
editorial (leader)
entertainment guide (radio and
   TV times)
features (e.g. food, gardening,
   fashion, motoring, travel)
financial/investment advice
gossip column

horoscope
human interest story
international news
letters to editor
notice of events
obituary
political news
profile (personality)
sports news
trade advertising
weather forecast
women's page
young people's page

Audiences

Tentatively listed from least to
most formal:

Oneself: younger self; older self
Trusted friend(s): same sex;
   opposite sex
Younger child(ren)
Older child(ren)
Imaginary reader: other time,
   other place
Character(s) in fiction
Self as expert to less well
   informed reader(s)
Unknown child(ren): pen pals
Parent(s); grandparent(s);
   relative(s)
Trusted adult: own teacher,
   previous teacher(s), parent of
   a friend, leader of youth
   group, Cubs, Brownies
Agony aunt
School staff – caretaker;

secretary; welfare assistant;
   bus driver; cook
Known adult(s) – supportive
   readers
Listener(s) – i.e. radio script
Media personality – pop star,
   chat show host
Authors of books
Publishers of books, comics,
   magazines, newspapers
Firms, businesses, agencies
Judges of a writing competition
Adults in authority: school
   governors; head teacher, PTA
   members, police
Unknown public readership –
   past, present, future, extra-
   terrestrial, deity
Hostile readership
High status adult – Queen,
   Bishop, Member of Parliament

Writing Purposes

Subsumed under I (informative), P (persuasive) or E (evocative):

advertise	P
analyse	I
announce	I
argue	P
challenge	P
comment	I
compare	I
congratulate	I
contrast	I
defend	P
describe	P/I/E
discuss	P/I
dramatise	E
entertain	P/E
evaluate	P/I
evoke	E
explain	I
express attitude/emotion	P/I
express opinion	P/I
hypothesise	I
inform	I
instruct	I
narrate	P/I/E
negotiate	P
persuade	P
plan	I
question	I
reach a conclusion	P/I
record	I
regulate	I
report	I
speculate	I
suggest	I/P
summarise	I
warn	P

Publishing Outlets

(1) In school (known audience):

assembly reading
class book – anthology of prose or poetry
class newspaper/magazine
class noticeboard display
corridor display
rules (pets, plants, equipment use, behaviour)
library display (book jackets, reviews)
foyer displays for visitors – parents' evening
messages to peers – seasonal greetings, get well cards, reminders, invitations, arrangements for meetings
personal folder – collection of own writing
reports to parents – outings, progress report
reports to governors' meetings
rules and instructions

(2) Outside school (unknown audience):

arrangements for visits
campaign in support of a specific cause
contacts with information agencies
contacts with famous people – media, politics, sport, authors
contacts with neighbouring schools
display in teacher's centre

E-mail to other schools –
home/overseas
information sheets for
parents
local media profiles on
school/ class projects

pen pal letters
publicity for school events
school brochure
school/class magazine for
sale
writing competitions

Appendix 2
LINKING IDEAS

The following are the main ways in which related ideas are linked in writing to create a coherent text:

(1) Addition

and, in addition to, equally, similarly, in the same way, by the same token, also, further, not only . . . but also, as well, even, besides, too, in particular, particularly, chiefly, especially, mostly.

(2) Exemplification

for example, for instance, to take (quote), a typical case, that is, that is to say, by way of explanation.

(3) Result and Inference

because of, consequently, in consequence, as a result, as a result of which, thanks to, in view of which, in that case, so, thus, therefore, for, then.

(4) Reformulation

in other words, or rather, to put it in another way, differently put, alternatively, as it were, so to speak, if you will.

(5) Disjunction

in fact, indeed, evidently, clearly, of course, admittedly, actually, now, turning to, as for, as far as X is concerned.

(6) Anaphora (Referring Back)

this, that, these, those, the foregoing, the above, here, such.

(7) Cataphora (Referring Forward)

below, the following, as follows, this, these, here, thus, like this, in this (the following) way.

(8) Pro-forms

he, she, it, him, her, they, them, his, hers, its, theirs, one, all, some, any, many, each, none, the same.

(9) Contradictives

but, on the contrary, on the other hand, against that, instead, in spite of.

(10) Contrastives

nevertheless, notwithstanding, however, yet, still, all the same, for all that, by (in) contrast, looking at it another way, on the one hand . . . on the other.

(11) Concessives

admittedly, assuredly, certainly, naturally, of course, true, it is true, to be sure.

(12) Time Indicators

then, just then, at that time, in those days, last Friday, last year, next Easter, in 1978, at the beginning of June, on the stroke of ten, at four o'clock sharp, four months ago, when these events began.

(13) Time Relaters

(a) Precedence: until (then), by (then), before (then), hitherto, up to that time, in the preceding (weeks, days, etc.), leading up to, prior to, at first, to begin with, at the outset, in the beginning.
(b) Co-occurrence: at the same time, in the meantime, meanwhile, simultaneously, at that very moment, (even) while (this was going on), as (these events were unfolding), all the while, all along.
(c) Subsequence: subsequently, afterwards, then next, thereafter, presently, by and by, after a while, later (on), in later days, in days (time) to come, in due course, eventually, finally, at length, at the finish, in the long run, in the end.

(14) Time Distributors

(a) Frequency: frequently, hourly, daily, weekly, etc., occasionally, now and then, every so often, again and again, from time to time, as the years (time) go(es) by, day after day, year after year, etc.
(b) Duration: briefly, for some moments, for many years, during those hours, second by second, minute by minute, etc., for hours/ days, etc., on end/at a stretch/at a time.

(15) Place Definers

(a) Juncture: at, in, on, on top of, here, there, where, against, touching.
(b) Spatial relationship: above, below, beneath, behind, facing, flanking, inside, within, on one side, to one side (of), to the right/ left (of), on the opposite side (of), in front (of), before, (all) round.
(c) Directions: across, along, aside, up, down, to, to and fro, for-ward(s), backward(s), downward(s), inward(s), outward(s), obliquely, sideways, longways, at an angle, to the left, (to the) north, south, etc.
(d) Proximity: adjoining, adjacent (to), (up) against, alongside, near, nearby, next to, (hard) by, close to, face to face, back to back, cheek by jowl, touching, neighbouring, (close) at hand, in the foreground.
(e) Distance: beyond, in the distance, in the background, past, far away (off), on the far side, at the further end, yonder, there, outside, to the north, south, etc.

(For further information see Nash (1980) on which the above is based.)

Appendix 3
PARAGRAPH STRUCTURES

In a great deal of published writing there is no consistent pattern in the paragraph structure. Indeed in newspaper reporting the propositions are often too short to merit the description paragraph, although even a single sentence may be given the conventional paragraph markers of new line plus indentation. However, in more extensive and/or more complex writing the thread of meaning must be carefully constructed so that the reader can follow it, and there are alternative logical structures which will guide young writers. The following categories are based on Gilliland (1972) who was quoting the work of Bissex.

(1) The Fable

>   Story-type illustration or fable

>   Conclusion or generalisation or moral

An anecdote or story-type illustration is followed by a generalisation stating or implying the significance of the illustration.

(2) The For Example

>   Generalisation

>   Story type illustration or fable

The opposite pattern to (1), a generalisation is followed by an illustrative story or anecdote.

(3) The Sales-talk

    Proposition 1
             2
               3
                 4
                   5
                     6
                       Generalisation

A list of items of any sort, e.g. causes, effects, implications or facts in any order is followed by a summative sentence. The impact comes from the cumulative effect of the list.

(4) The Count Them

    Generalisation
      Series of facts, names, examples: 1
                               2
                               3
                               4
                               5
                               6

An assertion or generalisation is made followed by a series of supporting facts; the reader's acceptance of the truth of the assertion must grow with the series.

(5) The Therefore

    Proposition (a)
      Therefore (b)
        Therefore (c)
          Logical conclusion

Though similar to (2), the statements here are a logical progression, and a grand conclusion follows the chain of logic.

(6) The Advancer

    Generalisation
      Detail
        More detail
          Finer detail
          Close-up

More generally now this process is likened to the zoom-in of a camera lens, selecting finer and finer detail.

(7) The Receder

> Letter
> Word
> Paragraph
> Book
> Library: shelf of books

The items included are in a sequence: particular to general or least important to most important. Type (6), The Advancer, is the opposite.

(8) The Come-on

> Attention-getter
> Main generalisation
> Related/unrelated detail

This is typical of advertising copy; after a catchy headline the body-copy is 'hype' rather than logic.

(9) The Switch

> First set of propositions
> but/similarly
> Second set of propositions

This suits a two-paragraph structure where there is a marked contrast, e.g. the seaside in summer, the seaside in winter.

(10) The Classic

> Generalisation
> Series of propositions developed:
> 1
> 2
> 3
> 4
> Recapitulation/transition

Although this is intended to describe the organisation within the paragraph, it is also the overall structure of the traditional school 'essay', which, because it is based on a series of sub-topics, particularly suits the 'boxes' plan described in Chapter 4.

Appendix 4
THE WRITING PROCESS

Pre-Writing Stage

(1) Context   Establish the context and the reason for writing.

(2) Preparation   Establish audience, content, form, agenda; decide on the medium to be used.

(3) Models   Examine appropriate models of real writing; identify the main principles.

(4) Planning   Create an ideational framework for the text using one of a range of plans.

Drafting Stage

(5) Samples   Experiment with alternative versions of a significant section of the text.

(6) Conferencing   Discuss the effectiveness of the plan and samples with writing partner/teacher.

(7) Drafting   Craft the text as an entity; use reference books.

(8) Redrafting   Revise in response to further conferences.

(9) Proof-reading Check text for accuracy.

Post-Writing Stage

(10) Publication   Present final text to a real audience.

(11) Review   Compare text with original guidelines; take note of appraisal comments.

(12) Reflection   Add the text to a personal portfolio; compare it with earlier writing; discuss future development.

BIBLIOGRAPHY

Abbs, P. and Richardson, J. (1990) *The Forms of Narrative*, Cambridge University Press.

Adamson, S. (1990) The what of the language, in C. Ricks and L. Michaels (eds.) *The State of the Language*, Faber, London.

Ahlberg, J. and A. (1986) *The Jolly Postman*, Heinemann, London.

Bain, R., Fitzgerald, B. and Taylor, M. (1992) *Looking into Language*, Hodder & Stoughton, London.

Banks, L. R. (1980) *The Indian in the Cupboard*, Dent, London.

Benton, M. and P. (1990) *Double Vision*, Hodder & Stoughton, London.

Bereiter, C. (1980) Development of writing, in W. Gregg and R. Steinberg (eds.) *Cognitive Processes in Writing*, Laurence Erlbaum, Hillside, NJ.

Beresford, J. (ed.) (1978) *The Diary of a Country Parson 1758–1802 by James Woodforde*, Oxford University Press.

Boomer, G. (1984) The ideal classroom for language development, in *The English Quarterly*, Vol. 17, no. 3, CCTE.

Booth, D. W. et al. (1984) *Write Again*, Globe Press, Toronto.

Boyd, A. (1988) *Broadcast Journalism: Techniques of Radio and TV News*, Heinemann, Oxford.

Briggs, R. (1980) *Gentleman Jim*, Hamish Hamilton.

Briggs, R. (1982) *Where the Wind Blows*, Hamish Hamilton.

Britton, J., Burgess, T., Martin, N., McLeod, A. and Rosen, H. (1975) *The Development of Writing Abilities (11–18)*, Macmillan Education, London.

Brownjohn, S. (1980) *Does it Have to Rhyme?* Hodder & Stoughton, London.

Brownjohn, S. (1982) *What Rhymes with Secret?* Hodder & Stoughton, London.

Bruner, J. (1986) *Actual Minds, Possible Worlds*, Harvard University Press, Cambridge, Mass.

Burningham, J. (1984) *Granpa*, Cape, London.

Burtis, P. J., Bereiter, C., Scardemalia, M., Tetroe, J. (1983) The development of planning in writing, in Kroll, B. and Wells, G. *Explorations in the Development of Writing*, John Wiley & Sons.

Butturff, D. R. and Sommers, N. I. (1980) *Reinventing the Rhetorical Tradition*, pp. 99–104, Canadian Council of Teachers of English, Arkansas.

Carroll, L. (1865) *Alice's Adventures in Wonderland*, Macmillan, London.

Carter, R. (ed.) (1990) *Knowledge about Language and the Curriculum: the LINC Reader*, Hodder & Stoughton, London.

Clegg, A. (ed.) (1965) *The Excitement of Writing*, Chatto & Windus, London.

Corbalis, J. (1986) *'The Wrestling Princess' and Other Stories*, Deutsch, London.

Corbett and Moses (1986) *Catapults and Kingfishers; Teaching Poetry in the Primary School*, Oxford University Press.

Cormier, R. (1977) *I Am the Cheese*, Victor Gollancz, London.

Coulthard, M. (1985) (2nd edn) *An Introduction to Discourse Analysis*, Longman, London.

Cowie, H. (ed.) (1984) *The Development of Children's Imaginative Writing*, Croom Helm, London.

Cox, B. (1992) English studies and national identity, in M. Hayhoe and S. Parker (eds.) (op. cit.).

Craft, R. (1975) *The Fair*, Collins, London.

Dahl, R. (1982) *Revolting Rhymes*, Cape, London.

Department of Education and Science (1975) *A Language for Life* (The Bullock Report), HMSO, London.

Department of Education and Science (1984) *English from 5–16. Curriculum Matters 1*, HMSO, London.

Department of Education and Science (1987) *Teaching Poetry in the Secondary School; an HMI View*, HMSO, London.

Department of Education and Science (1989) *National Curriculum: English for Ages 5–16*, HMSO, London.

Dhondy, F. (1990) *Ranters, Ravers and Rhymers; Poems by Black and Asian Poets*, Harper Collins.

Dixon, J. (1967) *Growth through English*, Oxford University Press/NATE.

Doughty, P., Pearce, J. and Thornton, G. (1971) *Language in Use*, Edward Arnold, London.

Dyer, G. (1982) *Advertising as Communication*, Routledge, London.

Ellis, S. and Friel, G. (1991) *Inspirations for Writing*, Scholastic, Leamington Spa.

Evans, J. and Moore, J. (1985) *How to Make Books with Children*, Scholastic/Evan-Moor.

Fergusson, R. (1985) *The Penguin Rhyming Dictionary*, Penguin, Harmondsworth.

Fish, S. (1980) *Is There a Text in This Class? The authority of interpretive communities*. Harvard University Press, Cambridge MA.

Freedman A., Pringle I., Yalden J. (eds.) (1983) *Learning to Write: First Language/Second Language*, Longman, London.

Ghadessy, M. (ed.) (1988) *Registers of Written English; Situational Factors and Linguistic Features*, Pinter Publishers, London.

Gilbert, P. (1989) *Writing, Schooling and Deconstruction; from Voice to Text in the Classroom*, Routledge, London.

Gilliland, J. (1972) *Readability*, Hodder & Stoughton, London.

Goodman, K. S. (1967) Reading: a psycholinguistic guessing game, *Journal of the Reading Specialist*, no. 6, pp. 126–35.

Goodman, K. S. (1976) *What's Whole in Whole Language?* Scholastic TAB Publications, Ontario.

Graves, D. (1983) *Writing: Teachers and Children at Work*, Heinemann, Portsmouth, New Hampshire.

Grossmith, G. (1975) *The Diary of a Nobody*, Penguin, Harmondsworth.

Grubb, J., Gorman, T. and Price, E. (1987) *The Study of Written Composition in England and Wales*, NFER-Nelson, Windsor.

Hardy, B. (1977) Narrative as a primary act of mind, in M. Meek, A. Warlow and G. Barton *The Cool Web*, The Bodley Head, London.

Harris, J. and Wilkinson, J. (eds.) (1986) *Reading Children's Writing: a Linguistic View*, Allen & Unwin, London.

Harrison, B. (1983) *Learning Through Writing: Stages of Growth in English*, NFER-Nelson, Windsor.

Hartley, J. (1982) *Understanding News*, Methuen, London.

Hayhoe, M. and Parker, S. (1988) *Words Large as Apples*, Cambridge University Press.

Hayhoe, M. and Parker, S. (eds.) (1990) *Reading and Response*, Open University Press, Milton Keynes.

Hayhoe, M. and Parker, S. (eds.) (1992) *Reassessing Language and Literacy*, Open University Press, Milton Keynes.

Higgins, Paul (1991) *Poetry Processor. Books 1–3, Teacher's Book*, Blackwell, Oxford. (Writing guidelines for secondary age-range.)

Hughes, T. (1969) *Poetry in the Making*, Faber and Faber, London.

Jackson, D. (1983) *Encounters with Books*, Methuen, London.

Joos, M. (1962) *The Five Clocks*, Mouton, The Hague.

Kinneavy, J. (1971) *A Theory of Discourse*, Prentice-Hall, Englewood Cliffs.

Kress, F. (1987) *Writing with a 'Pro': a Guide to Teaching Writing Skills with a Word Processor*, OISE Press, Toronto.

Kress, G. (1982) *Learning to Write*, Routledge & Kegan Paul, London.

Kress, G. (1991) Two kinds of power, in *The English Magazine*, no. 24.

Kroll, B. and Wells, G. (eds.) (1983) *Explorations in the Development of Writing*, John Wiley & Sons, Chichester.

Littlefair, A. (1991) *Reading all Types of Text*, Open University Press, Milton Keynes.

Lynn, J. and Jay, A. (1986) *The Complete Yes, Prime Minister*, BBC Books, London.

Magee, W. (ed.) (1989) *Madtail, Miniwhale and Other Shape Poems*, Penguin, Harmondsworth.

Marshall, S. and Williams, N. (1986) *Exercises in Teaching Communication*, Kogan Page, London.

Martin, N. (1983) *Mostly about Writing*, Heinemann, London.

Meek, M. (1988) *How Texts Teach what Readers Learn*, Thimble Press, Stroud.

Moat, J. and Fairfax, J. (1981) *The Way to Write*, Heinemann, London.

Moffet, J. (1981) *Active Voice*, Boynton, New Jersey.

Mosenthal, P., Tamor, L. and Walmsley, S. (eds.) (1983) *Research on Writing; Principles and Methods*, Longman, New York.

Nash, W. (1980) *Designs in Prose; a Study of Compositional Problems and Methods*, Longman, London.

Newman J. (1984) *The Craft of Children's Writing*, Scholastic, Toronto.

Oakley, G. (1987) *The Diary of a Church Mouse*, Macmillan, London.

Odell, L. and Goswami, D. (eds.) (1985) *Writing in Non-academic Settings*, Guilford Press, New York.

Owen, P. J. K. (1990) Defining reading standards: establishing the operational validity of assessments, in M. Hayhoe and S. Parker *Reading and Response*, Open University Press, Milton Keynes.

Parker, S. and Hayhoe, M. (1989) *Voyages*, Heinemann, Oxford.

Perera, K. (1984) *Children's Writing and Reading*, Blackwell, London.

Pirrie, J. (1987) *On Common Ground*, Hodder & Stoughton, London.

Protherough, R. (1983) *Encouraging Writing*, Methuen, London.

Richards, J., Platt, J. and Weber, H. (1985) *The Longman Dictionary of Applied Linguistics*, Longman, London.

Ricks, C. and Michaels, L. (eds.) (1990) *The State of the Language*, Faber, London.

Scardamalia M., Bereiter C. and Fillion B. (1981) *Writing for Results: a Sourcebook of Consequential Composing Activities*, OISE Press, Toronto.

Scieszka, J. (1989) *The True Story of the Three Little Pigs, by A. Wolf*, Viking Kestrel, London.

School Examinations and Assessment Council (1992) *Key Stage 3 Pupils' Work Assessed: English*, SEAC, London.

Schwartz, M. (1984) Response to writing, *College English*, Vol. 46, no. 1, pp. 55–62.

Sharp, H. (1984) *Advertising Slogans of America*, Scarecrow Press, Metuchen, NJ.

Smith, F. (1982) *Writing and the Writer*, Heinemann, London.

Smith, F. (1988) *Joining the Literacy Club*, Heinemann, London.

Stevenson, R. L. (1884) *Treasure Island*, Cassell.

Storr, K. (1967) *Clever Polly and the Stupid Wolf*, Penguin, Harmondsworth.

Swales, J. (1990) *Genre Analysis: English in Academic and Research Settings*, Cambridge University Press.

Tolkien, J. R. R. (1937) *The Hobbit*, Allen & Unwin, London.

Townsend, S. (1985) *The Secret Diary of Adrian Mole*, Methuen, London.

Wales, K. (1989) *A Dictionary of Stylistics*, Longman, London.

Wells, G. (1986) *The Meaning Makers: children learning language and using language to learn*, Heinemann, Portsmouth.

Wilkinson, A. (1971) *The Foundations of Language*, Oxford University Press.

Wilkinson, A. et al. (1980) *Assessing Language Development*, Oxford University Press.

Wilkinson, A. (1986a) *The Quality of Writing*, Open University Press, Milton Keynes.

Wilkinson, A. (1986b) *The Writing of Writing*, Open University Press, Milton Keynes.

ACKNOWLEDGEMENTS

Children's Writing

For the examples of writing quoted in this book, I wish to express grateful thanks to teachers and pupils (whose talent and enthusiasm gave me so much pleasure) of the following schools in the East Anglian region:

Chapel Break First School, Bowthorpe
Cringleford First and Middle School
Hethersett Middle School
Kinsale Avenue Middle School, Hellesdon
Lakenham Middle School, Norwich
Surlingham Primary School
Woodside First School, Hethersett

Alderman Peel High School, Wells
Broadland High School, Hoveton
Cliff Park High School, Gorleston
Diss High School
Gaywood Park High School, King's Lynn
Hellesdon High School
Sprowston High School
Thorpe St Andrews High School
Norwich High School
Notre Dame High School, Norwich

Published Writing

The texts used as models for 'real writing' have been reproduced with the kind permission of the following, who retain their copyright:

Books for Keeps: Book review: *Badger on the Barge*
Messrs Brooks & Bentley: 'Elizabeth at the Ball'
Champion Spark Plug: *Double Copper: the facts*
Eastern Daily Press: Editorial 'Sick society'
Electricity Association: *Safety in the Garden*
The Guardian: 'Burning less fuel is only sure solution'; 'Cut ironing time
    in half'; 'Questioners fail to crack "Mrs Big" in used car fiddle'; 'Ski-
    winged speedster'
Greenpeace: *Against all odds*
The League Against Cruel Sports: *1 Fox . . .*
Norwich City Council: *Norwich mini-guide*
Office of Fair Trading: *How to cope with doorstep salesmen*
Royal Society for the Prevention of Cruelty to Animals: 'The continentals
    love freshly butchered horsemeat'
South Central Colorado Tourism Region: *Revive your senses*
Stafford-Miller Ltd.: *Fluoride protection and the family: your questions
    answered*

SUBJECT INDEX

advertisement
    field of writing 18–19, 108–117
    classified 44
    display 110–116
affective
    influence on writing 24, 56, 69, 73,
        91, 96–7, 107, 109, 113, 116,
        122–3, 124, 147, 158
agenda
    teacher's 176
alliteration 23, 50, 109, 139, 173
anecdote, 21, 28, 97, 144, 149
angle (slant, pitch) 70, 72–73, 113, 127
appeal
    field of writing 18–19, 104–8
argument
    field of writing 18–19, 41, 92–98
    balanced 35, 92–93
    emotional 96–97
    illustrated 97–98
    partisan 93–96
assertion
    field of writing 18–19, 41, 98–104
    rhetorical device 58, 62
assessment 87, 189–90
    evocative 23, 129, 141
    informative 21, 54, 56
    National Curriculum 11
    persuasive 22, 90, 124
audience 7, 8, 9, 16, 41, 167, 186, 191,
    Appendix 1

bias 22, 44, 57, 83, 86, 89, 103
    scale of 57

biography
    field of writing 19, 23, 164–71
    as form 170–1
book jacket 38, 82
Bullock Report
    'A language for life' 3, 4
cameo
    definition 37–38
    forms 21, 70, 97, 102, 114, 116, 147,
        166, 167, 169, 170, 181, 188
camera lens
    see viewpoint
characterisation 36, 151–2, 155, 160–1
charter 101–2
chronology
    see structure
cliche 73–4, 75, 109, 115, 130, 147, 166
cliff-hanger 37, 154, 159, 163
collaborative writing 138, 171, 183–4
coloration of language 44, 51, 125, 127
complaint
    letter of 99–101
    action stages 101
conferencing 176
    strategies 181–2
cookery
    writing on 121–2
creativity 3, 27, 52, 108–110, 116, 130,
    174, 178, 186
crime reporting
    see journalism
critical reading/writing
    promotion of 88–9, 127, 172–3
criticism
    field of writing 19, 78–85

deadlines
working to 44, 68, 164, 166, 177
declamation 50, 91, 97, 98
description
field of writing 18–19, 117–126
in story 152
of action 125–6, 153, 159–60
developing skills
techniques for 87–8, 126–7, 171–2
dialogue
see speech
diary 38, 42, 160, 165, 167–9
dictionary 43, 88, 183, 185
display
as publication 136, 142, 186–7
see also audience
drafting 26, 164, 180–1
solo 183
collaborative 183–4
re-drafting 180, 184, 191
drama
field of writing 19, 23, 37, 155–164
improvised 162–3
in planning 29
rhetorical device 69, 71, 73, 76, 78, 93, 98, 134, 167
tension 146, 149, 157

early finishers 70, 116
emotion
see affective influence
empathy 29, 99–100, 133, 143, 150, 153–4, 166, 169, 172
encyclopaedia 54, 55, 88
epitaph 38, 165
essay 76, 93, 105, 202
evocative
primary purpose 18–19, 23, 128–173
experience
see personal
explanation
field of writing 19, 57–61
exposition
field of writing 19, 75–78

fairy tale 97, 129, 147–8, 150–2, 163, 172
feature article
42, 75–78
example of teaching process 78
fields
in model of primary purpose 18–20
form
definition of 7, 9–10, 13, 17, 19–20

genre 4, 8, 17

closed and open, definition of 10
literary genres
detective 31
fairy tale 147
fighting fantasy 35, 151
historical 23, 153
western 148
Green Cross Code 62, 64
Guardian News Service 74, 92–3, 117, 125
guidebook 118, 171

handwriting 167, 178, 179, 184
headline 48, 58, 69–70, 72, 103, 108, 110, 114
humour 24, 116, 141
hyperbole ('hype') 49, 50, 91, 111, 113, 115, 118, 119

illustration
to support text 54, 57, 59, 66, 68, 82, 85, 109, 110, 137
imagery 23, 51, 73, 109, 119, 121, 134–5, 138
imaging 29, 66, 113, 132, 137, 146, 153, 183, 185
impartiality 58, 87
impersonal voice 20, 42, 56, 68, 72, 81
independence
promoting 116, 158, 177, 184–5, 191
informative
primary purpose 18–19, 21, 53–89
instruction
field of writing 19, 61–66
leaflet, 53, 65
manual 53, 62, 88
interest
see personal
intro. (introduction) 70, 76, 84
invitation
wedding 10

jargon 55, 60, 75
journal
reading 165, 169, 173, 187
scientific 43
journalism 22, 42, 56, 67
crime 74–75
investigative 173
radio 143
sports 73
sub-categories Appendix 1
see also news

less able children 27, 28, 165, 167, 188

letter
  business 10
  as cameo form 38
  complaint 99–101
  personal 14, 43, 44
  twenty purposes for, Appendix 1
log 169
  see also journal

map
  as plan 32, 66, 118, 150
menu 122
memoir 165
memorandum 38
metaphor 49, 51, 73, 115, 121
mind's eye
  see imaging
minutes
  of a meeting 38
model of primary purpose 17–25, 53–4,
    75, 78, 165
  secondary purpose 18, 21, 54, 75, 78,
    90
models
  use of published forms as 67, 87, 126,
    157, 191
  teaching strategy 178–9
  teacher as writer 174, 178–9

narrative
  see structure, chronological
narrator 31, 153–4, 156, 162–3
National Curriculum for English 1, 4, 6,
    11–15, 43
news
  categories of 67
  human interest 163
  leader (editorial) 102–3
  newsworthiness 68
  slants 72–3
  personal writing as 165
  structure of news items 44, 68–71
  TV style 56
non-chronological writing
  see structure

objectivity 54, 57, 87, 166
  identifying 80
onomatopoeia 50, 73, 121, 139, 173
opening
  see intro.
options
  in composition 10, 17, 20, 21, 40–52,
    126, 140, 180

paragraph
  see structure
parody 74, 89, 117, 127, 147, 160
passport 38
performance 141, 164, 172, 190
person
  see viewpoint
personal
  writing 2, 6, 8, 10, 14, 42, 48, 80,
    164–71
  interest/experience 53, 62, 77–8, 118,
    122–3, 126, 132, 136, 160–1, 175
  opinion/response 81, 84–5, 93, 97,
    165
  vicarious 129
persuasive
  primary purpose 18–19, 22, 90–127
  secondary purpose 65
petition 99
pitch, *see* angle
planning 26–39, 179–80, 187, 191
  conceptual 33–36, 65
  experiential 28–29, 65, 168
  iconic 30–33, 65, 118, 150, 170
  synoptic 36–38, 159
plot 148–9
  shapes 150–1
  sub-plot 150
poetry
  field of writing 19, 23, 109, 130–42
postcard 38, 165, 166–7
poster 38
precis 68, 166
  telegraphese 167
presentation 119, 141, 179
pressure 164, 177
  see also deadlines
profile
  of personality 170
prompts 37, 135
proof-reading 184–5, 191
propaganda 19, 85–87
publication 186, Appendix 1
  see also audience
pun 49, 69, 103, 187
punchline 71, 93, 95, 105, 114, 117, 141
puppets 163
purpose
  model of primary purpose 17–25,
    53–4, 75, 78, 165
  secondary purpose 18, 20, 21, 24, 54,
    65, 75, 78, 90

reader
  persona of 21, 22, 23, 68, 80–81, 86,
    90, 96, 126, 129–30

reading 29, 45, 52, 73, 87, 158
reflection
    plot stage 149
    appraisal 190
    see also review
register 43, 55, 59–60
report
    as written form 17, 54
    science 55, 58, 79, 166
    weather 21
    see also journalism, news
reporting
    field of writing 19, 66–75
research skills 88, 126, 153, 176, 191
resistant reading 6, 44, 85–7, 98, 104,
    108, 113, 116, 117, 127, 172–3
review
    appraisal 39, 152, 189–90, 191
    form of writing 79–85
    basic pattern 83
    complex pattern 84
    non-literary applications 85
    structure of 81–4
rhetoric 48–52, 127
    rhetorical question 21, 50, 81, 95, 98,
        100
rhyme 23, 50, 109, 131, 139, 173
rhythm 50, 109, 139

samples
    drafting strategy 41, 100, 127, 180–1,
        191, 203
scientific writing 42, 43, 55–6, 58, 79,
    166, 169
secretarial features 6, 88, 181, 185, 190
sense impressions 119–22, 146
Shakespeare, William 17, 51, 134, 139,
    161, 172
'showing'
    literary construct 146, 149, 155, 156
    see also 'telling'
slant
    see angle
small print 60–1
speech
    direct 69, 71–2, 73, 98, 145, 153,
        159, 161, 167
    reported (indirect) 56, 68, 72–3
sports reporting
    see journalism
Stevenson, Robert Louis 145–6, 156–7
story
    field of writing 19, 21, 23, 142–55
    strapline 69, 108, 111
stream of consciousness 45, 154, 162

structure 8, 45–52
    advert 113–4
    appeal 105
    argument 93
    chronological 14, 27, 69, 105, 124,
        126, 142, 148–50, 161, 167, 171
    description 123–4
    essay 93, 105
    feature article 76–7
    ideational 26, 93, 95, Appendix 2
    letter of complaint 101
    news item 68–71
    non-chronological 14, 47–8, 63, 65
    paragraph 47, 76–77, Appendix 3
    review 81–4
    sentence 45–7, Appendix 2
suspense 50, 145, 150, 153–4
synopsis
    written form 37, 98, 144, 146
syntax 8, 45–7, 185, 191, Appendix 2

technical terms 59–60, 74
'telling'
    literary construct 146, 149, 155, 156
    see also 'showing'
tense 45, 55, 72, 84, 153
text support
    see illustration
thesaurus 43, 88, 122, 126, 183
tone 8, 62, 68, 100, 103, 105, 106
    range of 43, 63, 91
topic 7, 8, 16, 41, 67
travel writing 18, 42, 118–9, 171

values 24, 44, 57, 86, 103, 104, 108,
    129, 133, 154, 159, 173
viewpoint 41–2, 121, 123, 127, 146,
    154, 162, 172
    camera lens 118, 120, 146, 201
    first person 41, 55, 56, 69, 78, 95,
        144, 153–4, 162, 167, 181
    impersonal 20, 42, 56, 68, 72, 81
    multiple 154
    narrator 31, 153–4, 156, 162–3
    second person 42, 62, 125
    subjective 81, 89, 93, 98, 103
    third person 42, 69, 89, 144, 154,
        181
vocabulary
    options in choice 8, 43, 44, 59–60,
        62, 73, 120–1, 191
    scale of formality 44
voice
    active 20, 41, 55–6
    passive 20, 42, 55–6, 107

web chart
  plan 34, 68, 94, 96, 176
window
  plan 36, 94, 95, 202
Woodforde, Parson James
  diary 167
word-processing (WP) 62, 107, 165, 178, 180, 188–9
  workshop manual 53, 62
writer

persona of 42, 43, 54–6, 75, 81, 89, 91, 100, 154, 167, 172
  seeing oneself as a 187–8
writer's block 40, 41
writing
  functions, Britton's model of 2
  generator 7–15, Appendix 1
  process 25, 174, 182, 191, Appendix 4
  purposes, Appendix 1

CHILDREN'S WRITING INDEX

Reception news ('I went out ...') 165

year 2 appeal (whale hunting) 106
  book review ('Fungus the Bogeyman') 83
  petition (whale hunting) 99

year 3 concrete poem (pig) 137
  free verse ('Out in the sun ...') 134
  story (balloon ride) 143
  story ('The Grumpy Leaf') 143

year 4 argument (fox hunting) 97
  instructions (how to pack a sledge) 64
  news report: crime (jewel robbery) 71

year 5 description (picture) 123
  description: impressionistic (fairground) 124
  description: objective (ghost train) 124
  science report (gravity) 55

year 6 advert (toy) 114–5
  advert (toy) 115
  description (caravan park advert) 120
  playscript ('The Mad Axe-Man') 159–60
  snapshot poems (Victorian village) 135–6

year 7 alliterative poem ('Hawks hover..') 139
  argument (anti-smoking) 95
  free verse ('Life As An Owl') 132–3
  limerick (Paul) 141

year 8 charter (pupils' rights) 102
  couplet (Claire) 140–1
  diary (Robinson Crusoe) 169
  feature article ('Getting started in trucks') 77
  haiku (family album) 138
  postcard (Dear Zoe) 167

year 9 appeal (anti-vivisection) 107
  argument (dangerous dogs) 94–5
  autobiography ('First Day') 171
  diamante poem ('Love-Hate') 139
  film review ('The Naked Gun') 84–5
  free verse ('Stereo') 134
  letter: complaint (workhouse) 99–100
  list poem ('Fear is ...') 132
  description: process (zip fastener) 59
  story: crime (murder of Neil) 144
  story: romance ('Rebecca ... and Robert') 144
  story: suspense ('Dracula') 153

year 10 TV script ('The Good Book Show') 164